Moire O'Sullivan is a mountain runner, adventure racer, outdoor instructor, author and mum. Moire previously worked throughout Africa and South-East Asia for international aid agencies. It was while living in Vietnam that she and her late husband Pete met Tom, the intrepid street dog. Moire now lives in Rostrevor, Northern Ireland with Tom and her two young children.

Also by Moire O'Sullivan

Bump, Bike & Baby

Mud, Sweat & Tears

The
Hound
From Hanoi

The Vietnamese street dog who built a family

Moire O'Sullivan

SANDSTONE PRESS

First published in Great Britain by
Sandstone Press Ltd
Willow House
Stoneyfield Business Park
Inverness
IV2 7PA
Scotland

www.sandstonepress.com

Sandstone Press is committed to a sustainable future. This book is
made from Forest Stewardship Council® certified paper.

ISBN: 978-1-912240-58-6
ISBNe: 978-1-912240-59-3

Tom's portrait © Sinead Murphy from Photography & The Dog
Cover design by Antigone Konstantinidou
Typeset by Iolaire, Newtonmore
Printed and bound by Totem, Poland

To my dear Pete
Rest in Peace

Contents

Prologue

Pete asked me to write this book.

'Wouldn't it be great to walk into a bookshop and see a picture of our dog on a paperback?' he'd say.

I wasn't convinced. I write about mountain running and adventure sports, not pets.

It didn't take long for Pete to convince me, however, that our 'Hound from Hanoi' deserved to have his memoirs told. Our dog had travelled more places and lived through more hair-raising experiences than most humans we knew. There was definitely a story there.

I spent most of 2018 writing *The Hound from Hanoi*, each completed chapter being passed to Pete for his gentle nod of approval. It was only when I was doing the final edits on this book that Pete became unwell. It didn't seem anything serious; just a piece of work that was stressing him out a little and making him lose sleep. We didn't think much of it.

Unfortunately, Pete never showed any signs of recovery. Instead his worries continued to multiply, his insomnia spiralling out of control. Within months he was diagnosed with depression. He was put on a cocktail of medication and prescribed counselling sessions. Nothing seemed to work.

Then, on 27 December 2018, Pete took matters into his own hands. Unable to cope with his oppressive negative thoughts and feelings, he left the house early one morning and never came back. Mountain rescue found his body five hours later in the nearby forest where he would often run.

Nothing prepares you for the loss of a loved one, let alone to suicide. For the next few months I was in pure survival mode, bracing myself for the next raw emotion to batter me just when my guard was down.

While all of Pete's loved ones were busy coming to terms with his death, the *Hound from Hanoi* manuscript lay in a file of my computer, untouched. I didn't know what to do with it. It wasn't until I considered what Pete would have wanted that I realised that I had to release it to the outside world.

Reading through these pages again after Pete's untimely departure, it has struck me that this book is not just about our dog. Though I never intended it at the time of its writing, *The Hound from Hanoi* is a magnificent testament to Pete and to all that he loved in the world.

This book is also an appeal to those suffering from depression to please never give up hope. You may believe that the world would be better without you, but despite what this horrific illness might tell you, nothing could be further from the truth.

1

A New Home

Every dog needs a loving, stable home. Ten years ago, this was the one thing I didn't have.

It was early 2009, and I was living in Dublin, witnessing the demise of the Celtic Tiger. Everywhere I turned, there was frightening talk of pay cuts and job losses, mortgage defaults and home seizures as the Irish property bubble burst.

'There's no point hanging around here with everyone so depressed,' my boyfriend Pete told me on a near-daily basis. 'I'm going to find myself a job somewhere else and get the hell out of here.'

When Pete said 'somewhere else', he didn't mean some other Irish city. He didn't consider taking the boat to England like emigrants of the 1970s escaping Ireland's long-stagnant economy. He meant packing a single bag and jetting to the other side of the world as he had done before at the tender age of eighteen, fleeing Ireland for the United States. Twenty years on, Pete was intent on doing exactly the same again.

I was quickly learning that Pete didn't do things by halves. After just a few calls, he reconnected with an old friend in Vietnam, who needed someone just like Pete to work for him.

'Come with me,' Pete said to me after another one of my what-am-I-going-to-do breakdowns.

I hesitated. Vietnam seemed like a terribly long way to go just to find employment. What if I went all that way and still remained jobless, homeless and depressed? What if I missed Ireland too much and pined for its shores?

'What have you got to lose?' Pete said, sensing my reluctance. It was a valid question. Neither of us had borrowed copious amounts of money from the banks when they were desperately throwing cash around. Neither of us had property tying us to our country of birth. We had no children to care for, no pets to rehome. All we had was our redundancy money, which was just about enough to cover a plane ticket and a couple of weeks' rent.

What I feared was that our relationship wouldn't survive the drastic move. We had been together less than a year, taking advantage of the heedless days of Ireland's boom, spending money on frivolous things, having tons of flirtatious fun. Yet, as a dating couple, we had still lived relatively separate lives. Relocating to Vietnam meant that a lot would have to change. I would see an awful lot more of Pete, and he of me, and I wasn't sure whether we'd both like what we discovered. At the same time we would have to adapt to another culture, language and lifestyle. How would we cope if one of us loved Vietnam, and the other one felt only homesick?

'I'll give it six months,' I said to Pete, after going over in my mind ad nauseam all the pros and cons. Even if it didn't work out, at least I could consider it an adventure, to explore a part of the world that I had never been to before.

Pete looked visibly relieved when I finally gave him my answer. 'Great,' he said. 'Let's book return flights, and if it's not working out by, say Christmas ... well, I suppose we'll see.'

Six months. That gave us just enough time to cast our fledgling relationship into the Vietnamese waters and see if it would sink or swim.

So we moved to Vietnam. After a month in our new home of Hanoi, much to my surprise, our relationship seemed to be bobbing along. We had found a beautiful open-plan apartment overlooking the city's Trúc Bạch Lake. Pete's new job was interesting, and lucrative enough to sustain us both while I continued my search for work. More importantly, the country was thriving. There was investment, growth, employment and construction, a sharp contract to the bleak Ireland we had fled.

As I sat sipping chilled Chardonnay on the balcony overlooking our new city, I gazed across at Pete opposite me, reclining on a bamboo chair with a matching glass in his hand.

'More wine?' he said, catching my wandering eye. I nodded, silent and content. Maybe hanging out in Hanoi wasn't as bad as I had originally thought.

'What do you fancy for dinner?' I said, after an unexpected tummy rumble. 'I could cook if you like.' Pete shrugged his shoulders, easy enough with the idea. 'I saw a market at the end of the street and was hoping to check it out,' I continued. 'Maybe I could pick up some ingredients there for, I don't know, a stir-fry?'

'Sure,' Pete said. 'Do you need a hand?'

I shook my head as I readied myself to leave. I wanted Pete to stay and enjoy the sunset. He had done enough for me already, bringing me to this amazing place.

Leaving the serenity of our apartment, I braced myself as I descended the stairs to the road below. Opening the front door, I was immediately hit by the torrent of traffic that is Hanoi's transportation network. Buses, lorries, motorbikes, rickshaws, cars and cabs flooded past me, a wall of rubber, metal and fumes barring my passage to the other side. I stood there, mesmerised by the mania. It took a split second before I remembered the market I planned to visit was located on the same side of the street as our apartment.

I turned, having received a momentary reprieve. I knew that one day I would have to learn to traverse a Hanoian street, but for the moment I was happy to watch this traffic turmoil as a tourist from the safety of the pavement.

A five-minute walk transported me to the market's gates. Once inside its confines, the smell of rotting produce bombarded me straightaway, stifling sickly-sweet gases entrapped under its sun-scorched tarpaulin roof. The noise of boisterous food vendors heckling prospective buyers quickly replaced the deafening din of the road users outside. Flustered, I vowed to make my purchases quickly and to retreat as soon as I could back to the sanctity of our flat.

Meat and vegetables were the sole items on my shopping list. I spotted the butcher's stall in front of me and headed straight for it.

As soon as I got within striking distance, I stopped dead in my tracks. Starring hard at the fly-infested corpses strewn across the butcher's wooden blood-stained table, I tried to convince myself otherwise but no, it was a dog all right. The sharp teeth protruding from its head were undeniably canine. The body's dimensions were those of a small domestic pet. It was just that I didn't expect to see 'dead dog' on display on that day's specials list.

The way the body was positioned made it look oddly at peace. It was lying on its back, with all four of its legs dangling in the air, paws bent. If it had been still alive, it would have been an invitation to me to approach the bench and rub its furry belly. A scratch on this dog's stomach, however, would have drawn no looks of adoration from it, no licks of unending affection. The dog was as rigid as a plank, riddled with rigor mortis.

There was not even a patch of fur on this animal for me to stroke. The butcher had skilfully stripped the poor doggie of its entire coat, leaving behind a shiny, leathery skin. Even its snuggly ears and soft waggly tail had been relegated to the bin. I couldn't help but see my own beloved childhood canines lying there lifeless on that table, and immediately felt faint.

Coming to my senses, I realised that the butcher was watching me, intently. Slowly, he took his cleaver and gestured to the canine carcase, snarling a toothless grin.

'No,' I said. 'God, no.'

But the butcher could not understand me, and seemed intent on making a sale.

I shook my head profusely, backing away from his stall while contorting my face in disgust. Surely such body language was universally understood, even here in Asia. The butcher fixed his eyes on me as I reversed quickly away, disappointed that I didn't fancy serving up a leg of dead dog for dinner that night.

I made a hasty retreat in the direction of the nearest vegetable stall. There I browsed its exotic fare, trying all the while to erase from my mind the image of the dead dog. The abundant variety of fresh fruit and vegetables would have made anyone happily forgo meat. I quickly filled my shopping bag with water spinach, bamboo shoots and bitter melon, before making eye contact with the vegetable vendor.

'Bao nhiêu?' I said, with a confidence that took me by surprise. Miss Phuong, our new Vietnamese teacher, would have been proud of my latest vocabulary advances. My grasp of the local language, however, stopped there. The lady shouted a sentence at me that bore no resemblance to any I had learned thus far. Not wanting to lose face, I stuffed a fistful of dong notes into the seller's hand and hoped she would give me back some change.

I glanced over my shoulder to the butcher, who had apparently lost all interest in me. Instead he was busy carving up some canine fillets for an eager customer who had just arrived at his stall. I had wanted to buy some pork for the stir-fry I had promised Pete, but didn't dare approach his counter, still littered with animal figurines, again. I was too scared I might offend this knife-laden butcher by refusing his local dog delicacy. If there was one thing I had already learned in this country, it was that you don't want to offend the Vietnamese, even accidentally.

I walked the short distance from the market back to our apartment block and climbed the four flights of stairs to our flat. Catching my breath, I slid open the front door and threw my shoes inside the entrance. Dropping my market purchases in the kitchen, I spied Pete through the glass doors, still sitting on the balcony. I hesitated to go outside to him, back out into the hot, humid weather that I had just escaped. Pete had left the air-con on inside, and our home was wonderfully cold and sterile. It was the perfect antidote for the humid walk, oppressive traffic and putrid market smells that still inundated my senses.

I was so traumatised by my dead-dog encounter, however, that I had no choice but to join Pete on the balcony. I pushed open the glass door and was instantly hit by the clammy heat I had tried so hard to avoid.

'Hey there, what's up?' Pete said. 'Did you get everything you need?'

'Did you know they eat dogs here?' I said, answering neither of his questions.

'I thought they only did that in China,' Pete replied, slowly placing his wine glass back on the table. 'Why do you ask?'

'The feckin' butcher at the market,' I said, no longer able to hide my distress. 'He just tried to sell me dog steaks.'

I yanked my chair back out from under the table and threw myself into it. Without asking, Pete poured a glass of wine and pushed it in my direction. He had begun to recognise my look when I desperately needed alcohol.

'Have you eaten dog?' I asked, unsure if I wanted to know. I did know that Pete had lived in China for a while in his twenties, so there must have been times when dog was served up on the menu.

'God no,' Pete replied, nearly choking on his drink at the mere mention. 'I like my dogs alive.'

I clinked my glass against his, congratulating him on the right answer. I had still a lot of things to learn about my boyfriend.

'I thought dog meat was meant to give men strength, vigour and virility?' I said cheekily, the wine quickly loosening my tongue. 'Surely you'd like a bit of that? I can always go back to the butcher and buy some if you like.'

Pete appeared to contemplate my offer for a moment, then thankfully declined. He probably thought he already had enough of those qualities, so had no need of a top-up via some canine dining.

'Why don't we just sit here and enjoy our wine instead?' he said. 'Then maybe I can help you rustle up that stir-fry you were suggesting?'

The mere mention of my ill-advised cooking plan unexpectedly made my stomach lurch. 'Ah, would it be okay if we eat out instead? I'm sure those vegetables I got will last until tomorrow.' I also planned to get some pre-packaged frozen meat from the relative safety of the nearby supermarket the following day. 'What about some street food?' I added, as Pete downed the dregs of his glass.

He hesitated.

'Come on, it'll be fun.'

'Fun getting food poisoning?' he replied. 'No thanks.'

'Seriously Pete, I'm sure it's perfectly safe,' I said, surprised that I was now the adventurous one. 'Why don't we go downstairs and try out the hot-pot stalls below the flat? If we don't like it, we can always go to a proper restaurant further on down the road.'

I had secretly wanted to try Vietnamese hot-pot ever since

we had arrived. Every evening, like clockwork, Vietnamese hot-pot ladies arrived en masse outside our home laden down with utensils. They would first set about meticulously sweeping and scrubbing the pavements, before throwing down gigantic woven mats on the sparklingly clean slabs. On top of these, they set knee-high tables and tiny plastic stools, the type typically used in Irish playschools. The tables were then set with a simple gas-burning cooker, surrounded by plastic bowls and chopsticks.

I had watched hungry Vietnamese labourers pass these hot-pot ladies at the end of the day and murmur their deepest dinner desires. These workers would then take a seat at the low-level tables and wait for food to materialise. From out of nowhere, I had seen plates of thinly sliced raw meat and fish conjured up, together with a dazzling array of vegetables. These were placed on the table in front of the ravenous customers, together with a saucepan of steaming stock. Into this cauldron the diners themselves threw the uncooked morsels for them to be boiled. Then, at their own leisure, the diners picked out their freshly cooked meat and veg, and gobbled the whole thing up.

After some persuasion, Pete reluctantly agreed to my dinner suggestion and we made our way down to the street. By then the torrent of daytime traffic had subsided to a trickle, and Pete was able to shepherd me safely across the tarmac to the lakeside dining area.

The first obstacle Pete faced was making himself comfortable on the miniature plastic stool. It soon became obvious that they had not been designed with six-foot Caucasian males in mind. The Vietnamese were not only smaller in stature than Pete, but infinitely more flexible. After several aborted attempts at squatting without tipping over, Pete threw the toy chair to one side, sitting instead awkwardly cross-legged on the mat. Instead of a calm yogi pose, he looked distinctly squashed and grumpy. It was not a good start to our dinner date.

'So how do we go about getting some food around here?' Pete said, hoping his raised voice would attract someone's attention. I silently looked around to see if I could spot a hot-pot lady who might come and take our order.

We didn't have to wait long before one arrived tableside. She said something in quick Vietnamese that neither of us understood.

'Ah, menu?' Pete said, tracing a square in the air with his fingertip.

Instead of a piece of paper, his request was met with a further onslaught of local lingo.

'This is hopeless,' Pete said, rapidly losing patience. As he struggled to stand up to leave, I desperately tried to remember some vocabulary from the weekly Vietnamese language lessons we'd been taking. I don't give up that easily.

'Thịt bò?' I said, imploring her to understand.

'Vâng,' she replied, before marching away from us back to her makeshift kitchen on the roadside.

'What did you just say?' Pete asked me when she was out of earshot, unsure if he should settle himself back down again.

'I just said, "beef." That's all,' I replied. 'It seems to have done the job, no?'

'As long as she doesn't think we ordered raw dog, I really don't mind what she brings,' Pete said. 'I'm starving.'

'Don't remind me of that poor animal,' I implored.

'I'm sorry,' Pete said. 'It's just that all this talk of dead dogs reminds me of my poor Reggie.'

'Reggie?' This was the first time I had heard Pete mention the name.

'My dog, when I was a teenager,' Pete said. 'He died when I was at university.'

'That was over twenty years ago,' I said, surprised that he'd still be upset by a dog's death nearly two decades on. I'd also had dogs when growing up, but my parents had taught me to handle their demise stoically.

'Yeah, but he was the best dog ever!' Pete proclaimed, just as the hot-pot lady emerged from the shadows, carrying a pot of piping hot stock. She proceeded to place it carefully between us on the gas burner before scurrying away to retrieve the rest of our order. The aromatic steam spiralled upwards, moistening Pete's cheeks ever so slightly.

'My Dad brought home this pup one day,' Pete started to explain. 'He was meant to be just a family dog. But, seeing that we lived on a farm, Reggie was soon put to work.'

I was always on a mission to find out more about my boyfriend, and this canine conversation had started him down a road I was happy to follow. 'Did Reggie herd sheep?' I asked, knowing that many rural Irish farms keep such flocks.

'No – we had a dairy farm, and my Dad also planted wheat,' Pete said. 'Da would send Reggie and me out to the fields to pick stones out of the ground so they didn't catch in the harvesting machinery.'

'I'm sure the dog was a great help moving rocks,' I said, with obvious sarcasm.

'He was!' Pete said, practically jumping out of his yogi

pose, oblivious to my attempt at humour. 'Reggie was the best company ever for stone-picking.'

The hot-pot lady returned and covered our kiddy table with produce, briefly interrupting our discussion. I carefully picked up a pair of chopsticks, intending to skilfully use them to pick and place the food she had given us into the boiling stock. Instead I fumbled with them, dropped them, then gave up entirely, opting instead to up-end the entire contents of various plates straight into the pot.

Despite nearly four weeks of practice, I had zero dexterity when it came to these wooden tools. Fortunately, Pete was seemingly too caught up in resurrected thoughts of his deceased dog to register my chopstick uselessness.

'I was sent to boarding school when I was a teenager and I had to leave Reggie at home,' Pete continued. 'One day, my Mum phoned and asked how I was doing, if I missed anyone at home.'

'And you said?'

'I think she wanted me to say that I missed her terribly and that I desperately wanted to come back to the farm,' Pete said. 'But all I did was break down and blurt out, "I really miss Reggie". I don't think my mother ever forgave me for choosing my dog over her.'

I picked up my chopsticks again, determined they would not defeat me. Anchoring them together, I pivoted the top one and made a stab at the food floating on the pot's surface. Borderline starvation rendered me successful. I pinched out strands of meat and spinach leaves, and divided them out between us. We then slurped up the contents of our bowls and emptied them within seconds.

'So why don't *we* get a dog?' I said, surprising myself with the question.

'You're not serious,' Pete said.

Pete was right, it was a ridiculous idea. Vietnam was still so new to both of us, I had yet to find a job and neither of us knew how long, or even if, our own relationship would last. Still, something felt so right about my suggestion. Maybe I craved a sense of stability, something I thought a dog could provide. On reflection, I was probably more like a crazed woman desperate for a child, certain the arrival of an infant would make her present life better.

'Why not?' I replied, before cautiously adding, 'sure we'll probably be staying here for a while?'

Much to my chagrin, Pete refused to confirm or deny our future whereabouts.

'Then again,' I said, changing tack, 'maybe we could help save one of those beasts from that mad butcher's knife at the market.'

Secretly, I missed having an animal companion of my own. I had craved a pet when I lived in Dublin, but had travelled too much for work to actually take care of one.

'No, it's not that,' Pete said, looking around for the hot-pot lady so that we could get the bill and hightail it out of there. 'I couldn't have another dog after Reggie. It would be... disloyal.'

I was taken aback; I had never heard Pete being so sentimental.

'Let me keep an eye out at least,' I said, ignoring what Pete had just said. 'If I find a dog that's suitable, maybe we could have a quick look? Well, what do you think?'

2

The Search

Despite Pete's reluctance, I resolved to find us a dog. I didn't want to fork out cash, however, because of my diminishing bank balance; I wanted one going for free who would appreciate a good home.

I soon realised my search couldn't be for just any dog. Living in an apartment, up four flights of stairs, meant we could only accommodate one relatively small in size.

I started asking around everyone I knew, but finding a dog alive and well in Hanoi is easier said than done. In desperation, I logged on to the website that all expats turn to when negotiating the various peculiarities of living in Hanoi: The *New Hanoian* is the one-stop shop for everything expats need to know, acquire or share. Via this site, we had procured crockery, located a flat, joined a running club and found a Vietnamese language teacher. As we'd sourced such a disparate array of objects on the *New Hanoian* already, I figured that it must be the place to locate one lonely, Vietnamese puppy.

I scanned the classifieds section for any dog-related ads. I saw all manner of items for sale – everything from Honda motorbikes to fish tanks to second-hand yoghurt makers. I purposefully ignored the dodgy notices from lonely men and women looking for 'good massages' and 'cuddle buddies'. I occasionally clicked on house-moving adverts, to see if a dog was also part of the clear-out deal. All too soon, however, I found I could scroll down the list no more. Dogs were not given the slightest mention despite hundreds of items listed.

Obviously the hounds of Hanoi were all happily housed, or had already been served up on a succulent platter. Even when I posted an advert explicitly labelled, 'Wanted: Dog', I failed to receive a single answer. My hound had evidently yet to learn how to turn on a computer and log on.

While my search for a canine companion reached an unforeseen impasse, Pete and I turned our attention to a more pressing concern. We were spending a small fortune on taxis to get around Hanoi's expansiveness. Pete came home one day from work, his wallet devoid of Vietnamese dong for the umpteenth time.

'We need to get a motorbike,' he said as soon as he came through the door.

'Motorbike? Do you even know how to drive one of those things?' I replied, drying my hands on a dishcloth after washing up our respective two bowls and plates. I made a mental note to go back to the *New Hanoian* and find us some more kitchenware.

'Kinda,' he said. 'Someone always had a motorbike knocking about on the farm when I was young. Actually, me and my mate Denny used to bomb around on back roads on his dirt bike. I'm sure the motorbikes here are just like the ones at home.'

I turned back to the sink and the dishes to hide from Pete my look of horror. I wanted to tell him not to be so stupid, that motorbikes are really dangerous, but I didn't want to make the classic mistake of telling my man what to do.

'Where would you even get a motorbike anyway?' I asked, concealing the fact that I'd already seen hundreds for sale on the expat website.

'The guys at work said you can hire them for like fifty US dollars a month,' Pete replied. 'The only thing is, I need to get a license first.'

'How do you get one of those?' I asked, turning around to see Pete shrugging his shoulders.

'Seeing that I'm at work all week,' Pete said, cringing ever so slightly, 'I was hoping you could figure that one out.'

The whole idea of riding a motorbike filled me with inexplicable dread. I felt I was being forced to work out how to procure a license for something I didn't want either of us to have permission to drive. However, I did accept that having a motorbike was probably the best way to get around Hanoi. All the Vietnamese seemed to have one, even tiny pretty girls who seemed far too dainty to be wearing a crash helmet and revving a throttle at traffic lights. If they could drive one, I figured that burly Pete and I could as well.

Pete found out from his colleagues the documentation we needed. Once I managed to get it all together, I made my way bright and early the following morning to the driver licensing office in downtown Hanoi. I entered the building and joined a queue, the only white girl in a long line of Asian commuters.

When I arrived at the counter, I presented the lady behind the glass with our paperwork. I gave her completed application forms, together with originals, copies and translations of our passports and Irish driving licenses. But instead of the lady accepting my paper offering with serenity and calmness, it was received with bitter consternation. She started to point angrily at various sections on the form while spitting rapid-fire Vietnamese.

My statement of 'I just would like some motorbike licenses for myself and Pete, please,' was met with even more irate words beyond my comprehension. I looked at the growing line of drivers behind me, fearing this could, if I wasn't careful, descend into an international incident.

Quickly, I dug out my phone and called Ms Phuong, my Vietnamese teacher, who would surely understand what the hell was going on. As soon as I connected, I thrust my phone in the direction of the administrator. Ms Phuong had barely the chance to introduce herself before she also received an earful of abuse. Once the lady had finished with Ms Phuong, she shoved the phone back into my face. I held up the earpiece to hear the shaky voice of my Vietnamese teacher on the other end.

'You have brought your application to the wrong office,' Ms Phuong whimpered. 'You are at the driving test centre. What the lady has been trying to tell you is that you must instead exchange your Irish licenses for Vietnamese licenses, not get new ones. For that you need different forms and you need to go to another office on the other side of town.'

I thanked Ms Phuong for her intervention, forced an apologetic smile at the administrator, and slunk my way back out on to the street. Opening the door, the full heat of Hanoi hit me with a vengeance.

Though Ms Phuong had really tried to help me back there, I felt that the majority of Vietnamese were more like the administrator, unwilling to welcome foreigners into their country. Even though I liked Vietnam, I was beginning to get the impression that I wasn't really wanted there.

After a stressful taxi ride across town, I finally located the correct office where the exchange process could take place. I was not in the door five minutes, however, when I was sent straight home with a different form that needed filling in. The following day, I marched back to the same place with every piece of paper possible, stamped with every insignia imaginable. The clerk flicked through my file of official documentation, slowly nodding his head. I allowed myself to think the impossible: that Pete and I might actually get Vietnamese driving licenses that day.

'Photo too big,' the clerk said, handing me back my file.

'What?' I said.

'Too big,' he said, pointing vigorously to the universally accepted passport-sized picture that I had taken back in Ireland. 'Need small.' He seemed satisfied with Pete's photos, which he had had specially taken at his Hanoi workplace. Pete's application was good to go, while mine was unfortunately rejected.

'But where?' I said, terribly close to dropping to my knees to beg him to change his mind.

'Photo shop,' he said, stating the obvious before diverting his attention to the customer standing behind me. Our conversation, as far as he was concerned, was done.

I staggered out of the office, about to scream with rage. Then I came to my senses: having an angry-looking mug shot on my driving license wouldn't be wise if a Vietnamese cop ever stopped me at a later date. I put on my most serene expression, and went searching for a 'photo shop.'

I accidentally visited a pharmacy, then a bakery, before finally stumbling randomly across a small Kodak processing store. Through an intricate mixture of hand-signals and jumbled-up vocabulary, I managed to explain to the shop attendant that I needed my photo taken for a driving license. He took the shot, then emailed it somewhere. Thirty minutes later, a man pulled up on a motorbike, photos in his hand. He gave them to me. I took one look and handed them straight back.

'Not me,' I said, cursing myself for thinking that something as simple as getting some passport photos would happen without a hitch in this country.

The man took a look, shook his head, and pushed them back in my direction. At his insistence, I took a second look.

'You're not serious,' I whispered, as I absorbed my Vietnamese version. I no longer had brown hair, but instead what appeared to be a jet-black mane. My skin had become as flawless as Ms Phuong's, with a slightly browner tone. The developers didn't know what to do with my blue eyes, having never encountered an iris that wasn't brown. Instead, in the photo, they had made them a piercing shade of blue, straight out of a Disney film.

I stuffed some money into his hand and glanced quickly at my watch. It was 10.20 a.m. For some inexplicable reason, the office closed at 10.30 a.m. I hadn't a second to lose. I bolted out of the shop, ploughing into pedestrians and street-vendors unfortunate enough to impede my way. To get to the photo shop I had originally crossed the street via a considerable detour, using a set of traffic lights that vehicles actually obeyed. If I was going to make it before the office closed, such an elaborate diversion was no longer feasible.

I had no option but to run the gauntlet and dash straight across the street. Miraculously, as if I were Moses himself parting the Red Sea, the motorbikes swerved to the left and right of me. In a moment of sheer desperation, after weeks of unsuccessful attempts, I had finally learned to properly cross a congested Vietnamese street.

At 10.26 a.m., I burst through the office doors, dripping in nervous sweat. I pushed my way through to the clerk who had earlier rejected me, and proudly presented him with my slightly smaller, made-in-Vietnam photos. My application was complete.

When I arrived home, Pete was overjoyed to hear that we would soon be the proud owners of brand-new Vietnamese driving licenses. I was unable to share in his excitement after the rigmarole I'd just been through, so while he went off to find a motorbike for hire, I logged back on to the *New Hanoian* to find myself a normal pedal bicycle.

Back in Ireland, I had ridden my bicycle everywhere. If it was good enough for me at home, I reasoned, it would do me just fine in Hanoi. Despite the licenses arriving a few days later, I refused to ever make use of mine. To this day in fact, I still have no idea how to drive a motorbike. Anyhow, the Vietnamese used regular pedal bikes for years before all those new-fangled motorised Hondas ever came along.

I scrolled down the website's classifieds to see if there were any bicycles for sale. I dared not raise my expectations, given the random junk people always seemed to post up, but soon glanced across a new ad that stopped my mouse-finger dead in its track. Not a bicycle, but a 'Schnoodle, going to a good home'.

Schnoodle? What the hell is that?

Out of curiosity, I opened a new window and typed 'Schnoodle' into the browser. My screen instantly filled with pictures of cute, little puppies. A schnoodle is a type of dog, a cross between a schnauzer and a poodle, and this one was looking to move house. My hound had finally worked out how to get in contact.

I hit reply to the advert immediately and told its author that I was very interested indeed. They soon emailed back with a phone number and address, telling me to contact them if I wanted to visit said schnoodle.

Pete soon arrived home with his brand-new hired motor-bike. He didn't have time, however, to show me his latest wheels.

'Pete, I've found a dog!' I said. 'Come look!' I shoved my laptop right under his nose, the cutest picture I could find of a schnoodle dog emblazoned across its display.

'That's nice,' Pete said, flopping down on the sofa. 'But it's not Reggie.' He handed me back my computer.

'You're not going to find a replica sheepdog like Reggie out here in Vietnam, you know,' I said, slightly exasperated.

'Why are you so set on getting a pet anyway?' Pete asked. 'I really don't understand.'

It was a good question. Like Pete, I was also brought up with pets around. Although we'd had dogs, my first pets were primarily of a feline kind. When I was six months old, my eldest brother dragged home a stray cat. She landed on all four proverbial feet as soon as she hit our doorstep. It wasn't long before the creature was christened 'Mother Cat' as she popped out a litter of four. My parents let us keep the entire brood, upon which we bestowed the illustrious names of Eeny, Meeny, Miny and Moe.

We worked out that Moe was a female when she too started reproducing. My siblings and I were of course overjoyed with these additional playmates, and we set about naming them in earnest. The obvious solution was to call each of these brown and white kittens after our favourite chocolates, so we ended up having a plethora of cats called Yorkie, Milky Way, Smarties and Maltesers.

After seven years of multiplying moggies, my parents wisely decided to move house. Eeny and Yorkie, now safely neutered, were the only ones allowed to come with us. The rest were rehoused or ran away, depending on how smart or wild they were.

I knew that getting a cat now would be completely out of the question: Pete only had to sniff a cat's hair from fifty paces to descend into a sneezing frenzy. He is so allergic he can barely sit in a room that a cat frequents before he has to make a hasty retreat to swallow some anti-histamines. Fortunately for Pete, although I was an established cat-lover from my early years, as a teenager I defected to the other side.

Soon after my family moved, my mother took it upon herself to rescue forlorn-looking dogs within our locality. One evening, she walked to the shop to buy some groceries. In addition to some milk and a packet of biscuits, she arrived home with a black, shaggy mongrel. 'She's obviously been abandoned,' Mum would state if we asked when the dog would be returned to its proper owners. After a week, we named the dog Bertha, and she lived with us for nearly a decade.

Once Bertha had passed, Mum heard a Labrador puppy barking in our next-door neighbour's garden. 'The poor thing,' Mum would lament. 'That dog is all on its own all day. It must be terribly lonely.' Next thing we knew, Mum had paid the neighbours a visit and proposed we look after their puppy, Max, on their behalf. Mum would do all the feeding, walking and poop-a-scooping while Max relocated under our roof. The neighbours were more than welcome to come and visit any time but were freed from any pet-minding hassle. It was a win-win situation.

With Bertha and Max, I learned to appreciate having dogs at home. They were great for security, excellent reasons to go for fresh-air walks, and brilliant cleaner-uppers of food spilt on the floor. They were also wonderful company, and though I may not have felt the undying love that Pete had for Reggie, I definitely missed having a pet about the house.

I stared at Pete in silence, wondering how I was going to convey all this to him while convincing him to change his mind.

'Just a quick look Pete,' I implored instead. 'Please.' When rational arguments fail me, my last recourse is to beg.

Pete looked back at me, his eyes softening just a little. 'All right then, just a quick look. But only if we take the motor-bike,' he said, before swiftly adding, 'okay if I drive?'

3

The Perfect Hound

Pete handed me a helmet. 'Put that on,' he said as he shoved on his own headgear, fastening the buckle under his chin with a satisfactory click.

I looked at the hard hat he had just given me. It was red, shiny and round, and I instinctively knew it was not safe. 'Where did you get this thing? Some ex-Vietnamese Army store?' There was no padding inside it to cushion my head if we had any sort of collision. The strap was so flimsy it was obvious it would shred instantly on impact.

'It's fine,' Pete replied. 'I promise, I won't crash. You just need to wear something on your head so we don't get stopped by the cops.'

Even when I put on the tin cap, I remained unconvinced. I looked at Pete, who had by now mounted his motor and was ready to take off. Pete's shape and size were all wrong for the vehicle. He looked like a giant, cumbersome bear about to ride a tiny tricycle around a circus ring.

'Look, do you want to see this dog or not?' Pete said,

revving the engine impatiently. When he put it that way, I saw no option but to join him on his moped.

I hoisted my left leg over the rear seat. It took a while to find somewhere safe to place my feet so I didn't scorch the skin off my shins on the bike's hot exhaust pipe. Once perfectly balanced, I gave Pete the all clear to turn the throttle – and we were off to see the schnoodle.

I held on for dear life as Pete drove up the main road. My vice-like grasp proved unnecessary. As promised, Pete maintained a sedate pace, executing every manoeuvre with utmost care.

The swarm of bikes around us still frazzled my frantic nerves. I had the distinct impression that we were holding up the traffic, as to my left and right motorbikes blasted past us at break-neck speeds. We obviously needed some more practice at this if we were going to blend in with the locals.

Pete and I both breathed a sigh of relief as we reached our final destination still intact. We had arrived outside a house in the popular Tây Hồ residential area. There was nothing extraordinary about the place, just another home in the concrete jungle where expats seemed to congregate. I knocked on the door, wondering if the response would be a friendly bark. Instead, a slim blonde lady in her mid-forties opened the door to us.

'You must be Pete and Moire,' she said, in a distinctive Australian drawl. 'I'm Susan. You've come to see Mister T?'

'If Mister T is the dog in the ad?' I replied.

Susan was standing in the doorway, blocking our view into her home. I strained my head around her, trying to see if this supposed hound was for real. There was a distinct possibility that Susan was another crazy expat who had come to Vietnam to escape a dismal life elsewhere, and the dog was a figment of her imagination.

Just as I started to lose hope of acquiring a new pet, I heard a distinctively canine yelp from over her shoulder.

'Mister T, stop chewing that thing!' Susan shouted, forgetting us as she ran back into her house. Pete and I followed, hot on her heels, then stopped as we caught sight of a tiny white hairy thing lying on the floor, tearing apart a tea towel.

'Sorry, he's just a puppy,' Susan said. 'Reckon he's about three months old.' She grabbed the rag from Mister T, then handed it to a young boy who had materialised from upstairs.

'This is my son, Oliver,' she said. 'Oliver, this is Pete and Moire. They've come to see Mister T.'

Oliver said nothing. He seemed subdued by his mother's news.

'Is Mister T your dog, Oliver?' I asked her silent son. As much as I wanted a pet, I was not interested in separating a boy from his beloved dog.

Susan quickly intervened. 'No, Oliver already has a dog, don't you hun? He's got a Labrador, Spike.'

As if on cue, Spike entered stage right, plonking himself at Oliver's feet.

This could get complicated, I thought.

'Let me tell you the whole story,' Susan said, motioning us to sit down. She pointed to a leather sofa, positioned beside a window, on which Pete and I both took a seat. All around us were cartons stacked haphazardly and items covered in bubble wrap.

A visit to an animal rescue centre to adopt a stray would

have been so much less complicated. Or maybe I should have just gone back to the butcher's stall and asked him how much for an un-slaughtered dog.

'Oliver and I are planning to move to Thailand next month,' Susan started to explain. That was why the place was half-packed up into various cardboard boxes. 'I've already done all the paperwork so that we can bring Spike with us, but it really costs a fortune when you add up the flight and vet bills. I can't afford to bring two dogs, so that's why I'm looking for someone who will take Mister T off our hands.'

I looked over at Oliver to see his reaction. He had the tea towel that Susan had just rescued and was dangling it precariously over both his dogs' muzzles. Mister T was the only one taking the bait, jumping up and down like a mad thing, trying to snatch it back off his young master. The pup showed absolutely no interest in Pete or me. If this was the hound that wanted to live with us, then he really was playing hard to get.

'Would it not be cheaper to take Mister T instead of Spike?' I said, trying to help Susan out. I had heard that dog importation charges depend on weight: smaller dogs cost less to transport.

'We've had Spike for years,' Susan said. 'There's no way we'd leave him behind. Mister T only arrived a few weeks ago when we rescued him from a barbecue street-food stand.'

'You're not serious!' I said.

'Yeah, I was just wandering through the Old Quarter, when I saw the cutest white thing struggling to get out of a cage outside a kerbside restaurant. I crouched down for a closer look, only for the poor pup to start scratching at the wire like mad trying to get out, whimpering as if its life depended on it.'

'The poor thing!' I said, eager to hear this dramatic tale. 'How did you manage to rescue him?'

'I just asked one of the stall employees how much he wanted for the dog, gave him a couple of dong then asked him not to grill the animal,' Susan replied, matter of fact. 'Then I brought Mister T home.'

This revelation changed everything.

I had already seen many dogs caged up outside barbecue stalls on the streets of Hanoi, three or four of them thrust into a cage that should not even legally contain one. I had wondered if these dogs were destined for the dinner table like lobsters in a seafood-restaurant tank, ready to be picked out by a selective diner. Maybe I should have just wandered around those restaurants like Susan and ordered myself a take-away puppy straight from the waiter.

Most of these confined dogs seemed to be of one type: brown and black, of medium size, with sufficient meat on them to make up a meal. I glanced over to Mister T to see if he fitted the bill. He was small, white and fluffy. Judging by his miniature size and shape, he wouldn't even qualify as an hors d'oeuvre.

'Are you sure he was going to be eaten?' I said, wondering if Susan had inadvertently snatched someone's beloved pet.

'I wasn't going to wait around to find out!' Susan said, angrily raising her voice.

'No, no, what I mean is, it's great you rescued Mister T,' I said backpedalling at speed. 'It's really such a shame you can't keep him.'

Although I was busy chatting with Susan, I wasn't really listening to her. My attention was fixed instead on what was playing out behind her. Mister T was lying on his back, attempting to play fight with Spike, who was idly pawing him away. Oliver was perched on a seat, watching the brawl quietly from above. Spike looked like he didn't have the time or energy to indulge in play with this exuberant pup. In fact, it seemed Spike couldn't wait to get rid of this latest addition to the household.

I glanced over at Pete, who had been noticeably silent throughout our stay. I had no idea what he thought about this dog or the crazy situation I'd dragged him into.

'Listen Susan, thanks for showing us Mister T,' I said, deciding to take the initiative and wrap up our visit while we were still ahead. 'He looks like a great dog. I think it's best that Pete and I talk this over, and we'll get back to you if we decide to take him.'

Pete and I stood up and moved towards the door.

'That's no problem,' Susan said. 'You'd really be helping us out if you give him a home, but I totally understand if you can't.'

We were of course no sooner out the door than I was demanding Pete's opinion.

'He's a lovely looking dog,' Pete admitted, as he went to put back on his bike helmet. 'Awkward situation they're in.'

'Don't you want to help them out?' I said. 'Someone's got to take him.'

'Let's go home and think about it,' Pete said as he mounted his motorbike and turned the ignition key. I continued to stand there on the roadside, my red shiny helmet dangling aimlessly from my hand.

'No Pete,' I said, suddenly refusing to move from the spot. 'I think we should go back in there right now and take him.'

'Are you serious?'

I had never been more serious in my life. 'Think about it, Pete,' I replied, trying to explain to him why my gut was telling me to take Mister T straight home with us. 'It took me ages to find a pet that we could potentially adopt. And Mister T looks like the perfect size for our apartment.'

Pete stayed seated on his motorbike. Its engine idled for what seemed like forever beneath him.

'There are so few dogs available,' I continued, trying not to plead. 'Someone is bound to rock up later today and take him away before we come back again.'

Pete had never seen me this adamant before. I hoped his reluctance to commit was about the dog, not because he didn't like seeing this new belligerent side of me.

After what seemed like an eternity, Pete turned off the engine. 'Okay,' he said, resignation in his tone. 'We'll take him home, if you insist.'

My excitement at being a brand new pet-owner was, however, short-lived.

'How are we going to bring Mister T back to the flat?' I said, motioning to Pete's wheels. 'There's no way I can carry home a dog I hardly know on the back of a bike that you can barely drive.' Thoughts of Mister T putting up a fight and squirming out of my arms came to mind. It would be so easy for him to fly off the motorbike at full throttle and become traffic fodder.

Pete and I agreed that we would drive home and ditch

the bike, then come back to Susan's in a taxi. Whether a Vietnamese taxi driver would permit a live dog in the back of his car was something we'd just have to deal with later.

I ran back to Susan's door and banged on it once more.

'We'll take Mister T,' I shouted as soon as I heard her unlock, before adding, 'if that's okay with you?' As soon as I saw Susan's expression, I realised she was pleased with this news. 'How much would you like for him?' I asked, assuming that payment was required. I'd quickly learned that everything in Vietnam comes at a price, but I figured, for Mister T, it would be worth parting with some hard-earned cash.

'No, it's fine,' Susan said. 'You don't need to pay me for him.' On hearing those words, Oliver seemed like he was finally going to speak. Before he could say a word, Susan shot him a glance, barely perceptible to the eye, which made him immediately shut up. I couldn't help feeling a little sorry for the kid. It seemed like he didn't get much say in this household. It was all a little awkward.

I tried to insist on paying something, but Susan refused to budge. Mister T was going for free, whether I liked it or not.

'Well then, maybe we can buy something off you that you're not bringing to Thailand?' I suggested as way of compromise. 'Are you selling any kitchenware by any chance?'

Susan happily produced a range of cups and plates that fit the bill. Pete, meanwhile, spotted a potted plant and a beanbag that he planned to deposit in our sitting room. We added Mister T to our final purchase list before we drove off at high speed to drop our motorbike and pick up a taxi to transport our newly acquired goods home.

Within the hour we were back at Susan's, this time with a bottle of wine in hand. I had convinced Pete that we needed to at least give *something* to Susan in exchange for her rescue dog. Susan was ecstatic with the unexpected gift. She waved us inside, unpacked some wine glasses and poured us all a round.

Over our afternoon tipple, Susan gave us a rundown of Mister T's preferences.

'He likes to eat tinned tuna,' she told us, giving us a couple of spare cans. 'And this is his favourite chew toy,' she continued, handing me a tooth-marked tennis ball attached to a mangled rope. Mister T immediately sensed his beloved plaything was relocating and jumped up from where he was snoozing to scamper over to my feet. I hung the ball over his jaws until he playfully grabbed hold of it. He tugged on the toy with mini growls, trying to slay the thing. It was the first time Mister T had come this close to me and we both seemed quite at ease.

'He's still a puppy,' Susan explained, refilling our wine glasses, whose initial contents we had already drained. 'Don't worry, we've already toilet trained him, so he won't make a mess in your place. Just put a piece of newspaper down on the ground and he'll do his business on it.'

I was surprised how calm and obedient Mister T was given that he was technically a street dog. Maybe he was not wild or feral because he had been rescued so young and had been living in a loving home.

Once we had finished the bottle, Pete and I decided it was time to hightail it back to our flat. As I stood up with Mister T's belongings, the pup practically jumped into my arms.

Mister T seemed to instinctively know he was on the move again.

'So how much do we owe you?' I said, gesturing to the mishmash of belongings we'd just purchased from her. But before Susan could utter the total, Oliver intervened.

After his enforced silence, had Oliver finally found his voice? Had he worked up the nerve to tell me that Mister T was staying firmly put with them, and that the deal was definitely off?

'That'll be fifty-two dollars,' he said, all of a sudden standing tall before me, extending his hand with a confidence that had been noticeably lacking all day.

It took me a while to process what he had just said.

I counted out the bills one by one, wondering if I should ask him to reduce his asking price. But when I looked up and saw Oliver's confident, business-like face, I instinctively knew that he didn't do discounts.

Oliver's face beamed broadly as dollars hit his palm. It was amazing to see in that instant the transformative effect money can have, even on sulky teenagers. Maybe that was why he had been so depressed-looking throughout our visit: his mum had given Mister T away for free, when in Oliver's mind he could probably have made a small fortune from this doggie deal.

Our taxi was still parked outside, despite our impromptu drinks. Pete bundled our household goods into the back seat of the vehicle, while I remained standing on the kerb, trying to conceal Mister T as best as I could. When it became apparent that hiding him wouldn't work, I got into the taxi, placing the dog brazenly on my lap. The driver looked in his rear mirror and caught sight of his canine customer. I pointed to Mister T while nodding my head, half-questioning, half-stating, 'It's okay?'

Much to my surprise, our driver barely batted an eyelid.

With Mister T now on my knees, I could finally get a closer look at him. Susan had said that he was a schnoodle, and he indeed resembled the schnoodle dogs that I had seen on the Internet. He didn't have the tight, curly coat that I would have expected from a poodle mix. Instead Mister T's hair was long and straight, with just a hint of a wave. He had a flowing horse's mane to serve as a tail, and his ears were soft and covered with beautiful white-beige locks. Mister T was the most adorable thing I'd ever seen, apart from his mouth. His teeth were all crooked from an obvious lack of dental treatment, and his lower jaw jutted out, crying for orthodontic care.

Despite these oral defects, I was glad that we had finally acquired a pet. I was excited to bring him home and begin looking after him.

'So what are we going to call him?' Pete said as we sped our way back to the flat.

'What's wrong with Mister T?' I said, absent-mindedly stroking our new dog.

'I don't see much of a resemblance with that actor from the A-team,' Pete said.

I took a second look at our mutt. Pete did have a point. 'Have you any better suggestions?'

Pete took a moment. He looked like he was trawling through his contacts list. 'The dog does have a fine head of white hair,' he said. 'Remind you of anyone we both know?'

I thought long and hard. 'You're not talking about Tom what's-his-name?' Tom was a manager at the organisation where Pete and I had first met and started dating. The resemblance was striking.

'Uncanny, wouldn't you say?' Pete replied, trying hard to suppress a grin.

So, Tom the dog, formerly known as Mister T, came to live with us in Hanoi.

4

Puppy Trouble

The taxi left the three of us right outside our apartment block. I stepped out of the car as Pete ran up the steps to unlock the main front door. I was still holding Tom tightly, a warm bundle of sweaty dog hair in my bare arms. Despite my fears, Tom hadn't tried to jump out of the taxi and flee back to his former family. He seemed quite content to go with the flow and see where he ended up this time.

I put Tom back on to his feet before we climbed up the four long flights of stairs to our apartment. Tom skipped up the steps without looking back, seemingly curious about this new adventure. Pete slid open our front door as I in turn royally welcomed Tom to his new abode.

'Come on in Tom,' I told our newest household member. 'Make yourself at home.'

Pete and I took off our shoes before entering our home, a useful custom we had both picked up in Vietnam. It meant our floor was pristine, devoid of the dirt that can be picked up while tramping around outside on the dusty streets. Wanting to keep our floor spick and span, I went hunting for some newspaper. As Susan advised, I laid a sheet down at the entrance to our balcony, a spot that was visible from our entire open-plan first level.

'Here you go, Tom,' I said, pointing to the tabloid. 'You can pee and poo on that.'

Tom didn't even acknowledge my gesture. Instead he started checking out his new pad. He wandered over to the sofa and gave its legs a good smell, then made his way over to the TV and its table and trotted the entire way around them. He swept past the newspaper at the balcony exit without the slightest sniff before checking out the dining and kitchen area.

'Do you think he's hungry?' Pete said, as we watched him licking the tiles directly beneath the bread bin.

'It's worth a try,' I said.

I picked up one of the cans of tinned tuna Susan had given us. Finding an old bowl left behind by a previous tenant, I scooped the fish into the dish and placed it at Tom's feet. Tom stuck his nose into it and swiftly turned away.

'Nope,' I said. 'Doesn't appear to be hungry.'

Pete stood there, staring at the pup we had just allowed to invade our personal space. I was just waiting for Pete to ask me, 'So what do we do now?'

Thankfully, Tom gave us a hint. I had accidentally dropped his ball-on-a-rope toy on the floor on our arrival. Tom proceeded to pounce on it, and with theatrical growls, tried to shake the living daylights out of it.

'Come on, boy,' I said, 'that's the spirit. Do you want to play?'

I bent down to grab the toy out of Tom's mouth, but our

new dog was having none of it. With a quick-footed shimmy, he slipped between my legs and darted below the sofa, safely out of arm's reach.

Tom's playfulness served to lighten the mood a little.

I had been really worried that Tom wouldn't be happy moving house again within such a short space of time, but as I saw him hiding under our couch, ball in his mouth, tail wagging wildly, I knew he was young enough to start afresh with us.

Pete and I eventually relaxed and went about our usual weekend routine. This entailed cracking open a bottle of chilled white wine, in addition to the one Pete and I had already downed at Susan's, and savouring it on the balcony. We took our seats outside on a hot and humid afternoon. Pete was pouring me a cool glass of Chardonnay when I noticed something amiss back inside the flat, in the sitting room.

'Did you spill the wine?' I asked, pointing to a puddle I had just spotted on the tiles.

'How could I have?' he replied. 'This is a new bottle. I just opened it out here right now.'

I looked at Pete suspiciously as I got up from my seat and walked over to the liquid that had sprung up out of nowhere.

'You're joking me,' I said, recoiling swiftly from the stench. A pungent ammonia smell stung the back of my mouth. 'Tom, did you do this?'

'What?' Pete shouted from outside. 'What's he done?'

'That's dog pee,' I said, pointing to the wet patch. 'Tom, did you pee on the floor? Did you not see the newspaper?'

Tom was still crouching beneath the sofa, exactly where I had left him. His tail was wagging softly as if nothing had transpired in the interim. Despite the fact that Tom was the obvious culprit, I detected not a hint of shame. So much for being toilet trained!

'Oh God, that's disgusting,' Pete said, coming in to investigate. 'Quick, clean it up!'

I knew I must immediately heed Pete's command. Pete had a highly sensitive nose and could gag at the slightest odour. If I wanted to keep Tom as our pet, I had to get rid of the spillage quickly.

I grabbed reams of kitchen roll and a bottle of bleach, and scrubbed the tiles clean again.

'Tom, Tom, come here doggie,' I said once I was finished, crouching down and patting my knee to beckon him. Tom edged himself out from under the settee, and approached me with caution.

I patted his head and ruffled his ears. He was only young; it wasn't his fault.

'Now Tom, if you want to pee again, it's on the…news… paper,' I said, physically leading him over to the printed material. I pushed Tom's snout deep into the headlines, and silently begged him to comprehend. Pete meanwhile watched my instructional session from afar, seated back out on the balcony.

I wondered how long he was going to put up with this puppy piddling before he escorted Tom to the nearest deli.

I rejoined Pete outside and went to take a drink of the wine he had poured me. I took one look at the yellow liquid in the glass and put it back down again. Its resemblance to dog urine was too uncanny for me to now take a mouthful.

'Sorry about that,' I said, feeling responsible for the puppy's actions.

'It's okay,' Pete said. 'But let's make sure it doesn't happen again.'

'How? If he's not already toilet trained, I've no idea how to teach him.'

Pete twisted his glass for a moment. My guess was that he didn't know either.

'Tom should live out here on the balcony then,' Pete said. 'At least then if he pees or poos, it's all done outdoors.'

I was taken aback. What was the point in having a dog who was not allowed inside?

Growing up, all my dogs were firmly part of the family. They were allowed to roam freely throughout the house, both upstairs and down. When we wanted to sit and watch TV, we would tell our dogs to push over if they took up the whole of the sofa. Some of them would follow my mum into the bathroom and happily sit by her side, waiting for her to finish peeing.

Pete's dogs, on the other hand, were working animals, and their home was definitely outside. Their kennels were old converted oil drums located in the recesses of an abandoned shed, with a shred of blanket thrown in for warmth. God forbid any of them had ever ventured into the farmhouse and tried to curl up by the kitchen fire.

Despite our difference in opinion, I sensed I didn't have much say in this decision. Seeing that I didn't want to fight with Pete, if I wanted Tom to be our pet, this dog had to relocate.

I called Tom outside to the balcony. Obediently, he jogged up to my side. But as soon as he crossed the balcony sill, he started panting wildly.

'It's too hot for him out here,' I said. It was thirty degrees Celsius in the shade, too high for a hairy hound like Tom. 'Look, he's struggling to cool down.'

Despite my protests, Tom soon found his own solution to the heat Pete insisted he lived in. Tom wandered over to the potted plant that Pete had brought back from Susan's. I had watered it as soon as we arrived, and the excess liquid had drained straight through its dry soil. Tom walked over to the pot and plonked himself in the pool of surplus water lying at its side. His tongue was still lolling out of his mouth, but at least his undercoat was damp.

'Problem solved,' said Pete.

I sat there, staring angrily at Pete. How could he be so cruel to such an unfortunate little puppy? He must have been horrible to that Reggie, who Pete swore so adamantly he'd loved.

If Pete treated poor animals this way, what would happen if we decided to stay together, maybe one day get married and have kids? Would he also force them to live outside so he didn't have to deal with their vomit or dirty nappies?

Pete finished the wine that I had refused to drink. He seemed oblivious to my fury.

'Fancy watching some TV?' he said after a while. I agreed, reckoning that TV would be a safe and conciliatory way to spend the rest of our day. Pete and I both got up and started moving inside to plonk in front of the telly. Tom stood up to join us too.

'No Tom,' Pete said, using his foot to block Tom's path. 'You stay out here.' Pete slid closed the glass doors. A physical barrier separated us.

Tom peered through the window, wagging his tail with apprehension, seemingly confused by this invisible barricade. I willed him to go back to his puddle and settle down, but instead, he lifted his paw, and gave the door a scratch. Nothing. He lifted his other paw, and delivered another scratch. Still no movement in the barrier. Soon he was standing erect on his two hind legs, frantically trying to tunnel himself a way through the impenetrable glass door.

I watched Tom trapped on the other side of the glass, caught in a dilemma. If I let Tom in, Pete would be pissed off. But if I kept Tom outside, I doubted Pete would tolerate the incessant scraping-on-glass sound for much longer.

Eventually Pete thankfully made the call on my behalf. 'For God's sake, just let him in. But if that dog uses this place again as his personal toilet, I swear he's going back to Susan in the morning.'

Tom trotted over to us on the sofa and sat down beside us at its feet. My hand soon slid down, Tom quickly repositioning himself in the perfect place for me to pet him while I watched TV. Tom was so soft and fluffy and such lovely, easy company. He wasn't a bother at all. I couldn't believe how someone could be so cruel as to cage him up, and how fortunate we had been to find him.

Night-time thankfully came without further incident, and it was soon time for us all to go to bed.

'So where is Tom going to stay?' Pete asked me, as he locked up the flat. I didn't know if this was a trick question, to find out who I was sleeping with that night.

'I assume he'll sleep down here in the sitting room,' I said, confirming that Pete was still top dog.

'Good,' Pete said. 'I'm not interested in letting Tom share a bed with us.'

Fortunately, there was a suitable obstacle between the sitting room on the first level and our bedroom above, namely a steep spiral wooden staircase. Its twists and turns would easily impede any lonely puppy trying to sneak into our boudoir. With our sleeping arrangements agreed for the night, Pete and I bid farewell to Tom and left him alone downstairs.

The plan seemed to work. Once it was lights out, I heard Tom mounting the first step, his sharp claws scrabbling around on the hard wood. But the steep climb to the subsequent step proved too much, and I heard him dropping back to the floor tiles. After a few unsuccessful attempts, he gave up and nodded off.

The next morning, I descended the staircase to see Tom happily positioned at its feet. He was wagging his tail, seemingly glad to see me. It was so ridiculously cute. I bent down and ruffled his coat.

'Have a good night, doggie?' I asked him. His happy demeanour seemed to indicate the answer was yes.

I did a quick scan of the floor to see if he had had any more accidents. There were no puddles in sight, but still I couldn't help noticing the place smelled distinctly of dog pee. I walked over to the newspaper and checked its contents, but it was also devoid of debris.

'Good doggie,' I said, patting his back, assuming he had now remembered his toilet training. 'Want to go do your business outside?'

I latched on his lead and brought him down to the main

street. The lake outside our flat was calm and still that morning, a sheet of mirrored glass. Its waters hid its history well. Trúc Bạch is the lake where United States senator John McCain was captured when his plane was shot down during the Vietnam War. The North Vietnamese later incarcerated him in the infamously cruel Hỏa Lò Prison for more than five years, or the 'Hanoi Hilton' as the Americans nicknamed it.

Despite trundling up and down the lake's banks for ten minutes, Tom refused to do anything. I knew there was no way his baby-sized bowels could be holding on for this long. A terrible feeling swept over me that Tom *had* used our home as his personal toilet the previous night, relieving himself on the tiles. The warm Asian night air would have dried up the puddles, but the stench remained.

'Quick Tom,' I shouted as soon as the penny dropped. 'I've got to spray some air freshener before Pete gets up.'

I tugged on his lead and dragged Tom back to the flat.

We arrived too late: Pete was already up and downstairs, and he didn't look happy at all.

While we were gone Pete had opened the sliding doors and the familiar smell of Hanoi had flooded our sitting room. The smell of dog urine had miraculously wafted away on the breeze. Was Tom about to receive a momentary reprieve? And if Tom was already off the hook, why did Pete look so grumpy?

I slipped off my shoes and unlatched Tom's lead. 'Hey there,' I said casually. 'I just gave Tom a quick walk.'

Pete seemed uninterested in my morning's activities. Instead his gaze was fixed on our sitting-room floor.

'Tom didn't do anything last night,' I said, lying through

46

my teeth. 'Yesterday must have been a one-off accident.'

Pete stayed ominously silent.

Had I missed something when I came down this morning? Had Tom really messed up big time?

'What ... is ... that?' Pete said, pointing to something at my feet. I bent down to take a closer look before picking the offending item up off the floor. It was a white ball of silky, smooth fluff. On closer inspection I realised it was a tangled tuft of Tom fur.

'It's just dog hair,' I replied, relieved that it was only something small. Nothing really to worry about.

'It's EVERYWHERE!' Pete screamed.

I stood up straight and surveyed the house from above. Oh God, Pete was right. Thanks to the breeze blowing in from outside, dog hair was now drifting across our floor like wind-blown tumbleweed.

'But sure, that's no problem,' I said. 'You're only allergic to cat hair.'

Pete was standing there with both hands on his hips. It looked like he had no interest in testing out my theory about his range of allergies.

I sighed. Pete could be such a pain at times. Why couldn't he just accept that there are always teething problems with new pets? I felt like I was on the cusp of having to choose between my new dog and my relatively new boyfriend. Was I going to have to get rid of one of them so that I could live in peace with the other?

At that moment, I just wasn't sure which one would be the least stressful to live with long term.

'Don't worry. I'll pick it up,' I said, getting down on all

fours. Now was not the time to start a fight, I thought. Spying the multiple fluff balls I realised, whatever Tom had been up to the previous night, he had definitely had a good time and really let his hair down. Pete refused to assist in this clear-up, monitoring my cleaning from afar.

His silence weighed heavy on my mind. I couldn't help wondering whether having a pet was going to work for us. It was a shame – Tom was such a cute dog. It wasn't his fault that he moulted or couldn't control his bladder.

Despite all this, I couldn't help feeling responsible for him. I had promised Susan that I would take care of her beloved Mister T. With this thought in mind, I resolved to help Tom clean up his act, so that he would be forever welcome in my home.

5

Toilet Training

The next morning, I settled down in front of my computer. The weekend was over and Pete was thankfully back at the office. It meant that I had a full five days to figure out how to toilet train Tom before Pete was forced to spend another weekend in close confines with the dog.

I typed into Google, 'how to toilet train a puppy'. A glut of suggestions loaded. I read that I was supposed to bring Tom outside at least every two hours. I then needed to say a cue word like 'toilet' or 'clean' that told Tom that it was time to go. Once he successfully urinated, I was to give him a treat to serve as encouragement for the next time.

It all sounded easy enough. Really, what could go wrong with such a simple, logical plan?

I led Tom down to the street and crossed over to the lakeside. I then directed Tom to the nearest tree that was sprouting up between the pavement slabs. Motorbikes whizzed past us, coming a bit too close for comfort. I prayed their engine noise didn't distract Tom from his all-important business.

Tom sniffed the tree I brought him to, then the concrete that enclosed its roots. He proceeded to encircle the entire trunk, before sitting firmly down on his backside, panting. His pink tongue hung lazily out of his mouth, like a backpacker who had had too much cheap Tiger beer. I was sweating too, from the morning heat that was already proving oppressive. I might have also been sweating from the stress of Tom's training. By this stage, I was probably more nervous than the dog about this whole toileting business.

'Toilet Tom,' I said. 'Tom, Tom, toilet.'

Tom did nothing. I stood there wondering what next to do. I shoved my hand deep into my pocket and jangled the dog treats that I was ready to give Tom once he had managed to do his business in the great outdoors.

'No toilet, no treat,' I said to Tom, wondering if bribery would be a better strategy.

Tom was oblivious to the deal I was proposing. He was too busy licking up scraps he had just found on the sidewalk from the previous night's hot-pot dinners.

I stayed outside for over an hour, suffering more and more from the heat. After a while, I plonked myself down on the pavement and just sat beside Tom. I patted his head, stroked his back, then tickled his underbelly, caresses that went down with Tom very well. For a dog that had been caged up, he was exceedingly affectionate. In the end, it was actually kind of nice hanging out with Tom waiting for something to appear from his rear. Despite my delaying tactics though, still nothing materialised.

'Come on, boy,' I said, disappointed I had failed so spectacularly. 'Let's go home.' Tom stood up and jogged back to the flat with me, oblivious to the minor mayhem he was causing.

As soon as we got home, I positioned myself once more in front of my computer screen on the kitchen table, while Tom retreated to beside the sofa. I was sure there was some trick I was missing. Maybe I was meant to make him drink loads of water just before we went outside, or perhaps my cue word was wrong.

I was so busy clicking links that I failed to see the puddle materialising under Tom's hind legs on the other side of the room. We had not been back in the house five minutes when Tom, amazingly, remembered how to urinate.

'Nooooooo!' was the only sound I could muster up when I saw the pool. Why didn't I force Tom to stay outside for just a few minutes more? I was so angry with myself for my impatience.

'Well, there's no point in bringing you outside now,' I said to Tom, once I had calmed myself down. 'Let's try again in two hours' time. Promise me you'll pee outside then?'

Tom lay down beside my feet, and curled up into a tight ball. Maybe he was feeling the pressure to perform, when he was still too young to know how. I felt so sorry for him. It was not his fault that Susan had said he was toilet trained, so high expectations were set.

While I waited for Tom's bladder to replenish, I did some more Internet searches and found an organisation named Dog Training Ireland. Surely someone based back in my home country would understand my plight. I emailed them with my dilemma, outlining what I had done thus far. I couldn't help but also relate to them my increasing levels of frustration with this toilet training deadlock.

Soon enough, they got back to me, clearly worried by my correspondence's tone. They confirmed that what I was doing should, in theory, work.

'I would suggest you attend a Puppy Socialisation course as soon as you can,' Tara from Dog Training Ireland told me in her reply. I must have forgotten to inform her that Tom and I were actually living in Vietnam. It would prove difficult to attend one of her Dublin-based socialisation courses, several thousand miles away from Hanoi. Tara was really trying to help me out, God love her, and delivered one final suggestion. 'If you feel that you cannot commit the time needed to toilet train, chew train, and obedience train this puppy, then do let us know and we can help find him a suitable home.'

I nearly fell off my seat laughing. I'd need to be desperate to transport Tom all the way round the world and back to Ireland just so that he could be rehoused.

It did, however, make me imagine a day when I could bring Tom back to Ireland and take him for walkies there. I'd been struck by bouts of homesickness lately, wishing that the Irish government hadn't made such a mess of its economy, forcing me into such drastic exile. The thought of home was too much for me to handle though, so I packed away that dream reluctantly and returned to the job at hand.

Despite the hilarity of Tara's rehousing suggestion, she did inform me of a more serious issue: she told me, given Tom's age, it might take a further two months before Tom was actually house trained.

I didn't have two months! Pete would never tolerate 'accidents' for that long. Damn it, *I* would never last that long.

I delved back into the Internet to find a quick and dirty

solution. After an extensive search, I happened upon a technique called crate training. It was based on the premise that dogs refuse to dirty the place where they sleep. Using this technique, I would have to keep Tom enclosed in a crate when he was in the flat. Then, every hour, I would take him outside so that he could relieve himself there.

I found a pet shop close by where I was able to purchase a crate that suited Tom's exact shape and size. Taking it back to the flat, however, I was wracked with guilt. Susan originally found Tom holed up in a crate, I reminded myself. Was it not cruel to lock up Tom once again after his escape? Would it not make him have horrific flashbacks of that traumatic event?

In the end, however, I concluded I had little choice. Tom had to be toilet trained or risk getting forever kicked out of our house, to fend for himself.

My anxiety levels were on red alert as soon as I entered the flat. Already I had concocted an elaborate plan in my mind for how I was going to trick Tom to enter the box. Putting it into action immediately, I placed the container down on the ground and opened wide its gate.

'Tom, Tom, where are you?' I cooed in the most happy-go-lucky voice I could muster up. Tom appeared out from under the dining table and, obedient beyond belief, jogged over to my side. I didn't have time to explain to Tom that this new crate was his friend. I didn't even have to grab Tom by the collar and thrust him deep into the box. Instead, Tom dove straight into the container head first, practically slamming the gate shut behind him.

I bent down to see what Tom was up to in there. All I

could see was a white mound of fur curled up comfortably at the back of the cage. A little tail tapped its plastic bottom rhythmically. He seemed . . . happy.

'Remind you of your old home, Tom?' I said, patting the box's roof. Maybe he wasn't all *that* traumatised by his puppy days spent banged up.

When Pete came home from work later that day, he immediately asked after Tom.

'He's in the crate over there,' I said. 'Been in there all day, to be honest. It's meant to help toilet train him.'

Pete crouched down and peered deep inside. 'Tom, are you all right in there? Want to come out and play?'

'Already tried that,' I replied. Two hours had already passed since I had arrived home with the crate and Tom had shown no intention of leaving his new, cosy abode. Even when I did extract him later from the box, just before bedtime, Tom still refused to pee outside. I couldn't help wondering where all his food and water was going, as the crate was spotlessly clean inside. How a puppy could hold everything in for this long remained a mystery to me.

Pete and I agreed to leave Tom in his crate overnight, and to bring him outside again first thing in the morning. Tom seemed happy enough to kip right there in the box, so we switched off the lights and locked up.

If I thought Tom would be happy living in his crate forever more, I was tragically mistaken. At 1 a.m., I was awakened abruptly by what could only be described as wolf-like howling.

'Good Jesus,' Pete said, waking up with a start ten minutes later. 'What's that noise?'

'It's Tom,' I said, trying hard to hide my annoyance. I despised anything that disturbed my beauty sleep. 'Ignore him. I'm sure he'll stop in a while.'

Tom didn't stop. In fact, the howling only seemed to get louder.

'Do you think he's all right?' Pete asked after a few more verses of Tom's soulful rendition.

'I'm sure he is,' I said, desperate to get back to sleep. 'Just ignore him, I'm sure he'll calm down eventually.'

Instead of Pete ignoring Tom, his concern seemed to only increase in tandem with the dog's crescendos.

'Do you think I should go down and stay with him?' Pete said, now sitting bolt upright in bed.

'You're not serious?' I replied, refusing point-blank to get up. 'No, don't go downstairs. Then Tom will know that, if he howls, he gets your attention, and then he'll howl even more when you leave.'

Pete thought about it for a minute, then slowly lay back down again.

'It's just that, he sounds so...lonely,' Pete said, rolling away in our bed, turning his back on me. Through the shadows I stared, bewildered, at this hulk of a man lying beside me. Since when did he start caring about Tom's emotional needs? I thought Pete was on the verge of throwing this hound out of the house. Surely this night-time rendition was going to be the last straw?

After a few more minutes, Tom's howling thankfully stopped, and silence was restored to our household.

When I got up the next morning, I was unsure what part of the previous night's events I should be more disturbed by. Should I have been worried that we had a noisy dog who could interrupt our nocturnal sleep? Or should I have been alarmed by this sentimental part of Pete that had appeared unexpectedly in the dead of night? I thought I was the one who had the soft spot for dogs. Was Pete the real dog lover in our household?

'You must be bursting,' I said to Tom as I opened up his gate. I found Tom's lead and snapped it to his collar. Tom skipped down each step behind me, his little legs struggling to keep up with my long stride.

I stopped in front of the main door and pulled its key out of my pocket. Tom patiently stood to attention at my feet while I set about turning the lock. I looked down at Tom, and was just about to open up when I saw a patch of yellow liquid growing on the tiled floor below.

'No Tom, no, no, no,' I shouted, instinctively yanking on his lead to see the full extent of the flood damage. We had been right on the brink of Tom peeing outside, but instead he had just done his business right inside our flats' threshold. I couldn't believe it!

I searched inside my pockets for a tissue of any sort, but drew a blank. 'Feck, feck, feck,' I muttered under my breath, pulling Tom away from the door and back up to our flat. I had to find something to clean up Tom's mess asap before one of our neighbours stepped right into it.

'That was quick,' Pete said as soon as Tom and I got back to our flat.

'Don't talk to me, Pete,' I said, dumping the dog. 'He's just gone and peed in the hallway downstairs, right in front of the door.'

'Did you not see him lift his leg or something?' Pete asked. 'Could you not have stopped him?'

'He didn't cock his leg or anything. He just squatted and peed like a girl.'

I didn't have time to check whether Tom really was a boy or whether he hadn't yet learned to pee like a male. Instead I rushed upstairs to the bathroom and grabbed a full toilet roll.

I bolted down to the main front door, hoping no one had encountered Tom's urine yet. Fortunately, the puddle was still intact, and the toilet roll just about soaked it all up. I threw the soiled tissue into the communal dustbin then made my way back to our flat.

Just as I started to climb the staircase, I saw one of our neighbours coming down the steps. I attempted a smile at the short, suave man who I had never met before. I was not in a friendly, conversant mood, however.

'Was that your dog I heard last night?' the man asked me in a distinctly French accent, stopping me before I could dodge him.

'Yes, sorry about that,' I said. 'He's just a young pup. We got him over the weekend.'

'Ah yes, he was howling a lot at 1 a.m.,' the French neighbour replied. 'It's normally okay, but I'm a pilot, so I prefer to sleep whenever possible.'

Maybe I should have let Pete go downstairs after all and sing Tom sweet lullabies.

'I'm so sorry,' I said, shrugging my shoulders. 'I promise, we won't let it happen again.'

With that assurance, the pilot pottered off in his sleep-deprived haze to fly his aeroplane.

I was livid with myself when I finally arrived back at our flat. Perhaps Pete was right. Maybe Tom wasn't the right dog for us. Or maybe our living arrangements just weren't conducive to minding any sort of pet.

'Now the neighbours are complaining,' I said, slamming the door behind me. 'I just met the guy from upstairs, some French pilot, who couldn't sleep because of Tom's howling last night.'

'You should have just let me—'

'I know, I know,' I said. 'Next time, I promise to let you keep Tom company as soon as he starts wailing.'

Pete looked back at me blankly. I had no one to blame but myself. I was just surprised that Pete hadn't called for Tom's dismissal as well.

I spent the rest of the day locking Tom into his crate, dragging him out an hour later, physically carrying him down the stairs to stop him peeing in transit, then parading him up and down the street. But Tom expelled not a single drop on the roadside.

When Pete came home from work later that day, I was close to giving up. Nothing had worked. I was mentally making plans to pack Tom off to Dog Training Ireland, for them to deal with him.

Pete sensed my growing frustration, and suggested we go for a quiet drink. 'Let's head to the Irish pub at the end of the road,' he said. 'We can bring Tom with us and see if he, I don't know, does anything?'

Reluctantly I agreed and went to get my shoes.

When we arrived at the pub, I pulled a few chairs onto the kerbside outside and sat down with Tom still attached to his lead. Pete soon arrived back from the bar with two ice-cold Tiger beers and a bucket of salted peanuts. The bite of the beer helped to soothe away some of the day's frustration.

'I've been thinking,' Pete said, after he finished his first mouthful. 'Maybe I've been a bit harsh with Tom.'

'No, Pete, it's my fault,' I quickly interrupted. 'I shouldn't have made you take the dog in. It was a bad idea.'

I looked down at Tom. He was lying beneath me with all four paws splayed out on the ground, as if he had just parachuted from a great height and landed badly. It seemed like he had a certain set of poses like this one that helped keep him cool in this hot and humid climate.

'It's just that his whining last night,' Pete said, ignoring what I had just said, 'it reminded me so much of Reggie.'

I turned to face Pete, but he was looking elsewhere. His gaze was far out towards the lake, as if watching for Senator John McCain to parachute back into its waters.

'Reggie used to howl just like that whenever there was a storm,' Pete continued. 'One night, he was so scared he broke into the house, ran up to my bedroom, and hid under my bed. Perhaps I wanted to find an excuse not to have another dog, so I wasn't disloyal to Reggie.'

'Hence your issue with Tom's hair and toileting?'

'Yeah, maybe,' Pete said, nodding his head thoughtfully. 'I know that Reggie can never be replaced, but that doesn't mean I can't learn to love another dog.'

With that surprising admission from my boyfriend, the floodgates opened and Tom peed all over the road.

6

Vietnamese Ladies

With Tom's monumental discovery of how to urinate in wide-open spaces, Pete and I relented. If Tom promised to do his business outside from then on, he was allowed to stay with us.

With this commitment now firmly in place, one of the key things I needed to do was get Tom vaccinated. I tracked down a vet in Tây Hồ, close to Tom's old abode, who could tend to all Tom's needs. I called for an appointment, and brought him along the next day.

As soon as we arrived, Tom and I were ushered behind closed doors into a spotlessly clean surgery. A friendly Vietnamese lady vet greeted us, dressed head-to-toe in baby-blue hospital scrubs.

'How can I help you today?' she asked, her eyes darting from me to Tom.

I gave her a brief history of how Tom had become my dog. 'Do whatever you need,' I told her. 'I just want him fit and healthy.'

I hoisted Tom on to the table top, where he proceeded to

freeze to the spot. Immediately I started worrying that Tom might snap or nip the vet, this unsuspecting petite lady who had surely his best interests at heart. I soon realised, however, that Tom was too immobilised by fear to be able to make such a sudden move. The vet set about her inspection, checking his ears and eyes. She pulled up his gums to reveal his small yet impressive set of fangs. She then started poking and prodding him in other more personal places. Tom's rear leg started to tremble ever so slightly with each successive touch. Despite this being his first ever visit to the vet, he was remarkably well behaved.

'He looks in pretty good shape,' the vet told me once she had completed Tom's check-up. It was amazing news, considering none of us had any idea how Tom was treated during the first few months of his thus-far brief life. She listed all the vaccinations she would give him that day; then instructed me to hold on to him tight. Even when the vet produced her sharpest set of needles, Tom was surprisingly compliant. His ambivalence was probably due to the fact that he had absolutely no idea of the pain injections can inflict. The vet swiftly pricked Tom and inserted the concoction of drugs he needed under his skin. Though Tom barely moved throughout, it was only when he started to drool a steady stream of saliva that I realised that this, his first vet experience, would permanently traumatise him.

'His coat is a bit long for this time of year,' the vet told me once she had binned her syringes. 'You might want to get him trimmed so he doesn't suffer from the heat.'

Ah ha! So that was why Tom had been panting like mad every time the air-con was switched off at home. He just badly needed a haircut. I soon learned the vet not only delivered medical care, but provided grooming services as well. I agreed to leave Tom with her and to return later after Tom had had a shower and shave.

I headed up the street to indulge in a cup of strong coffee and some delectable desserts while I waited for Tom. One of the advantages of Vietnam's French colonial past was its appreciation of the café culture. Hanoi is littered with restaurants and cafés serving exemplary fine French cuisine, so it was not long before I found a suitable place to pass the time.

I was buzzing with sugar and caffeine by the time I returned to the vet an hour later.

'Tom is nearly finished,' the receptionist informed me. 'You can go in and see him if you like.'

She pointed me towards the grooming room, and I pushed open its door. What I saw next, unfurling before me, was the closest thing I have ever seen to puppy porn. Tom was perched on a high table, his tongue hanging out of the side of his mouth, with what could only be described as heightened pleasure. Around him were standing three stunning Vietnamese ladies with long black hair, each one holding a miniature hairdryer. They smiled and giggled as they spewed hot air towards Tom's body, their long slender fingers fluffing up his shortened coat into the latest style. Tom seemed to be enjoying this level of female attention far too much for my liking. He looked like the ultimate street dog turned suave city slicker.

In my absence, Tom seemed to have also worked his charm on the other veterinary staff. Even the receptionist seemed besotted by Tom when I went to pay his bill.

'What a handsome dog!' she said, reaching down to pet my former street mutt. 'I hope you're going to come back one day and sleep with us too,' she whispered seductively to him, petting his new soft spotless hair.

'Excuse me?' I said, feeling like a parent whose child has been just asked to an over-eighteen drug-fuelled rave.

'We have kennels here at the back,' the receptionist went on to explain, her voice tinged with remarkable innocence given her recent invitation. 'So if you want to go away for a while, Tom is more than welcome to come and stay with us.'

I nodded my head. This was obviously an issue of translation. I glanced down at Tom, his close-shorn coat now revealing a svelte, curved body that had all the time been lurking underneath his unruly fur, unbeknownst to me. He looked well pleased with himself.

If I thought that Tom's charm was limited to the Vietnamese veterinary staff, I was very much mistaken. Every Wednesday morning before Pete went to work, our Vietnamese teacher, Ms Phuong, visited our apartment for our weekly language lesson. She had been coming for several weeks already, but this was her first encounter with Tom.

As soon as I answered the door to Ms Phuong, Tom leapt up with excitement. He galloped towards this young Vietnamese lady, and frantically jumped up and down on the spot trying to get her attention. I desperately tried to calm Tom down in case Ms Phuong didn't like animals. Instead of shunning our little pup, Ms Phuong knelt down and showered him with hugs and kisses.

'What a good doggie you are!' she said, all smiles for our new household addition. 'What is your name? What is your name?' Tom was too busy licking her hands and making her giggle to divulge such personal information. I couldn't help but feel a tinge of pride at being Tom's owner when I saw Ms Phuong's besotted reaction.

'He's called Tom,' I said to Ms Phuong, deciding to answer on our dog's behalf. 'Sorry if he's annoying you.'

'No, no, it's fine,' Ms Phuong replied, slipping off her petite, ballet-like shoes. 'I also have a dog at home.'

I was surprised by this revelation. I thought most Vietnamese hated the idea of dogs as pets, preferring them on their dinner plate. Then again, Ms Phuong was the sort of dainty young lady who probably loved puppies and daisies and everything that was sugared and spiced.

Pete, on hearing Ms Phuong's voice from upstairs, made a dramatic entrance from the top of our spiral staircase. He was dressed smartly in his office wear, with his perfectly matching shirt and pants. I loved it when he looked this handsome and dapper.

'Xin chào, Ms Phuong,' he said, flashing his widest, most charming smile.

'Xin chào, Mr Pete,' she replied, her porcelain skin blushing ever so slightly as she bowed back in return.

For a split second, I felt like I was intruding on them.

It was hard, however, not to be enchanted by Ms Phuong's beauty. Her long, flowing hair extended luxuriously all the way down her slender back. Her fine facial features were flawless without the slightest need of make-up. When she smiled, the whole world seemed to stop turning for just an instant.

I was not sure if Ms Phuong realised how captivating she

was. I wouldn't have minded it, but it seemed as if she had inadvertently captured my Pete as well with her magical charm.

Pete, Ms Phuong and I sat down at our dining-room table and took out our language books. We only had an hour scheduled, so it was down to business straightaway.

'Today we will learn about tones,' Ms Phuong said. 'Can you turn to page ten and repeat after me? The first tone on the page is called high rising.'

I looked at it and smugly recognised it as an accent aigu in French. This should be easy, I thought.

'An example would be Má, which means "mother". Can you say Má?' Ms Phuong said.

'Maaaa' both Pete and I repeated back simultaneously, without the slightest inflection. We sounded more like a flock of sheep than anything remotely Vietnamese. I thought I would be better at this. Fortunately Ms Phuong smiled back at our effort, politely ignoring our bleating.

'The next tone is called low falling.'

Again, I figured my command of French would come to my rescue. It looked just like an accent grave.

'An example would be Mà, which means "that".'

'Maaaa' Pete and I again said in unison. It sounded remark-ably similar to our attempt at 'mother'.

Things went from bad to worse when our teacher intro-duced us to three more tones that looked nothing more than scribbles. Ms Phuong proceeded to inform us that Mả means tomb, Mã means horse, and Mạ is rice shoots. Despite making various facial contortions and guttural sounds, neither Pete nor I could mimic her intonation. She then informed us that we had both successfully said the word 'Ma' on several attempts, which is the word for ghost in Vietnamese. At least we had mastered one word in the local language.

'Now, let's move on to your homework from last week,' Ms Phuong said.

I pulled out my copybook with my long list of answers neatly laid out. Pete looked at me, then Ms Phuong. He had been really busy at work lately, and Tom's arrival hadn't helped matters, but this was the third time in a row that Pete had not done his homework.

'Mr Pete, can you give me the answer to number one?' Ms Phuong said, oblivious to Pete's incomplete assignment.

I shielded my homework with my arm to stop him from cheating. I didn't want to give Ms Phuong any reason to compliment Pete by him giving her the correct answer.

'I'm ... not ... sure,' Pete said, trying to peek over my shoulder. 'It's just that − I'm sorry Ms Phuong, I didn't have a chance to do the work you gave us.'

'Mr Pete, that's very disappointing,' she said. 'Do you want me come over there and ... punish you?'

A wicked grin spread right across Pete's face. Was that *exactly* what he'd like Ms Phuong to do to him?

I, on the other hand, was too shocked by this scene to know how to react. Was Ms Phuong's grasp of the English language not as perfect as I thought? Was this a truly innocent error on her part? Or was she fishing for a foreign husband, and considered Pete the perfect catch?

Ms Phuong continued on with the lesson regardless, even though I was itching to get her out the door. When our sixty minutes were finally up, Tom seemed quite sad to see Ms

Phuong depart. I, on the other hand, couldn't wait to see the back of her.

Most conveniently, Pete needed to head out to work just as Ms Phuong left.

'I'll accompany you downstairs,' he said.

Isn't that so chivalrous of you, I thought.

As soon as they had disappeared, I sprinted over to the balcony and watched them depart. I saw Ms Phuong perched on the cutest Vespa moped, a Vietnamese Audrey Hepburn if I had ever seen one. Pete was right behind her, wheeling out his cumbersome Honda, sweating as he tried to kick it off its stand. They exchanged some words, which Ms Phuong giggled at, before donning their respective helmets. Then, with a flick of the wrist, Ms Phuong glided off up the road, her silk scarf streaming out behind her in the breeze. Pete put-putted off in the opposite direction, coming close to running over a stray cat in the process.

Though I was still unsure how committed I was to our relationship, I couldn't believe how jealous I felt when seeing Ms Phuong and Pete speak to each other this way. Their interaction made me feel wildly possessive. Was it because I really loved Pete and subconsciously wanted to stay with him forever? Or was it just that I didn't want anyone else having a piece of him?

I was still standing in shock on the balcony, when I sensed Tom by my side. He must have felt my dismay, even though there was no way he could have understood. Kneeling down, I buried my face in his fur. Tom just sat there, obediently, letting his coat absorb my nascent angry tears. The fact that he was there just when I needed him most made me realise why dogs are indeed our best friends. Once I had calmed down, with Tom's help, I filed Pete's flirtatious behaviour away in my mind, in case it was needed for another day.

Ms Phuong had not long departed when there was another knock on the door. I wiped my face clean before sliding the door open to see another Vietnamese woman, the polar opposite of Ms Phuong. She was short, squat and stocky. She looked as if she could have harvested an entire paddy field single-handedly before coming to our home.

She thrust her hand out in my direction. 'Hello. My name is Xuan.' Xuan was Pete's answer to Tom's floating dog hair: our new housemaid.

Regardless of my reservations, I knew I had no choice but to employ our own personal cleaner. Tom's hair had defeated me. Even with his new crew cut, and despite my best efforts, balls of his hair still periodically floated across our living room. Xuan was now the person in charge of rounding them up.

I was unhappy with the arrangement for several reasons. Firstly, if I had work to do, I often did it at home. I preferred not to have someone bustling around, cooking and cleaning while I was trying to concentrate on my computer screen. Secondly, thanks to my inconsistent workload in comparison to Pete's clockwork schedule, I was technically the one responsible for household cleanliness. The arrival of Xuan felt like a massive hint from Pete that I didn't keep the house clean and tidy enough to meet his exacting standards.

I showed Xuan into our home, inviting her to have a look around to see if she wanted to work for us. I secretly hoped she'd see the state of our dog-infested place and beat a hasty retreat.

No sooner was she in the door, however, than her shoes

were off, her sleeves were rolled up, and she was filling a bucket with hot, soapy water.

'You don't need to start working today,' I said, trying to delay the inevitable.

'No problem,' she said. 'Where is your mop and iron?'

I slunk off to get them, trying not to mope too much.

Within the space of two hours, the place was spotlessly clean. She had cleaned the floors, washed the dishes, dusted the plants, changed the bedding, done the laundry, as well as ironed and hung up all our clothes. I peeked inside Pete's wardrobe and saw all of his shirts lined up as if in a shop window display. I had downright refused to iron his shirts on his behalf, stating it contravened my feminist convictions. As a result, Pete had instead enlisted another woman to do his dirty work.

I had to admit she had done a great job, but I was damned if I was going to admit that to Pete.

'How much do I owe you?' I said, opening up my wallet.

'Ten dollars,' she said, flinching ever so slightly. It was a paltry amount for me, but an excellent wage for Xuan. I guessed it was worth it if it restored household harmony and kept Tom's fluff balls at bay.

Once Xuan was gone, I opened up my laptop to write down this expense. Pete had recently instituted a shared spreadsheet system to keep track of our household bills. It was still way too early in our relationship to consider merging our financial lives so, after lengthy negotiations, we had come to an agreement outlining who would pay for what, when. If I was not working, Pete paid the rent and sixty per cent of our expenses. If I found a job, the ratio reverted to fifty-fifty.

This would seem simple and fair enough, but Pete was an accountant who dealt with foreign currencies on a daily basis. The fact that our expenses were in a mixture of Vietnamese dong and US dollars meant he could really go to town. It had provided him a chance to show off his superior Excel programming skills, as though it were an elaborate mating call. Little did Pete realise that Excel spreadsheets failed to turn me on.

He had developed a spreadsheet that needed a degree in mathematics to understand. Columns included transaction currencies, functional currencies, settlement currencies and complicated exchange rate calculations. I still didn't get the column named 'USD Net Impact to Pete'. It seemed an awful lot of effort just to split a ten-dollar fee.

There was part of me, though, that didn't want to pay my share of Xuan's wage, seeing that I objected to having a maid in the first place.

As I was closing my laptop, Tom came over to me wagging his tail. He sat himself down in precisely the right spot so that he was just within petting distance. He probably sensed my frustration. But it wasn't just the maid and spreadsheet that were vexing me. It had started to dawn on me that, though I liked Vietnam, my stint in the country had not worked out as I had planned. In particular, the lack of employment was killing me. I got pieces of work here and there, but nothing that could sustain me. Without Pete's income, I would have had to head home. It was embarrassing that he had to support me.

The only positive thing was that I had Tom to keep me company during the day while I waited for Pete to return from work. I leant over and patted Tom on his head. He in turn flopped down and rolled on his back, exposing his soft, pink belly. I scratched his undercarriage until his back leg started scratching the air out of misplaced pleasure.

'Come on boy,' I said. 'Let's go for a walk.' At the mere mention of the word 'walk', Tom jumped to all fours. He had learned one word of English, finally.

If I thought the walk would do me some good, I was very much mistaken. I led Tom to the end of the road to give us both a good stretch of the legs. At the crossroads, opposite a street-food stall, was a cage full of rabid dogs that I had not noticed before. As soon as they caught sight of Tom, they unleashed their vehement might. They started barking violently at Tom, as if it was his fault that they were locked up while he was free to roam the streets. Tom didn't react in the slightest to their vicious snarls, but I took instant fright. I figured it was best to give these dogs some peace before they came under the imminent butcher's knife.

'Come on Tom,' I said, backing away. 'Let's go home.'

On the way back to our apartment, Tom squatted for a quick pee on the pavement. I watched him proudly, as a teacher does when she sees her pupil performing well. Suddenly, from behind me, I heard a woman screaming in Vietnamese – surely nothing to do with me. Then a hot-pot lady was coming straight at Tom, brandishing her broom at him.

Tom scurried between my legs in the opposite direction, his lead soon extending to full stretch. I stood there dumbstruck as she diverted her attention away from Tom and started to hurl abuse at me instead.

I had absolutely no idea what the problem was. I was not sure what to say. It was only when she started scrubbing hard at Tom's pee with her broom that I worked it out: she must have cleaned the place to set up for dinner and Tom had just contaminated her dining spot.

I returned home with Tom, mortified by what had happened. But Tom was not to blame – the problem was me, and my relationship with this place.

It would have been so much easier if I could learn the language and understand what was going on around me, but my language lessons were proving fruitless. I couldn't pronounce the words, I couldn't remember the important phrases, and I definitely couldn't understand when the words were spoken to me, or yelled at me, which seemed to be more frequently the case.

I didn't seem to be getting on very well with Vietnamese women either. The hot-pot ladies hated me, the female vets wanted to steal my dog, and Ms Phuong was on a mission to elope with Pete.

I needed to do something to escape this situation. I needed to either find a full-time job or just move to a new country and get the hell out of there.

7

New-Found Love

Despite his initial hygiene issues, Tom ended up settling in to our home remarkably well. He loved hanging out in his plastic crate. He ate whatever food we gave him. He stopped using our flat as his personal latrine. I eventually managed to train him not to mount the staircase but to stay on our flat's first floor. I even taught him not to jump up onto our chairs and sofas, but to keep all four paws firmly on our tiles.

The only obstacle I encountered while training Tom was Pete. Once Tom had started peeing and pooing outside, and thanks to Xuan cleaning up his errant fur balls, Pete developed a real soft spot for the dog. So when I tried to be firm with Tom about something I didn't like, Pete would subsequently come home and teach him to do the complete opposite.

I tried to teach Tom to walk properly on the lead, stopping dead in my tracks when he pulled in the slightest. But as soon as Pete took him for a dander, Pete let Tom drag him here, there and everywhere.

'I'm just giving Tom his freedom back,' Pete told me when I insisted he brought Tom to heel. 'He needs some time to explore after all those months caged up.' I sighed with exasperation, knowing that when I brought Tom on a walk next, he'd expect to have free rein.

I also tried to stop Tom from jumping up on me excitedly and scratching me with his claws. Pete, on the other hand, loved it when Tom leapt up to greet him as soon as he came through the door.

'He'll rip your pants,' I told Pete, as Tom scraped madly at Pete's trouser threads.

'I can buy new ones at the market,' Pete replied, as he knelt down to Tom's level and was rewarded with Tom's tongue licking his inner ear. 'Anyhow, this is the best part of my day,' Pete revealed. 'Work isn't great at the moment, so at least I can look forward to Tom greeting me when I get home in the evening.'

As the days went by, I felt like Tom and I were vying for Pete's attention. I would be so happy to see Pete coming home after him being absent the whole day. However, Tom also missed Pete and wanted to demonstrate his undying love for him. At times I felt like Tom's displays of affection and undivided attention towards Pete upstaged my own. He could barely contain himself when he saw Pete after any sort of separation. One day, after Tom had performed his 'Pete welcoming ritual', Pete stood up to take off his shoes. I was about to have my turn, to embrace Pete and ask him how his day was, when I saw a spatter of fluid on the floor.

'Where did that come from?' I said, pointing to the spray. Pete shrugged, ignorant as me. I thought about it for a second then looked down at our canine housemate. 'Tom,' I said, with an ominous growl. 'Was that you?'

Tom looked back at me, oblivious to my anger, idly shaking his tail.

I was not convinced by Tom's denial, however. I went over to the sink, grabbed a sheet of white kitchen roll and let it float gently down on top of the wet spot. As it soaked up the liquid, lo and behold, the paper turned yellow.

'Tommmmm!' I barked. 'Did you pee?'

I waited for Pete to join in with the damning chorus, but instead he jumped to Tom's defence. 'It's just a sprinkle,' said he who had originally recoiled at the slightest smudge of dog urine. 'Don't worry, I'll clean it up.'

I stood back in shock as Pete mopped up Tom's accident. Admittedly, he donned rubber gloves, used half a bottle of spray disinfectant and the entire roll of kitchen towel to clear up the minuscule drops. But that Pete even considered wiping up Tom's pee was a sure sign of a major change in heart.

It wasn't long before Tom had a formidable ally in our home. No matter what he did, Pete stood up for him as his guardian and protector. It was only a matter of time, however, before Tom tested this relationship to its limit.

One weekend after Tom's arrival, Pete and I arranged to meet up with friends in town. We returned to the flat in the early hours, after a boozy late-night dinner. I turned the key and practically fell through the doorway, waking Tom up with my drunken giggles. Holding on to the wall tightly, I attempted to take off my footwear. Just as my first shoe hit the ground, I noticed something terrible.

'Oh no!' I shouted, taking in the carnage that was wrought in our absence.

I stared down at our shoe rack and surveyed the evidence.

While we were gone, Tom had dragged every single shoe off its respective shelf. My favourite sandals had been hauled off to one side, where Tom had chewed right through the toe strap.

'That feckin' dog,' I said, picking the sandals up to survey the damage. 'He's gone and feckin' destroyed them.'

What made matters worse was that I knew I'd never find a replacement pair in Vietnam. I may have been a small size back home in Ireland, but I was a giant by Vietnamese standards. I had already looked, and shoe sizes on sale in Hanoi stopped short of my comparatively gigantic western foot length.

Just as I resigned myself to losing my favourite pair, I spied another beloved item of mine lying defeated on the ground. 'Please tell me Tom didn't touch that too,' my brain begged.

I picked my cherished rucksack off the floor, the one I wore when biking. It was the perfect size to carry a coat and puncture repair kit, so I always used it whenever and wherever I cycled. I had brought it all the way from Ireland, knowing that that type of bag was simply not available to purchase elsewhere on the planet. My heart plummeted as I touched the bag and felt the warm goo of dog saliva.

'That dog is so dead,' I whispered. While we were out, Tom had chewed through the buckles, making it impossible to close the bag properly ever again.

Pete wobbled over to have a closer look at my beloved rucksack and sandals that were now dangling distraught from my hands. 'Tom, you're in deep trouble you know?' he said in a slurred voice that noticeably lacked gravitas.

Tom looked up at both of us with half-moon eyes, before crouching down and delivering a short, sharp yelp in tandem with a fluttering tail wag. I may have been mistaken, but I was convinced Tom wanted to play right there and then.

If ever there was bad timing.

Pete took the offending items off me and guided me to our couch. It was obvious what was going to happen next. This was what Pete did time and time again when he wanted to placate me.

'Listen, he's only young,' Pete explained. 'I'm sure he'll grow out of it.'

'For feck sake's Pete, I'm not sure I can wait that long.'

I was well aware that getting rid of Tom was no longer an option. Pete was falling in love with the dog, deeper and deeper with each passing day. So much for Pete thinking he'd be unable to love a dog after his first pet, Reggie. Now Pete was not only being disloyal to Reggie but clearly cheating on him.

The next day, I had sobered up enough to do a thorough inspection of my beloved sandals and rucksack. Though Tom had indeed destroyed sections of them, they were still wearable. I continued to sport my sandals with their missing strap and my rucksack that lacked a buckle until I managed to get to a country where replacements could be found. Somehow, I also started to see those shoe and bag deficiencies fondly, reminding me of the good old days when Tom was just an adorable, innocent pup.

Cute though Pete's attachment to Tom was, it soon became somewhat of a hindrance when the two of us decided to go away for the weekend. Hạ Long Bay had been on our list of places to visit in Vietnam ever since we had arrived. Both guidebooks and friends alike had regaled us with stories of how a wondrous place it is. Situated in the northeast corner of Vietnam, a four-hour drive from Hanoi, it is a scattering of islands topped with rainforests surrounded by a serene, emerald sea. The way to see it is via a boat tour, a twenty-four-hour floating expedition around the rocky outcrops.

We booked onto a boat for an overnight trip, opting for a high-end, no expenses spared romantic cruise. Pete and I were both looking forward to the break. Part of me was hoping to rekindle the fun we used to have in Ireland before the economy crashed. I also wanted to remind us of the things that made us fall for each other in the first place and made us agree to travel together to Vietnam. With Tom attracting so much of Pete's attention, I was intent on reminding Pete who his one true love really was.

Soon enough though, the penny dropped with Pete that we couldn't bring Tom along. It could have been a real issue. Pete might refuse to go on the trip on the grounds of it not being dog friendly.

When he found out dogs were prohibited, Pete asked, 'What are we going to do with Tom?'

'We could always leave him at the vets,' I said. 'Don't they have kennels there?'

Pete looked doubtful. He obviously needed some more persuading, so I reminded him of Tom's superior grooming experience there, and convinced him that Tom would have that same level of care. I told him that if Tom did suffer any major illness or trauma while we were absent, I was sure the in-house vet would run to his bedside.

Pete eventually relented and agreed to my suggestion, on the condition that he and I both went to the vets and escorted

Tom into his kennel on the Friday night before we left early on Saturday morning. By this stage, I would have agreed to anything just to get Tom out of the picture so I could spend some quality alone time with my man.

Pete was visibly upset when he handed Tom over to the kennel staff the night before our departure. They had to physically tear Tom's lead out of Pete's hand to officially take charge of our dog. Pete hesitated at the door, waving a prolonged, solemn good-bye. In sharp contrast, Tom didn't even think twice about his kennel stay, scampering off instead to locate those three female groomers and their hot hairdryers. Tom looked like he had already made his own weekend plans.

'Come on,' I said to Pete, dragging him away by the arm. 'Let's go have a drink.'

The kennels were right beside Daluva's cocktail bar, the creator of some of Hanoi's most decadent and potent cocktails. Friday night was happy hour until 7 p.m. We had timed our kennel drop to perfection so that it coincided with half-price drinks.

'Two margaritas,' I shouted as soon as I reached the bar. The bartender whipped them up within seconds, and Pete and I downed them in a similar timespan. I signalled to the barman another round of the same, even though I could already feel the potent effects of tequila and triple sec leeching into my brain.

This time Pete and I decided to take a seat at a table to savour our drinks more slowly.

'Are you sure you're okay with leaving Tom for the weekend?' I said, the margarita giving me the bravery to broach the subject. Pete twisted the thin stem of his glass.

'Yeah,' he said after a minute's thought. 'No, it'll be fine,' he said, this time with more conviction, as if trying to convince himself rather than me with his response.

'I do think it will be good for us to get away though,' I said, finding myself already at the bottom of my second glass. I thought I was drinking slowly, but the cocktails were exceedingly tasty. I waved at the bartender for another round. Pete didn't try to stop me. 'I think we need to have a break maybe, spend some quality time together.'

The sudden infusion of alcohol had obviously dug down deep into my subconscious, unearthing unknown insecurities. All I could think about was how much Pete loved to spend time with Tom. All I could see was the way Pete's eyes danced when he caught sight of Ms Phuong. Was there even any room in Pete's heart for me? Would it not be better if I left so that Pete, Tom and Ms Phuong could set up their own little cosy family? It all felt so believable and real given the units of alcohol I had just consumed.

Pete seemed a little mystified by what I was saying until I somehow blurted out the name of our Vietnamese teacher.

'Oh yes, Ms Phuong promised to punish me.' He guffawed. 'I can't wait for our next lesson!'

'You better be joking Pete,' I said, automatically crossing my arms. 'Because I won't put up with this behaviour any more.'

Pete looked at me sideways, confused. A waiter brought us our third round of cocktails and set them on the table, breaking the silence between us. Neither of us touched the drinks.

'What behaviour?' he said. 'I'm only kidding about getting punished, you know.'

'I saw the way you were flirting with her when you guys left the flat together last week,' I shouted, losing my self-control and my dignity.

'You don't think...' Pete stuttered, before getting to his feet, losing his balance slightly as he rose. 'You don't think there is something going on between Ms Phuong and me... do you?'

This was where I should have just conceded that I was feeling a little left out, that my mind was playing tricks on me. I knew I was being silly thinking that he loved Tom more, that he wanted to settle down with Ms Phuong rather than me.

Instead, I blurted out, 'Well, *is* there something going on?'

'That's ridiculous!' he slurred. 'Right, I've had enough.' With those words, Pete stumbled past the other happy-hour customers and straight out through the front door.

I didn't bother to follow him, convinced he would come back inside once he had cooled down. But after five minutes of waiting, I realised Pete was gone, without the slightest good-bye.

I staggered to the bar and threw a handful of dollars on to the counter. I then found the bar's exit, and when I could see no sign of Pete on the street outside, found the first taxi free to take me home.

On the ride back to our apartment, my anger with Pete grew more and more. By the time I fell out of the taxi, words could not describe my all-consuming fury. The first thing I noticed on entering our home was that there was no Tom there to welcome me. Even though I wasn't a huge fan of his frolicking greetings, I sorely missed them now. What made matters worse was that Pete wasn't home either.

For the first time in a long time, I was home alone.

I texted Pete, asking him where he was, but got zero reply. Soon, I was too livid with him to care where he had ended up...just as long as it wasn't on the muddy bottom of Trúc Bạch Lake that lay outside my window.

My head was starting to pound after our exuberant happy hour, so I decided to lie down on the sofa and close my eyes. I quickly descended into a deep, dreamless sleep.

It was still dark when Pete finally walked through our door, waking me up with a start.

'Where did you go?' I said, rubbing my eyes, momentarily forgetting that we were still mid-fight.

Pete silently made his way over to the sofa, and sat down at its edge. 'I went to see Tom,' he said, his head hanging slightly.

'But the kennels closed right when we left at 6 p.m.,' I replied.

'I know,' Pete conceded. 'The security guard wouldn't let me in.'

He couldn't be serious, I thought. 'So you left me in Daluva and tried to break into the kennels to rescue Tom?'

'Pretty much,' Pete replied.

I looked at my watch. It was past 9 o'clock. 'That was over three hours ago.'

Pete bit his lip. There was evidently more to this story. 'I went to the Pan Pacific and had another drink,' he told me, looking a little ashamed. Pan Pacific was a luxurious hotel at the end of our street that was far too fancy for us to frequent. I didn't bring Tom by there in case he peed in its vicinity. 'Then

I tried to check in for the night, because I was too mad with you to see you. When I found out it was a hundred dollars to stay, I decided to come home instead.'

I couldn't contain myself any more and blurted out a laugh. The situation was too ridiculous to be angry over. Fortunately, my chuckle proved contagious, and soon Pete could see the funny side.

'I'm sorry,' I said. 'I know you're not having an affair with Ms Phuong. It's just that she's so pretty and charming. I suppose I'm just jealous of her, and jealous of the effect she has on you as well.'

'I'm sorry too,' Pete said, joining in with the mea culpas. 'I shouldn't make you feel like that. You've got to know, though, I'm not interested in her at all. I just find it funny how flirtatious she is, without even really knowing it herself.'

Reconciled, I gathered my arms around Pete and pulled him into an all-encompassing embrace. His body was familiar and warm. I hated fighting with him, but making up with him afterwards made it all worthwhile.

'So do you want to cancel our trip and go get Tom in the morning?' I said, finally providing some sort of peace offering.

'No, it's fine,' Pete said. 'Let's go and check Hạ Long Bay out as we planned.'

In the end, Pete regretted not taking me up on my offer. The drive to the boat was arduous and boring, a whole four hours canned up in a minivan. When we finally arrived at the coast, our boat was quite literally a junk, nothing more than a floating set of planks with fake rigged-up sails that didn't work. Our luxurious cabin turned out to be a darkened cave, with room for little more than a bed.

We had also failed to consider that an overnight boat trip meant being holed up with other shipmates for an entire twenty-four-hour stint. Though they were all pleasant enough, Pete and I felt claustrophobic as we were forced to make small talk and socialise with strangers.

After seeing the largest of the Bay's rocks, which were in themselves impressive, there remained little else to do on board. Neither Pete nor I were interested in sunbathing or swimming, so we retreated to our cabin for some solitude. Unfortunately, our bed was directly positioned above the boat's motor, so we were subjected to the constant drone of its roar and the smell of its diesel fumes.

Every couple of hours we were summoned on deck for a spot of fine dining. The kitchen staff must also have been bored, as we were presented with all manner of foods that they had elaborately butchered. We were given prawns for starters that were twisted into peculiar shapes. Pineapples and papayas, carved into weird theatrical birds, surrounded the fish main course. The food was brought out in slow progression in an effort to kill time as we floated aimlessly around the Bay. Fortunately Pete and I eat anything otherwise we would probably have starved, seeing as we were trapped on this vessel with no lifeboats. Even at bedtime, neither Pete nor I were able to sleep. Though they had turned off the motor, the constant bobbing around on the water meant we felt seasick for the entire night.

Pete nearly kissed dry land when we finally disembarked. When we arrived home in Hanoi, we took the first taxi we could find to pick up Tom, and apologised to him for abandoning him for the weekend. The kennel staff led Tom out of his cage. He was panting with excitement.

'I think he's happy to see you, Pete,' I said, as Tom's lead was rightfully placed back in Pete's hand. Pete stooped down to give Tom a hug, but Tom had other plans. He darted straight out the door, pulling Pete behind him.

'Looks like he wants to get outta here,' Pete called after me.

I followed them outside to see Tom sniffing excitedly around the kennel entrance. He had never shown interest like that before. Soon it looked like Tom had found a particular scent that he was dead set on chasing. The smell seemed to lead Tom to a telegraph pole, which made him stop dead in his tracks. Then Tom did something he had never in his short life done before; he cocked his leg up and peed.

To this day, neither Pete nor I have any idea what happened on Tom's wild weekend away. What we do know, however, is that our trip away marked the end of Tom's time of 'squatting like a girl'. After twenty-four hours of hanging out with other adult dogs in the kennels, Tom had become a full-fledged male.

8

Near-Death Experiences

Life in Hanoi continued as normal, Tom becoming less of a young pup with each passing day. In particular I noticed that, when we ventured outside, Tom wanted to hone his leg-lifting skills. He was specifically dying to mark our front doorstep as his territory.

Little did he know that such demarcation was potentially suicidal. The hot-pot ladies liked to hang out at our very entrance as they waited for evening trade. If they arrived and smelled Tom's urine caked across the concrete, they would certainly serve him up for dinner if they got their hands on him.

It meant that if I wanted to let Tom outside to do his business, I had to emerge from our door like a greyhound at full sprinting speed. I had to make Tom run to the opposite end of the street, to get as far away from our front step as possible, before allowing him to let off his leg in safety.

While Tom was making his mark in Hanoi, I was having zero impact on the place. I continued to apply for work, but with no success. I either got a letter of rejection, or employers ignored me entirely. It was making me quite depressed.

Out of desperation, I started looking online at the jobs section with the Irish charity Pete and I had previously worked for in Dublin. Unsurprisingly, there were no vacancies back home in Ireland, which was still in the deep throes of recession. There would be no going back there for a while. However, there were places available in the organisation's overseas field offices in thirty or so far-flung locations around the world.

Vietnam was too prosperous a place for my former employer to have operations there. Instead, I trawled through the list of other countries with available job openings. I skipped through an array of foreign destinations, many of which were in Africa. All of a sudden, I stopped dead on a country I had longed to work in: Nepal's country office had a vacancy.

I visited Nepal once before on a short work assignment, and instantly fell in love with place. The capital Kathmandu was a fascinating hive of activity that I quickly longed to immerse myself in, full of rickshaws, ancient Buddhist temples and Tibetan flags fluttering in the mountain breeze. I had been entranced by the pungent smell of incense and the sound of spinning prayer wheels. Most of all, I was blown away by the formidable Himalayas that were visible from the capital. To the north, the peaks towered above the city, its snow-dusted summits beckoning mountain lovers to go trekking in their midst.

I clicked on the link to discover more about the job posting. Much to my delight, it was for a managerial position I had aimed for throughout my career: Country Representative, the person in charge of all their Nepal operations. It was my dream job in my dream location.

I simply *had* to submit an application, regardless of whether it was even feasible for me to take up the position.

When Pete came home from work, he was no sooner in the door than I accosted him with the advertisement I had printed out. He knew me well enough by then to realise this was an opportunity I would loathe to let slip by. I was worried though that I was reneging on the agreement Pete and I had originally made. The plan was to live and work together in Vietnam. Applying for such a post would entail a significant change to our original deal.

'Nepal?' he said, perusing the job description that I had shoved into his hand.

'It's still Asia,' I hastened to point out. I was hoping we could renegotiate our arrangement so that we kept within the continent of Asia in general, as opposed to a specific country.

'Country Representative?' he continued. I wished he would hurry up and tell me what he thought rather than just reading out random lines from the job spec.

He handed me back my piece of paper. 'It's your perfect job,' he said, without divulging in the slightest what he really thought.

'I know, isn't it?' I replied, unable to contain myself any more. 'So, is it okay if I apply?'

Pete thought about it for it a minute, before shouting, 'Tom! Tom, what do you think?'

I rolled my eyes. Since when did my career path depend on our dog?

Tom trotted over to us both and stared at us both as if asking 'What's up?' Pete knelt down to him and buried his face in his fur. Tom in turn pawed Pete's head and pretended to gnaw on Pete's hand.

I wished they would just get a room.

'Tom-Tom, do you want to move to Nepal?' Pete said as Tom playfully rolled on to his back.

I folded my arms across my body. 'Pete,' I said, knowing this could take a while, 'I'm asking whether *you* want to live in Nepal? There's no point in me applying for the job if you're not interested in going too.'

'Tom is part of this household as well,' Pete said, kneeling up to attention.

'Yes, yes, yes,' I said, trying to hide my frustration. I didn't want to argue. I just wanted an answer. 'Tom can come as well. What I want to know is, can I apply for the job or not?'

Pete patted Tom on his belly, before jumping back to his feet. 'Go for it,' Pete said, sounding more enthusiastic than I expected. 'I've always wanted to check out Nepal. If you like, I can help you with your application as well.'

Pete's offer of assistance was a godsend. He is much better than me when it comes to all things work-related and professional. Pete went through my CV with an expert eye and put in all the latest buzzwords. He rephrased my previous work experience so that it tallied exactly with the job specification demands. When I was invited for a telephone interview, he prepped me perfectly with potential questions that, amazingly, all popped up.

Despite all this meticulous preparation, the odds of me getting this job remained slim. I knew many other charity-sector professionals would salivate when they saw such an opportunity in Nepal. Applications would easily reach triple figures.

I was also sure there would be multiple candidates with far more experience than me, people who had already been Country Representatives in a variety of settings. The only advantage I had over them was my current flexibility. The position was unusual in that it was quite short-term, lasting only eight months, with no possibility of an extension. The charity also needed someone to relocate immediately as soon as they were offered a contract.

As I waited to hear back about my application, Pete continued with his own job. One morning, as usual, he left to go to his office. Less than an hour later, I heard his key turning in the door and the sound of him returning to our flat. It was highly unusual for him to come home before 5 p.m. I figured he must have forgotten something important and had returned home to pick it up. I went downstairs to the living room to check it was him, only to see Pete still standing by the front door, completely dishevelled, trouser legs torn, his torso covered in blood and mud.

'Oh good God, what happened?' I said, rushing to his side.

Pete was visibly shaken as I guided him into the safety of our home. Taking hold of my arm, he limped the short distance to our couch.

'Feckin' motorbike,' he mumbled, as he painfully took a seat.

'Did you fall off?' I asked, assuming straightaway that his pitiful state was of his own making. Pete's confidence on the bike, as well as his speed, had risen to dangerous proportions of late. Already several times I had begged him to slow down while giving me a lift, his driving had become so reckless.

'No, it was a bloody taxi's fault,' he said, finally finding his words. 'I was driving along Thụy Khuê Street, right behind this taxi, going at the same speed.' The anger in his voice rose as he recalled the events as they had unfurled. 'We were both driving past a hotel entrance. Then, just at the last minute, the taxi driver braked hard as if he had missed the turn,' Pete explained. My heart was in my mouth. Driving in Hanoi is notoriously dangerous, with stupid accidents like this happening all the time. 'He didn't indicate or anything, just swerved right in front of me,' Pete continued. 'I tried to stop, but braked too hard. The next thing I knew, the motorbike was sliding across the road without me. My whole right side got cut up on the tarmac skidding after it.'

A million scenarios filled my mind as Pete recounted his story. He could have been seriously injured, or worse, killed. I doubt anyone would have phoned an ambulance to make sure that Pete was physically okay, or even if an ambulance would have turned up if such a call had been made. If the police had actually arrived, I'm not sure they would have understood or even believed Pete's story, seeing that he's not from this side of the world.

I looked at Pete's slashed clothes that he had put on so clean and neatly pressed that morning. On closer inspection, through the cloth's gaping holes, I saw more scrapes and bruises than actual gashes on his extremities. Nothing, thankfully, seemed broken. Pete had been very lucky. We knew of other expats who had had motorbike accidents who had not come off as lightly.

Pete was too shaken to go to his office that day. He made a call to his boss who, without hesitation, gave him the day off. I think Pete was secretly glad that he had an excuse not to go into the office that day. More and more, he was coming home from work and complaining about his job.

After speaking with his manager, my poor injured man hobbled upstairs and undressed to have a shower. I heard him screaming as the hot water made contact, as it washed the grit and dried blood out of his freshly carved-out lacerations.

Pete eventually came back downstairs again, wearing pyjamas that hung limply over his wounds. He lay down on the sofa, easing himself down gently with the occasional pain-streaked grimace. I bandaged what needed covering, all the while feeling overwhelmingly protective of Pete. I was truly shaken by this incident, the idea of losing Pete in a stupid road accident being too much for me to bear.

Once I had finished, Pete beckoned Tom to his side. Tom looked distinctly nervous as Pete hoisted him up and laid him prone on Pete's belly. I didn't dare remind Pete that Tom was not actually allowed up on our upholstery. I figured coming close to death was an extenuating reason to override that rule that morning. Looking at Tom's uneasy expression it was pretty obvious that, if Pete's arm hadn't been wrapped tightly around him, Tom would have made a hasty retreat back to the safety of the floor. Tom had already suffered my wrath when I had caught him splayed out on our armchairs. Hanging out on Pete's body, Tom seemed unsure why I had not already scolded him for his close proximity to the sofa.

'I thought I was going to die and leave you all alone,' Pete said, smothering Tom with desperate hugs. I wondered if I should be annoyed that this comment was directed to Tom rather than me.

If Pete's road accident had happened before our drunken

argument, I would have taken offence, immediately questioning Pete's affections for me. But after sobering up, I had come to understand that Pete's love for Tom was not something I should be jealous of. If anything, having Tom around helped my own love for Pete to grow. Tom's presence allowed Pete's emotional side to emerge, a side that I found wonderfully endearing. And, truth be told, I preferred it if Pete squashed Tom rather than me while he recovered from his road-accident trauma.

'I suppose the bright side of my near-death experience was knowing I was going to see Reggie again,' Pete said, directing this statement now at me.

'Sorry, what?' I said, a bit confused by how Reggie had anything to do with this incident.

'I thought I was going to die and then see Reggie again in doggie heaven,' he said.

Pete must have hit his head on impact. That was probably why he was talking such rubbish. 'You know there's no such thing as doggie heaven.'

Pete looked back at me in abject horror. I might as well have told him Christmas had been cancelled and Santa does not exist. I realised I needed to provide him with evidence to back up my statement.

I decided to give him a religious explanation, backed by sound doctrine. 'I'm not saying that dogs don't have souls. It's just that, unlike human souls, animal souls depend on matter for life. That means they cease to exist when they die.' I sounded like a complete killjoy, but we had both been brought up in Ireland as Roman Catholics, and this was the dogma that we supposedly subscribed to.

Pete stared at me as if I had spoken a terrible heresy. He then elaborated his personal belief system, as enshrined in the as yet unrecognised *Gospel according to Pete*: 'When Reggie died, I know he went to doggie heaven. He is there right now, at the doggie-heaven bar, drinking a couple of pints.' Pete looked at me for validation, which I point-blank refused to provide. Undeterred, Pete continued, as if explaining a well-known fact to an ignorant child. 'So when Tom dies, he's going to hang out with Reggie as well, and have a couple of drinks with him. They'll probably discuss what it was like having the same master.'

'I suppose, when you die, you'll join them in that dog-friendly heavenly pub?' I was hoping Pete would hear what I was saying and realise how ridiculous it sounded.

Instead, Pete made a miraculous recovery and jumped straight off the couch. 'YES! EXACTLY!' Pete shouted, relieved that I had finally understood.

Actually, I was trying to work out where the hell I was going to find a medical specialist for Pete in Hanoi, to get him an emergency appointment for a suspected head injury.

9

On the Move

I let Pete recuperate on the couch for most of the afternoon, with Tom acting as his bedside nurse. However, it wasn't long before Pete and I were both hungry, and needed to find some grub.

'Fancy going out and getting some phở?' I said. I would have suggested staying in and cooking something up so that Pete could stay put on the sofa, but there was nothing edible in the house. I also figured Pete wouldn't be able to stomach anything heavy, but a bowl of Vietnamese noodle soup might just do the job.

Pete rose from his deathbed and slowly put on some proper clothes. He hobbled down the four flights of stairs, grasping on to the stair rail as if suffering from vertigo. I wondered if we'd ever make it the soup shop at the rate Pete was going. I didn't dare suggest we take his motorbike to speed up the journey; I was hoping Pete was permanently done with that mode of transportation.

The phở shop was located on a side street, a five-minute walk from our place. I'd happened upon it accidentally one day when I was roaming the streets with Tom. It had no signage on display, but it was obvious from afar what type of food it was selling. Outside, a street vendor diligently stirred a huge cauldron of steaming broth with a massive wooden spoon. Beside him, there was a large basket of white rice noodles, already softly cooked. My mouth watered as soon as we neared the stall.

'Phở bò, hai,' I said, hoisting two fingers in the air in case my Vietnamese was dodgy. I gave him 40,000 dong, the equivalent of two US dollars, to pay for two bowls of beef noodle soup. Pete and I then manoeuvred ourselves inside his shop to take up a free table. We were the only westerners in the place, but the Vietnamese clientele were too busy slurping soup to even notice our presence.

The plastic stools only came up to Pete's shins, which was a slight problem given his physical state. We squeezed ourselves into the kiddy seats and watched as our soup was prepared before us. The vendor tossed two nests of noodles into our bowls then threw some thinly sliced raw beef on top. This he drowned in boiling broth before serving up these steaming brews with beansprouts, fragrant green herbs, red-hot chilli and sliced limes on the side.

I grabbed some chopsticks from a container on the table, unwrapping them from their paper before breaking them in two. My months of living in Vietnam had turned me into a chopstick pro.

'How are you feeling now?' I asked Pete, plunging my chopsticks deep into the noodles, swirling them round to cool my soup.

'Sore,' he said, blowing absentmindedly on his phở. 'I think

I've had enough of that damn motorbike. I'm tempted just to take taxis to work from now on.'

I silently nodded. I understood where he was coming from. I had had a few near misses on my own pedal bike while travelling around Hanoi, and I went at nowhere near Pete's speed. The traffic was so chaotic you were risking life and limb going anywhere near a main road.

'But it's not just the accident that has thrown me for six,' Pete continued. 'I've been thinking, my job and everything, it's really not worked out how I had originally planned.'

I pulled a couple of coriander and mint leaves off their stalks and threw them on top of my meal. What Pete was saying didn't come as a surprise.

'So what do you want to do about it?' I asked.

'Your application for the job in Nepal got me thinking,' Pete said. 'Maybe we should just get out of here.'

'There's no guarantee that I'll get offered the position,' I replied. 'You know there are way better candidates out there.'

'I know, I know,' Pete replied, munching through some noodles that he had shoved into his mouth. It would have been nice if he had lied to me about my chances and said I was a dead cert. I knew, however, that the conversation was bigger than my Nepal job application, so it was probably best if we both told the truth.

'Vietnam does have lots of good things going for it,' I reminded him. 'You can't deny it's got great food and cheap beer.'

Pete nodded in agreement.

The Vietnamese had also lots of qualities I deeply admired. They have a fierce pride; something I assumed was instilled in them by the fact that no foreign invader had ever success-fully conquered their country. The Chinese, the French and Americans all left Vietnam defeated, despite what their own history tellers might imply. I was also amazed by the Vietnamese's incredible work ethic, as exemplified by our maid, Xuan, and her ferocious cleaning regime.

Regardless of Vietnam's various merits, Pete and I needed to figure out for ourselves if the place was good for us. One thing I had worked out about Pete and I was that, if we were unhappy with our jobs, regardless of the location, then there was no point in hanging around.

We drank up our phở and walked the short distance home.

We were not back in our flat five minutes when I received a phone call. 'Hi Moire, this is Kate,' the voice on the other side said. Kate was the human resources manager who was on the panel that had interviewed me for the Nepal job.

My heart stopped for an instant as it relocated to my mouth.

'I'm just calling to let you know the results of your recent interview,' Kate continued. Pete was standing beside me, excitedly mouthing to me words my head couldn't process.

'I'm happy to say we'd like to offer you the position of Country Representative in Nepal.'

I nearly dropped the phone. 'Thank you *so* much,' I said, giggling excitedly down the line. I sounded like some teen-ager who had just been invited to the school prom by her long-term, elusive crush. I took a deep breath and tried to sound professional. I was now a Country Representative after all. I needed to adopt a bit more decorum.

'If you could forward me the contract with the terms and

conditions then I can get back to you once I've read through it all,' I said. As if there was even the remotest chance of me refusing this offer. Just send me the damn thing and tell me where I need to sign, I thought.

'We'll forward the draft agreement later today,' Kate duly informed me. 'Of course, it will be conditional on you passing a medical exam.'

I knew this was standard procedure with overseas charities, given the health-care facilities in most developing countries. Kate didn't want me going to Nepal with any major pre-existing conditions they would then have to shoulder. I had no worries in that department, as I'd normally pass with flying colours. Then I remembered Tom: if he were also coming to Nepal, would he need medical clearance as well?

'There's just one other thing I need to ask,' I said to Kate, hesitating as I spoke. 'If I accept the job, is it okay if I bring my dog along as well?'

Pete's head craned towards my mobile's earpiece, eager to hear Kate's response. Interestingly, he didn't seem offended in the slightest that I'd asked Kate about Tom first. Technically I should have established if Pete could join me as my partner before enquiring about our dog.

'It shouldn't be a problem,' Kate replied, 'as long as you make the necessary arrangements yourself.'

I gave a thumbs-up to Pete, who rushed off to tell Tom the good news.

'Do you have a specific starting date in mind?' I asked Kate, trying to get the ball rolling. She informed me that they needed me to provide a signed contract and a completed medical assessment before they could book my plane ticket.

This paperwork normally took about seven days to finalise.

'I should be gone in a week,' I told Pete as I hung up. It all seemed so fast, but that was probably one of the reasons the interview panel chose me. I had sworn to them I could move immediately.

We soon realised there was no way Pete could look after Tom properly once I had left Hanoi; Tom would end up being locked up all day in the flat while Pete was at the office. 'You should bring Tom with you,' Pete said, helping me work through the emerging plan. 'I'll follow you in a couple of weeks, once I've quit my own job.'

If I had only a week, I needed to get moving if Tom was to fly with me. Neither Pete nor I had any idea, however, about how to move a pet across international borders. We should have quizzed Susan, Tom's previous owner and knight in shining armour, about her move from Vietnam to Thailand when we had the chance.

I called Tom's vet, the one who doubled up as Tom's groomer and boarding kennels. I assumed they moved pets for expats all the time. They told me to make an appointment so they could examine Tom. If he was in good shape, they could arrange for the Vietnamese government to issue an Animal Health Certificate. This was what the Nepal government would rely on to allow Tom entry to their country. Fortunately, all of Tom's vaccinations including his rabies one were up to date, so I anticipated the process wouldn't be too painful.

At the same time, Pete did some research online and found out something more troublesome. It turned out that different airlines have different policies when it comes to transporting pets. I needed to know the name of the airline I would be flying with to work out the exact process I had to follow, but I wouldn't know that until my job contract and my own medical examination were finalised.

I had an ominous feeling that this was going to turn into an administrative, logistical nightmare.

I got back in contact with Kate, the HR manager, and told her my dog-moving dilemma. She suggested we made a tentative flight booking from Hanoi to Kathmandu for the twelfth of the month, in ten days' time, so at least then I would know which airline I was travelling on. When I probed further, Kate revealed that the twelfth was the latest date I could arrive. The person I was taking over from, a guy called Phil, was leaving Nepal a couple of days later. To make matters worse, my line manager Lucia, who was based in Dublin, would be flying out to Kathmandu especially for the transition. I needed to arrive in time to see both my predecessor and new boss so that there was enough time for a proper handover. If not, I would be catapulted into the job without anyone senior there to help me. I'd be drowning before I even started.

Kate soon discovered that the most convenient routing was with Thai Airways, with a layover in Bangkok. Pete got in contact with the airline immediately to find out their rules and regulations governing pet transportation. When it came to organising things like this, Pete was always much better than me. I was happy for him to take the lead.

As soon as Pete got off the phone, he gave me the lowdown. 'The good news is that, if Tom and his crate are a combined weight of less than ten kilos, he can travel with you in the cabin.'

Neither Pete nor I had the slightest notion how heavy Tom or his crate was. To make matters worse, we didn't own a bathroom scales.

'I'll just bring Tom's crate along to the vet when I have Tom examined,' I suggested. 'I'm sure they have a weighing machine there.'

'To fit into the cabin,' Pete continued, 'the crate can be a maximum of fifty-five centimetres long, thirty-seven centimetres high, and thirty centimetres wide.'

We took out the tape measure we had bought when buying furniture to fit the flat. By a random stroke of sheer luck, the crate I got for Tom's toilet training also adhered to Thai Airways' pet-transportation policy.

I brought Tom along to the vet, who checked him over and gave him the all-clear. She told me that the Vietnamese Government's Department of Animal Health would issue Tom's certificate in about a week. I quickly did the maths. That meant I would probably receive his paperwork on the ninth of the month, giving me three days' leeway before my flight left. It was tight, but doable.

I also got Tom to stand on the scales when we were in the surgery. It turned out that he was a seven-kilogram dog, and his crate was exactly three kilos. With Tom curled up inside, they would just make Thai Airways' cut-off weight of ten kilos.

Everything seemed to be falling nicely into place. It looked like Tom and I would be winging our way to Kathmandu within the next couple of days.

In the meantime, I went along to a designated doctor in Hanoi to have my own check-up. However, unlike Tom, I failed to receive immediate clearance. I was instructed to scan all the completed forms and email them to a medical company based in London. Only when they had reviewed their contents could they give my employer the go-ahead.

As I ran around Hanoi hunting for various bits of paper, I was oblivious to the fact that Pete was busy contemplating the consequences of my leaving. I came home one evening to find him sitting on the flat's floor with Tom balanced on his knee. They looked like they were having a serious conversation.

'Now Tom, you have to look after Mummy when you're in Kathmandu,' Pete explained to Tom, ruffling his hairy head. 'Don't worry, Daddy will be there soon, and then we'll be a family again.'

On hearing those words, my eyebrows rose so far up my forehead they formed part of my fringe.

'Mummy? Daddy? What are you on about?' I said.

Pete ignored me as he continued to whisper top-secret instructions to Tom. It seems so obvious in retrospect, but I had been so focused on swotting up on the new job, confirming travel arrangements for both Tom and I, and packing up my things that I'd forgotten all about the emotional consequences of breaking up our household.

'Are you sure you're okay with this?' I asked Pete. 'With me moving and everything?'

Pete hesitated for the briefest moment. 'It's fine,' he said, hugging Tom close to him. 'It's for the best, I guess. And, like I said, I've always wanted to check out Nepal, maybe live there for a while. It's just that...are we breaking up?'

'What? Are you serious?' I hadn't expected that question.

'Sure haven't we passed the six months' probation we agreed on before leaving Dublin? And we're still together, no?'

Pete looked at me solemnly, his expression confirming that he was deadly serious. 'It's just that, you seem so focused on leaving. You don't seem that worried that we won't see each other for a while.'

He looked and sounded genuinely hurt.

To be honest, I could see where he was coming from. In my mind, however, our relationship had already survived our stint in Vietnam. We had managed to welcome a young pooing and peeing pup into our home and make him sanitary. I had learned that Pete's love for Tom did not diminish his own feelings for me. Our relationship had even endured my jealousy when I was convinced that Pete was going to run off with Ms Phuong.

I needed to assure Pete that I did love him, that we were a team, that we would go to Nepal together and have more adventures there. Admittedly I was still unsure at this stage if Pete and I would stay together forever, but I felt that our relationship was probably strong enough to survive another move to a different foreign country.

I also felt like that would be stating the bleedin' obvious. Weren't we both Irish? Since when did our nationality ever express what we truly thought and felt?

'Don't worry,' I said. 'If we do split up, you can have Tom.'

It was a horrible thing to say, but I found it easier to joke in awkward situations like this one rather than admit my true thoughts and feelings.

Pete hugged Tom a little closer, an embrace that seemed more akin to a desperate vice grip. Even if he was now second-guessing whether it was a good idea to move with me to Nepal, I knew that he would follow Tom wherever he went. Equally, I was sure that Pete, with his ability to make contacts and always say the right thing, would land on his feet and find something to keep him occupied once there.

On the ninth of the month, as promised, the vet handed me Tom's Animal Health Certificate courtesy of the Vietnamese Government. It was not until the following day that I got my own medical clearance. With the human doctor's seal of approval, I could finally confirm the airline ticket for my departure for two days' time.

I scanned Tom's Animal Health Certificate and sent it to the travel agent, for forwarding on to Thai Airways. Everything was finally going to plan.

That is, until I received a reply from the travel agent.

'I have forwarded your dog's certificate to Thai Airways. They have confirmed back that your dog will have clearance to travel in three days' time.'

Three days? No, that wasn't possible. We were scheduled to travel in forty-eight hours. I politely reminded the travel agent of my itinerary and of the necessity to expedite the process. She replied that it was out of her hands, and that I needed to talk to Thai Airways directly myself.

I dialled their number immediately. A very polite Thai lady answered and I tried to keep my cool as I explained my precarious situation.

'I understand your request,' she replied, formality in her tone. 'Our Thai Airways' Bangkok head office must approve your request first before we can allow you to travel with your dog.'

'And they can do that before the twelfth? I travel in two

days' time,' I said, hoping the travel agent had misunderstood Thai Airways' rules.

'This process normally takes three days,' she replied. 'I can put in a request for it to be prioritised if you like, but I cannot guarantee anything.'

The day of my flight arrived with no approval back from Bangkok. I was all packed up and ready to go, but I still had no idea whether Tom could join me or not. I refreshed my email account over and over again as I waited for my taxi to arrive. Despite clicking the mouse pad multiple times, no emails arrived.

Eventually, I couldn't wait any longer. I had a plane to catch to Kathmandu.

Pete and I agreed to go to the airport together, and bring Tom along in his crate. It was possible that Tom's authorisation was waiting at the airport rather than being emailed to me directly. As soon as I entered the departures terminal, I raced up to the check-in counter, threw my passport and ticket on the desk, and demanded to know Tom's travel status. The Thai Airways attendant tapped some keys on his computer.

'I'm sorry,' he said. 'Authorisation from Bangkok has not come through yet on our system.'

'But I've brought my dog with me to the airport,' I begged. 'Please let him come with me.'

At this stage, Tom and his crate were dangerously balanced on top of my other suitcases on the airport trolley. Pete was holding on to the crate for dear life.

I had a terrible feeling everything was going to start tumbling down around us.

Pete, Tom and I waited at the check-in desks until we heard the final boarding call. We approached the attendant one last time, but he shook his head at me before I could even open my mouth.

I turned around to face my entourage. 'I can't bring him,' I said to Pete, a lump stuck in my throat. 'The airline won't allow it.' I was already a bag of nerves from moving countries, taking up a new job, and leaving Pete behind. Having to leave Tom with Pete now, not knowing if we would ever be able to bring Tom with us to Nepal, was the final straw.

'Don't worry, I'll sort it out,' Pete said, a crack appearing in his voice. Knowing there was not much time left before my plane departed, I hastily threw myself into Pete's arms and buried myself in his embrace. I could no longer take the stress as my tears finally broke their banks and flooded down my face. Pete hugged me back desperately in return, as if we were trying to draw from each other enough strength to go our separate ways.

I stood and watched as Pete wheeled Tom away on the trolley and out the airport door. I was not sure if what I heard was the whine of a squeaky trolley being pushed away or of a mournful dog unsure of where his future lay.

If Pete was going to sort out Tom's departure, he would have to do it fast. Tom's Animal Health Certificate expired in a couple of days. If Tom was ever going to leave Vietnam, he needed to get out asap.

10

Kathmandu Chaos

I spent the whole flight out of Vietnam fretting about what was going to happen next. Would Pete be able to get Tom out in the coming days? Or would Tom have to stay in Hanoi until Pete was ready to relocate himself? Or, even worse, would Pete be able to get Tom out of the country at all, given all the administrative hurdles involved? What if Pete had to leave Tom behind in Hanoi forever, and find him a new owner before he went?

I wasn't sure how Pete would cope with that last worst-case scenario. I would have probably come to terms with Tom's rehousing, eventually, but I doubted Pete would ever recover from such a brutal separation.

It was not until I saw the Himalayan Mountains emerging beneath me that I snapped back to the present. I was moving for a purpose and I had work to do.

Arriving in the airport, I was met by the office driver who'd bring me to where I'd live during my stay in Kathmandu. I found him standing outside the terminal holding a placard emblazoned with my name. I approached him, signalling that the name written on his card was indeed mine. Putting it to one side, he brought his two hands together, palm gently touching palm. Bowing ever so slightly, he politely mouthed, 'Namaste.'

What with my hands brimming with my belongings and my total ignorance of Nepali, I failed to reciprocate his warm and welcoming gesture. Instead, I smiled back as broadly as I could, as it finally dawned on me that I had actually made it to my dream job and country. I was going to live and work in Nepal.

It was a relief to have a ride pre-arranged. As I followed the office driver back to his car, local taxi drivers swarmed around me trying to get my attention, shouting random prices to transport me into town. Their prices ranged wildly, and I had no idea which one was the proper rate. I doubted, however, their mini Suzuki cars would be capable of holding all my luggage: my entire life's possessions crammed into several bags. Fortunately they just about fitted into my company's four-wheel drive Land Cruiser.

Kathmandu itself was teeming with sights and sounds. Even on the short trip to my new house, my senses were bombarded. I watched the chaos of the capital's traffic swarming past my window, madly and badly driven motor-bikes, decrepit buses, overloaded lorries belching out black fumes, with miniature cars weaving their way through this vehicular swamp. I smelled the stench of a busy humanity, wafts of prayer incense intermingled with putrid sewage flooding the car's confines. Despite all these technically unpleasant surroundings, I was secretly happy to be in the midst of such madness. Kathmandu would be a challenge, one that I couldn't wait to get stuck right into.

The driver dropped me off at the place I would call home for the next eight months. He unbolted and swung open the heavy metallic gates to reveal a beautiful, simple house.

Phil, the guy I was taking over from, was there to meet me and to guide me around his soon-to-be former abode. I would not only be taking over his job, but also his home.

He descended the steps leading to the front door, and warmly shook my hand. 'How was your trip?' he asked me. 'Good, I hope?'

Despite my best intentions, memories of abandoning Tom at Hanoi airport suddenly invaded my mind. I wanted to appear upbeat and enthusiastic, but I just couldn't shake the trauma of my hasty Hanoian departure. Just as I was considering whether or not to disclose to Phil these recent happenings, he looked down at the luggage I had brought and asked, 'Did you bring your dog?'

I shook my head, the guilt now oppressive. Phil had gone to great lengths to check the Nepalese government's entry requirements for domesticated dogs, yet to no avail. I felt fully responsible for not getting Tom's paperwork approved in time, even though I could have maintained that I was technically not to blame.

'No,' I said sadly. 'It's a long story, but my partner, Pete, will try and get him shipped as soon as possible.' I tried to force a smile.

I looked around at my new surroundings and felt even more overwhelmed. The house would have been a perfect pad for Tom. It had a small garden, without any hot-pot ladies in the vicinity to dictate where he peed and pooed. The house itself was completely enclosed by a perimeter wall, which

Tom could run laps around inside to his heart's content. It was so much better than his current arrangement, holed up in a small flat in Hanoi, four storeys up.

Phil thankfully probed no further. 'Let me show you around the place,' he suggested instead. He led me through the front door, to a large sitting and living area, with a kitchen at the back. To the side there was an office and spare room, with a sweeping wooden staircase leading up to the main en-suite bedroom. It was the perfect size for a couple with a small dog. This realisation hurt profoundly.

Phil then brought me into the office and pointed to a large metal trunk in the corner. 'Your earthquake kit is over there,' he said. 'It's got everything you'll need if one strikes.' I opened it up to see tinned food, a tarpaulin, a machete and a shovel. There were batteries, torches, a satellite phone, rope and a whole host of other essentials.

Nepal is located on the boundary of two tectonic plates. These colliding plates have produced the Himalayan Mountains, and with them, the propensity for earthquakes. What makes matters worse is that Kathmandu is built on a former, now dried-up, lake. Sub-standard buildings now sit on this unsettled clay soil, which liquefies and amplifies with the slightest shock. It was well known that the smallest jolt and Kathmandu could be flattened in an instant, like a gigantic pack of cards. Little did I know that five years later, an earthquake would do exactly that.

I closed the box up and made a mental note to go through its contents meticulously at a later stage. I wanted to be prepared if a quake did indeed hit while I was there.

Phil then brought me to the adjacent corner, where a long

line of car batteries was jerry-rigged together. 'Power outages are common at the moment,' he explained. 'There's low rainfall at this time of year and the dams don't have enough water to produce sufficient electricity for the city's population.'

I knew this was the politically correct version of events. Nepal has massive hydroelectric potential but produces only half of what it needs. Investment in the power sector was negligible during the country's ten-year civil war, which had ended only a few years before. The conflict's devastating effects still resonated in the country's daily life.

'There's an official timetable I'll give you later telling you when the cuts are. Don't worry, it's normally just for a couple of hours a day,' Phil went on. 'These batteries are enough to light a few bulbs, charge your mobile, watch some TV, but anything big like the fridge won't work.'

'Good to know.' I'd been spoiled in Vietnam with uninterrupted electricity supply and was probably getting a little soft. Now I was feeling like I was in a proper developing country with real issues, where maybe I could actually do something useful to help out.

'Oh, and the water supply often gets cut,' Phil said. I wondered if he was trying to frighten me off or prepare me for the worst. 'We have a tank outside that should hold enough to tide you over.'

Once Phil was finished briefing me, I brought my bags into the house and dumped them inside the front door. I noticed then there was another similar doorway on the other side of the house, facing mine.

'What's in there?' I asked.

'Your neighbours,' Phil replied. He proceeded to tell me

that the landlord had basically split the place in two. From the outside, it looked like one building, but it in fact housed two families.

'They're a Dutch couple with two young kids,' Phil said. 'Really nice guys. I'm sure you'll get along just fine.'

Once Phil and the driver left me alone to settle in, I needed to talk with Pete, let him know I'd arrived safely, and find out if he and Tom were okay. It had been over twenty-four hours since we had last been in contact.

The easiest way for us to speak was via Skype. I crossed my fingers and hoped my connection worked. I was not sure if Phil had mentioned anything about Internet outages.

Pete picked up after a few rings.

'Hi Pete! I'm in Kathmandu.'

'Oh thank God you've arrived safely,' Pete said. 'I was really worried.' It was kind to say, but I should have been the least of his concerns given the situation I had left him in.

'How are you guys doing?' I asked. 'Did you get back from the airport okay?'

'Oh man, it's been a total disaster of a day,' Pete replied, exasperation in his tone. 'I called Thai Airways as soon as I got home and asked them what we should do.'

'And?'

'They put me on hold for ages and transferred me to a million different offices.' I was sure that put him in a really shitty mood. I immediately thought of the poor airline official who probably ended up dealing with Pete after he had had to go through such a phone ping-pong rigmarole. 'I *finally* got through to someone who told me I can send Tom to Kathmandu next week, unaccompanied. They will treat him as checked-in baggage and put him in the cargo hold.'

'He'll go as cargo?' I stuttered. 'Is that really safe?'

'They told me he'll be put in a pressurised, heated part of the baggage hold,' Pete reassured me, though by the sound of his voice he needed some convincing as well. 'The next available cargo flight going to Kathmandu is in four days' time. I just need to go to the airline's office here in Hanoi and fill in all the forms to book him on that flight.'

I knew straightaway this would be an activity Pete would despise. Anything to do with officialdom, like filling forms or being made to wait, made his blood boil. That was precisely why he'd made me deal with our Vietnamese motorbike driving licences all those months before. Much to my surprise, however, Pete sounded surprisingly calm when talking about arranging Tom's transportation. Perhaps Pete didn't mind so much if the administration was for Tom. Perhaps Pete enjoyed spending hours writing down facts, in great detail, about his darling dog.

The other thing that Pete needed to work out was some sort of mechanism to allow Tom to eat and drink while in transit. If Tom had accompanied me, I could have placed him on my knee in the cabin and hand fed him myself. If Tom was going to be placed in the hold, he needed to be self-sufficient for the entire trip. Pete told me that the vet could sell him a special water bottle that screwed into Tom's crate door. An inverted water bottle connected to a long plastic tube ending in a metal ball that only expelled water when pressed on, it resembled something you'd find in a hamster cage. I was certain Pete would devote several hours each day up until Tom's departure training Tom to drink from this foreign receptacle. I was actually close to putting money on Pete doing an actual drinking demonstration himself just so that Tom could fully grasp the mechanism.

Finding a food receptacle for Tom's crate proved a tad more difficult. Neither the vet nor the pet shop apparently sold such contraptions so Pete headed off to the local supermarket. After much wandering up and down aisles, he purchased a plastic soap dish from the toiletry section, stabbed a few holes into it and firmly fixed it to the crate's wire door with cable ties. He then filled the dish with some dry dog food, purchased from the same supermarket. Just in case Tom became extra ravenous on board, Pete taped the remainder of the dry-food bag on to the top of the crate. All Tom had to do was inform Thai Airways handlers to top up his bowl if and when he was peckish.

I breathed a huge sigh of relief. I knew I could trust Pete to find a way to move Tom safely to Kathmandu without one of us having to physically hold Tom's paw on a flight.

'That's great news!' I said. 'I'm so sorry his approval didn't come through in time.'

'Honestly, it wasn't your fault,' Pete rushed to point out. 'I should have just lowered my expectations and assumed something would go wrong.' I felt chastened as Pete said this, for not devising a foolproof plan in the first place. 'Listen, leave it with me,' he said. 'I'll make sure Tom gets on that flight.'

Pete loved that dog too much to leave anything to chance. With Pete in charge, I knew Tom would be winging his way to me the following week, without fail.

With matters in Hanoi under control, I turned my attention to Kathmandu. It was Friday, so I had the whole weekend to find my feet in this new town. Before leaving Hanoi, friends had forwarded me contacts of people they knew living in Nepal. I emailed some of them to see if there was anything happening in the next day or two and soon heard back from a Dutch guy named Roger who ran a hotel that was literally around the corner from my new home.

'There's a group of us doing a run tomorrow in the hills around Kathmandu Valley,' Roger told me. 'Want to come?'

I used to run a lot when I lived in Ireland, especially in the mountains, but my athletic habits had been severely curtailed while living in hot and humid Hanoi. I hummed and hawed over whether to go, unsure if my body could handle it, yet I was so desperate to get out into the hills that in the end I wished my body good luck and signed up for the jaunt.

At 6.30 a.m. the next morning, I was sitting in a hotel reception chair, flicking through a magazine and cursing myself for arriving so early. Before Roger's appearance, I was contemplating returning home and going back to bed, willing to concede that I had made a terrible error.

Then Roger bounced into his hotel lobby and introduced himself, shaking my hand firmly. 'You're in for a real treat with this morning's route.' Roger was a tall, thin man in his fifties, with an accent impossible to trace back to the Netherlands. He had probably travelled around the globe so much that his English was now a mixture of several international influences.

His infectious enthusiasm for that day's planned adventure meant I couldn't bail out. When two more runners, Billi and Richard, arrived at the hotel lobby on their mountain bikes, I knew escape was impossible.

We started off on a gentle jog out through the city's district known as Patan. Soon we were winding our way through narrow streets, past ornate red-brick temples packed with morning worshippers. We took wide berths past stray dogs, around women precariously balancing metal urns brimming with water on their heads.

On our way out of the city, we picked up two Nepali runners, Rajman and Bhimsen. Roger, Richard, and Billi greeted them in Nepali, then took off after them. I soon saw that, although Rajman and Bhimsen were both small and wiry, they were incredibly fast runners. 'Just watch,' Roger panted, chasing after them. 'They're going to kill us on the hills.'

Soon we crossed over the main Ring Road, Kathmandu's official corset. Urban sprawl had engulfed this barrier, and spilled out into the countryside. 'This all used to be paddy fields,' Billi lamented as we journeyed through more built-up areas. It took us another quarter hour before we finally reached open green countryside, full of rich and fertile terraced rice paddies. Finally we had reached 'real' Nepal. We ran on through tiny villages, taking it all in at speed: women tending the cattle, men drinking strong tea from shot glasses, and children carrying firewood, everyone busy about their day.

We hit the ridge at Suryabinayak and stopped to pay an impromptu visit to a local temple. All around us people were busy lighting candles and turning prayer wheels, hoping their fortune would change with each candle flicker and cylindrical spin. I saw goats being hoisted up some steps to a small courtyard. 'They're going to be sacrificed for good fortune,' Roger explained.

I felt a bit overwhelmed.

Fortunately, as we left the temple, Roger suggested we stop for some refreshment. That was exactly what I needed right then: a nice calming cup of tea. Roger led us to a teahouse conveniently located on a ridge. We sat down on the concrete outside and sipped our hot, spiced and sweetened drinks. On the horizon, barely perceptible, I made out a faint white line. The snow-capped peaks of the Himalayan Mountains were right in front of us. I could barely contain my excitement.

We completed the rest of the run at a relatively leisurely pace. Around midday, we emerged from a forest. Nearby was a village, and we were just in time to catch a local bus back into town. We crammed ourselves into its rickety back seats: we were sweaty, dusty, blistered and weary, yet none of us seemed to mind. Despite our evident dirt and smell, sari-clad women squeezed into the seats beside us, without a single complaint.

'So are you coming with us to Pokhara next week?' Roger asked.

I shrugged my shoulders. 'What's happening there?'

'An ultra-marathon on part of the Annapurna trail.'

I thought about it for a second. It would certainly be a chance to explore the area. 'Sure. Count me in.'

I spent the rest of the weekend recuperating from the morning jaunt, but deep down I was very happy. I really believed I was going to like my stay in Nepal.

On Monday morning, bright and early, I made my way to the office where Phil and my new boss from Dublin, Lucia, were waiting. They ushered me through to the meeting room, and started my handover briefing.

From the get-go, I felt swamped. There seemed so much to do, and so little time to do it. The reason the contract was only for eight months was that the organisation was closing its offices in Nepal, having decided instead to prioritise even poorer countries. I was therefore responsible for wrapping up its operations.

I was told of water and sanitation programmes and nutrition interventions that needed urgent completion. I was briefed on human resource issues that I had to prioritise. I had to dispose of assets, make sure final reports were submitted to donors, archive relevant documentation, and complete remaining audits.

All of a sudden, my worries about Tom paled into insignificance. My full focus needed to be on getting the long list of activities done. I simply didn't have the time or energy to be thinking about transporting a former street dog halfway across Asia.

11

Tom's Flight

Before I knew it, it was day three of my new job and my head was throbbing from information overload. I had jumped in the proverbial deep end and was experiencing a distinctly sinking feeling rather than a bobbing-along-nicely one.

With the office closure date approaching much faster than I could have anticipated, the scale of work seemed overwhelming. I was in deep trouble.

Admittedly, I was partly to blame. It had since dawned on me that I may have slightly exaggerated my professional abilities during the interview process. Maybe I wasn't as hot as I thought I was when it came to dealing with human resource issues. Perhaps I was a little bullish when describing my grasp of financials and donor accounting.

I staggered into the office early on Wednesday morning, planning to swot up on the issues I needed to deal with that day. Work didn't officially start until 9 a.m., so there was little risk of anyone disturbing me at that godforsaken hour. As I swung open my office door, all I could see were piles and piles of papers dominating my desk's skyline. I groaned at the thought of wading through them, knowing full well that the chances of me understanding their contents bordered close to zero.

I needed an appropriate diversion, so instead of tackling the mountain of papers, I switched on my computer and opened my email box. At least if I dealt with urgent matters, which emails tended to bring, I would get some sense of accomplishment to help kick-start my day.

Within seconds, a truckload of emails was dumped into my inbox, bold and blackened in their unread state. My eye scanned through their senders' names and summarised contents, until it stopped dead at one from Pete. 'Wish us luck!' was its title. I double clicked on it to see its subject matter. Oh God, I had completely forgotten! What with all the work mayhem preoccupying my mind, I had completely forgotten that Tom's scheduled departure date was that very day.

I scurried off a quick reply, telling Pete I would call him on Skype that night to hear how he got on. I was of course assuming that Pete would be successful in his mission and that, by the time I contacted him, Tom would be winging his way to me. The alternative outcome I didn't even dare contemplate: that Pete was forced to return to our flat in Hanoi, dragging Tom behind him, the inconceivable conclusion that I would never see Tom ever again.

I spent the rest of the day trying to get my head around a disparate array of donor funding contracts. I barely came up for air. Before I knew it, the day was over. I looked at the clock in the corner of my computer screen. It was 5 p.m. I remembered my promise, to check in with Pete before the office closed for the day. I clicked on his Skype call button.

Pete picked up almost immediately.

'Hey Pete. Tell me. How did it go?' I asked, cutting to the chase.

'Oh my God, Moire, it was an unmitigated disaster!' he gasped over the phone line.

That didn't bode well. 'What happened?' I asked, my stomach suddenly turning triple back somersaults. 'Did Tom get on the flight or not?'

Despite my clear question, Pete didn't immediately give me the answer I was desperately seeking. Instead he decided to provide me with blow-by-blow details of the trauma he had just undergone with Tom.

Before Pete left our flat that morning, he had kitted Tom's crate out in line with Thai Airways' stringent requirements. He filled out a raft of forms that demanded various intimate details about Tom. This highly sensitive information, once divulged in triplicate, was secured to Tom's crate with reams of parcel tape. Pete didn't even dare contemplate what would happen to Tom if this information accidentally peeled off mid-transit.

Pete also had to glue on a variety of stickers warning handlers that the crate contained live cargo. In addition, he had to affix a sign with several arrows pointing skyward, the orientation in which the crate had to remain. Heaven forbid that Tom undertook the entire journey travelling upside down on his head due to a handler mistaking which way was up. Once everything was attached, Pete could barely see the crate underneath all the official documentation and hazard labels. Tom was also a little unsure of venturing into his box, unable to recognise his old home. It took Pete a couple of friendly shoves of Tom's derrière before he could finally slam the crate's gate closed, locking Tom firmly inside.

With Tom bedded down in his carrier, they headed off to Hanoi airport. Though Tom's flight wasn't scheduled until 2 p.m., Pete had decided to turn up good and early five hours in advance, in case of any unforeseen delays. This was despite the fact that, unlike last time, Thai Airways' headquarters in Bangkok had already provisionally approved Tom's paper-work. At this stage, however, Pete was not taking anything for granted.

Thai Airways staff had instructed Pete not to bring Tom to the usual departures terminal designated for human beings. Tom had already lost the privilege of travelling that way after the mess I made of his travel arrangements first time round. Instead, Tom had to go to Thai Airways' freight office, a sepa-rate industrial building tucked away within the sprawling airport complex.

At 9 a.m. on the dot, Pete stood outside the freight office, looking up at the stark, grey warehouse. Tom lay in his cage by Pete's feet, motionless and worryingly quiet.

'It's okay, Tom,' Pete said, addressing the stickered crate from above. 'You'll be on the flight before you know it.' It was Pete who needed more reassurance than Tom, however, even though it was Tom's future residency that was hanging in the balance.

On the stroke of nine, a Thai Airways official arrived and opened up the building. Pete stalked the Thai Airways agent into his office, lugging Tom and his cumbersome crate with him. It was stuffy and hot in the office after a night of Asian enclosure. With no one else waiting in line, Pete marched straight up to the agent's desk and plonked Tom on the floor beside him.

'I'm sending Tom, my dog, to Kathmandu this afternoon,' Pete said, spreading the entire contents of Tom's folder on the counter that lay between them. Without saying a word, the agent surveyed the pages fanned across his table top before deciding which page to inspect first. During this period of deadly silence, Pete's eye gravitated towards the nametag pinned to the agent's shirt pocket. Mr Nguyen was the man who held Tom's future in his palm.

As Mr Nguyen picked up each piece of paper one by one, there was no hint from his blank expression whether Tom would be successful in his application. Pete didn't know whether to make small talk with Mr Nguyen to cajole him into making the right decisions, or to bend down to Tom and assure him that the process was in good hands. Tom, too, remained deadly quiet, as if holding his breath in preparation to hear the final outcome.

After what seemed like forever, Mr Nguyen nodded his head ever so slightly in the affirmative. 'Your forms and medical documentation are correct,' he said, before bending down to scrutinise Tom's crate. After checking that all the right stickers were in the right places, he judiciously stamped Tom's forms.

Pete chuckled to himself.

'I should not have come so early, Mr Nguyen,' Pete said, gesturing to the office clock on the wall. It was barely 9.30 a.m.

'No, it is good you come early,' the agent replied. 'This stage is fast. The customs agent take more time.'

'Customs agent?' Pete said, a little confused. 'I thought Thai Airways...I thought you dealt with the whole process. I thought we were...done.'

'No, no, not finished,' Mr Nguyen said, gathering up Tom's papers and forcing them back into Pete's hands. 'Thai Airways is responsible for the physical shipment of your cargo. Now you must go to your customs agent, to clear your cargo through government customs and immigration.'

'Customs clearance?' Pete said, nervously eyeing the same clock. 'How long does that take?'

'That depends,' Mr Nguyen replied. 'It depends on how good your customs agent is, how well he knows the customs officials.' He looked away, avoiding Pete's death stare. 'Maybe three to four hours,' he said, with a nonchalant shrug.

'I wasn't told about *this* process,' Pete snapped, leaning heavily over the counter that barely separated Mr Nguyen from Pete's growing wrath. 'Where do I even find one of these, these...people, these...customs agents?'

Mr Nguyen refused to react to Pete's looming physical presence and obviously mounting anger. The Vietnamese refuse to flinch when confronted with any invading foreign entity.

'You go to building over there,' Mr Nguyen said, pointing wearily out of his window to another depressing edifice across the way. 'That is where Mr Ho works. He usually does Thai Airways custom clearance.'

'Mr Ho? Okay. And what time will Mr Ho be there?' Pete asked, trying to maintain some semblance of composure.

'Sorry, Mr Ho is on holidays today,' the agent replied.

Little did Mr Nguyen know that Pete is prone to physical

violence when confronted with unexpected revelations such as this. It was only Tom's presence that forced Pete to maintain his composure. He didn't want to set a bad example in front of his impressionable young dog.

'Then who is doing Mr Ho's work today?' Pete said, forcing a bittersweet grin. 'Who is my customs agent now?'

'Mr Ho come back next week,' Mr Nguyen replied. 'You can come back and send your dog then.'

'No!' Pete roared involuntary, losing the plot despite his original resolve. Getting into an argument with any Vietnamese official, government or otherwise, is never a good idea, but Pete was so exasperated that he could not help but start a fight. 'Next week is no good. Tom's medical clearance will have expired by then. My dog has to go today.'

Mr Nguyen had probably witnessed such a scene a million times before: a foreigner failing to understand simple rules and regulations that were clearly laid out in the official freight shipping procedures manual. If only Pete had bothered to request said manual and read it from cover to cover, none of this would have ever happened.

Pete did not know what to do next. He isn't good at being utterly powerless in the face of unadulterated authority. Only the thought of leaving Tom behind in Vietnam forever made Pete stand his ground. He literally refused to move from Mr Nguyen's office until Tom's transit dilemma was somehow sorted.

'Okay, how much money do you have?' Mr Nguyen said with a hesitant sigh, all of a sudden taking pity on Pete and his stranded pup. Money can make things move in this country. The question was how much would it cost?

'Fifty dollars,' Pete blurted back, grabbing the lifeline Mr Nguyen was reluctantly throwing.

'Not enough,' Mr Nguyen retorted immediately. 'Go to ATM in main terminal, then try and get him through customs yourself.'

It was a considerable risk. Mr Ho, the real customs agent, was probably crucial to achieving a successful clearance. How could Pete possibly get Tom through this process when he knew nothing about the customs process and was mute when it came to Vietnamese?

'How much will I need?' Pete replied. He still had over four hours before Tom's plane left Vietnamese airspace. He still had a slim chance of getting Tom on that flight.

'Get as much as you can,' was all Mr Nguyen would offer as an answer.

It was becoming clear to Pete that the more money he had, the greater the chances were that Tom would physically get on that plane.

There was no time to lose. Pete stuffed the forms back into their folder, grabbed the handle of Tom's box, and raced towards the nearest ATM. Tom's crate banged angrily against Pete's leg with every stride he took. Tom himself must have been in a state of shock, barely making a sound as he was bashed against the container's sides as Pete sprinted towards the machine.

Once Pete had barged his way into the main terminal, he thrust his card deep into the ATM and extracted the maximum daily limit, an extra five hundred dollars to add to his current stash.

It was 10.30 a.m. by the time Pete lumbered towards the

freight terminal area where Mr Nguyen had instructed him to go. By now, Tom was cowering inside the back of his crate, fearing to make a wrong move. The Vietnamese sun was streaking towards its midday peak, showering down searing heat rays. The fact that Pete still didn't cope well with the Asian climate didn't help his case. His clothes were soaked with sweat, making him look suspiciously tetchy to the terminal's guard whom Pete now approached.

'Customs clearance?' Pete asked the guard.

'No English,' was the guard's definitive reply.

Undeterred by this welcome, Pete persevered. He delved into the folder that was now dripping in his own perspiration, and presented the guard with Tom's freight forms. Refusing to touch them with his own military hands, the guard scanned the forms from afar. A brief flicker of recognition appeared in his eyes before his hand rose to indicate the exact building that Pete and Tom should go towards.

A din of voices rose ominously in volume the closer Pete brought Tom to the actual customs building. Pete took a deep breath and pushed open a set of double doors to discover a den of mayhem inside. Hundreds of people were crammed into this constricted space, shouting and furiously shaking paperwork at a line of inexpressive uniformed officials sitting stoically behind a counter. It looked like a bad day at the New York stock exchange, when share prices were crashing and brokers were desperately trying to sell.

If there was ever a time when Pete needed Mr Ho, the Thai Airways custom agent, it was right then. How could a white Irishman with a cuddly domestic pet ever negotiate this bedlam?

Grasping Tom's crate handle firmly, Pete attempted to force his way forward through the frantic crowd. All around him, there was pushing and shoving, yelling and screaming. Several elbows were shoved into Pete's ribs as he forced his way towards the counter. Only Pete's superior six-foot stature and many years of playing rugby allowed him to advance at all. It still took over twenty minutes of close physical contact before Pete finally emerged from the scrum and found himself directly in front of the officials. Plonking Tom down between his legs, Pete readied himself to make his case.

If Pete had actually participated in procuring our driving licenses way back when we arrived in Vietnam, he might have had at least some experience to draw on as he stood in front of these stern customs men. It would have been excellent training. Instead, with an unrealistic sense of optimism, he handed Tom's well-worn and well-read documents over, buoyed with false enthusiasm.

It wasn't long before Pete was subjected to a tirade of incomprehensible Vietnamese.

'I'm so sorry, I don't understand!' Pete said over and over, which did nothing to calm down the tormented official seated before him. Instead of taking pity on Pete, the official's yells only became more venomous. The official's hand movements, telling Pete to piss off, only became more irate.

Despite the fact that he was obviously not wanted, Pete stood his ground. Eventually his intransigence somewhat paid off. The customs official took hold of a form from a pile on his desk and threw it in Pete's general direction. Pete picked it up off the floor and retreated momentarily, bowing submissively as he left.

On closer inspection, Pete noticed that the form was in pure, unadulterated Vietnamese. It was 12.30 p.m. Tom's flight was due to leave in an hour and a half. It was highly unlikely that Pete could master the local language and fill in the form correctly within this ninety-minute period.

Pete had had enough. He retreated to a semi-quiet corner and placed the crate on the cool concrete floor.

'Come on Tom,' Pete said with a heavy sigh, bending down to face the crate he had been lugging around all morning. 'I think it's time for us to go back home.'

Tom tried to push his snout out of the wire grate to console Pete, to thank him for his valiant efforts, but the stifling heat in the customs building had robbed Tom of his wet, welcoming lick. His tongue felt like sandpaper on Pete's fingertips. Even his nose was perilously dry from too many hours confined in his stuffy cage. 'I think we need to wait until next week when Mr Ho comes back from his holidays,' Pete said, his voice starting to break from the stress. 'I'm so sorry, but let's get out of here.'

Pete was about to get up and disappear out of the double doors, when he felt a hand being firmly placed on his arm.

'How much money do you have?'

On hearing these words, Pete rose up from the ground with a renewed sense of energy. Seeing Tom in this fragile, frightened state had made Pete realise that he had to get Tom out of this country right away. It was now or never.

Pete looked down at the Vietnamese man who had just reached out to him. Despite Pete physically towering over him, the man held his ground.

'I have fifty dollars,' Pete replied, refusing to divulge the real amount of cash he had in his possession.

'Not enough,' the man shouted back. 'Custom fee is forty dollar already.'

'Okay, okay,' Pete said. 'How much do you need?'

The man opened his mouth, then closed it again. He needed a moment to think. This could be a big payday for him, from this obviously loaded westerner who was so out of his depth, but he evidently didn't want to say something so ludicrously high that it would force Pete to make good his promise to leave.

'Two hundred,' the man yelled.

Pete hesitated. 'Okay, two hundred,' he said. 'But that's it. That's all I have.'

The man stared back at Pete. Did he know Pete was lying?

'Okay, I help you,' Pete's new Vietnamese friend said at last, seemingly content with the offer. He pointed to an empty waiting area at the back of the room. 'Wait there. I meet you in five minute.'

Pete was so dazed by this sudden change in circumstance that it took a while for him to comply. Eventually he bent down to pick up Tom's crate, and hobbled over to the quiet area. Once there, he opened up Tom's cage for the first time that day and let Tom hop up on to his knee. Pete hugged Tom tightly as if trying to draw strength and courage from his ever-resilient dog. For once, Tom didn't try to escape Pete's desperate hold. He too seemingly needed the comfort of Pete's firm and commanding embrace.

Five minutes later, as promised, the Vietnamese man returned. He had no time, however, for such emotional interludes.

'Quick,' he commanded. 'We fill form.'

When Pete failed to respond quickly enough, the man grabbed Tom's papers off Pete and took control. He filled in a raft of new forms the customs officials required, copying most of what was on the airlines' forms, but just on to different lines and boxes.

'Are you a customs agent?' Pete asked, impressed by his new friend's proficiency.

'Yes, yes, yes,' he mumbled back, not wanting to waste a second.

The clock on the wall showed 1 p.m. Tom had only one hour left before his plane left Vietnam forever.

'Forty dollars,' the man said, holding out his hand. Pete gladly handed over the cash then watched as his friend disappeared back into the frenzied crowd.

It of course occurred to Pete that he might never see the man ever again. The man could have been a skilled con artist, roaming the room for bewildered customers who were only too happy to cough up hard currency for some assistance. Then again, though forty dollars might be a large sum to some, it wasn't much to Pete. If Pete never saw the supposed customs agent and his forty dollars again, it wasn't the end of the world.

Pete was still wondering if he had just been duped when his friend dramatically re-appeared. He duly presented Pete with the forms he had just filled in on Pete's behalf, now signed and stamped by the customs officials. Pete could hardly believe his luck.

'Now you pay me,' the man said, holding out his hand for the remainder of his two hundred dollar fee.

'Not yet,' Pete said. 'Please, just tell me where I bring my dog now?'

'Don't worry,' he replied. 'You have all the forms. You just need to put your dog on the belt.'

'But where's the belt?' Pete said, by now worried that this process would never, ever end. 'Please, can you just bring me there? I promise, I'll pay you once we get my dog on to the plane.'

The customs agent's face softened a little. 'Sure,' he said. 'Come this way.'

He led Pete and his crate out of the double doors and finally into the fresh air. Together, they walked a short distance to a hangar-like building with large sets of conveyor belts lined across its mouth guarded by yet another official.

Pete was already looking forward to leaving the airport and never seeing another uniformed officer again.

The customs agent stepped forward and began to converse with the guard. While they spoke, Pete noticed one of the belts had a Thai Airlines logo fixed above it. It was a welcome, reassuring sign.

'See,' the customs agent said, leading him to the same conveyor. 'You trust me now?'

Pete couldn't help but smile. 'You've earned your money.' With that, Pete gave the man his dues. Without this mysterious Good Samaritan, Pete would have already returned home to contemplate how else to smuggle Tom out of Vietnam.

With one palm, the man accepted his payment. With the other, he grabbed hold of Pete's hand.

'I think you love your dog very much,' he said, shaking Pete's hand firmly. The close unexpected contact from this kind random stranger was too much for Pete to bear.

'Yes,' Pete said, stifling an unexpected sob. 'I suppose I do.'

Without warning, the conveyor clunked into operation

and the belt began to turn. The sound made Pete snap back to reality. 'Be a good dog now Tom,' Pete said, reclaiming his hands before bending down to Tom's level as his faithful friend prepared for his imminent departure. 'Try and sleep. You'll see Moire soon in Kathmandu.'

Despite his comforting words, all Pete heard in return from the back of the crate was the most desperate, desolate whine. All morning, Tom had been stoic about his travel plans, but now that the moment had finally arrived, the prospect of leaving Pete for what could be forever was too much to bear.

Fighting back his own emotions, Pete picked Tom's crate up by the handle and placed it on the belt. Slowly, he watched the container inch its way towards the rubber flaps. Suddenly, without warning, Tom appeared at the crate's grating door. Realising what was happening, Tom tried to escape back to his master, pawing the solid metal rods, but in vain. Desperate yelps and frightened barks joined the cacophony of Tom's scraping nails on his impenetrable gate.

Pete couldn't watch. That day Tom witnessed the closest that Pete, a man who doesn't easily shed tears, has ever come to an emotional breakdown.

Pete did not leave the airport immediately. Instead, he headed to the nearest bar in the terminal and ordered himself a stiff drink. Once his nerves were sufficiently numbed, he went and found Mr Nguyen at the Thai Airways office.

'Your dog is on the flight,' Mr Nguyen confirmed with a brief smile. The Thai Airways flight from Hanoi to Kathmandu had departed. Tom was on his way to Kathmandu.

With Tom now gone, Pete found himself all alone in Hanoi.

Tom the puppy after just arriving in our flat in Hanoi, Vietnam 2009.

Reggie, Pete's childhood sheepdog. Waterford, Ireland.

ABOVE: Moire and Pete visiting Ha Long Bay, Vietnam 2009.

LEFT: Pete with his beloved Tom on our balcony overlooking Hanoi's Trúc Bach Lake, Vietnam 2009.

Pete and his Honda Motorbike in Hanoi, Vietnam 2009.

Pete and Moire hiking to Poon Hill on the Annapurna Circuit,
Nepal 2010.

One-year-old Tom in his home in Kathmandu, Nepal 2010.

Moire on a mountain run on Kathmandu's ridge,
Nepal 2010.

Pete in Kathmandu's Durbar Square,
Nepal 2010.

Pete and Moire in a traditional Cambodian outfit photoshoot,
Phnom Penh 2011.

Pete and his beloved Tom back home safely in Ireland, 2014.

12

Himalayan Home

I put down the phone, reeling from what Pete had just told me. I was still not sure whom I should feel sorrier for: my partner or my dog. At the end of our call, Pete had hastened to reassure me about his own wellbeing. He told me that he would be perfectly okay once he had had a couple of drinks. In fact, Pete planned to go downtown later and get horrendously drunk at a party at the Irish Ambassador's residence. Only once he was fully liquored up would he be able to let go of the stress of spending five full hours in Hanoi's freight and customs terminal, and the trauma of saying goodbye to his beloved dog.

Despite Tom's traumatic departure, I was sure our dog would cope just fine with the travel. My confidence was based on the fact that, as soon as he was born, I was pretty sure he had been caged up for weeks on end, destined for the chopping board. A twenty-four-hour stint in a crate at ten-thousand feet was nothing when compared to such an initially dysfunctional upbringing.

Having reassured myself that Pete and Tom would both be

fine, I was suddenly hit by a whole new stressful dilemma. If Pete had had this much hassle putting Tom on a flight, what was it going to be like for me when I tried to collect Tom from Kathmandu airport? What were the Nepali customs officials going to say when I had the audacity to try and bring a Vietnamese mutt into their kingdom?

Tom's flight was scheduled to arrive in Kathmandu around midday the next day, after an overnight stop in Bangkok. I planned to go to the airport with our office driver, Ashok, who had originally collected me from my own flight. At least if I went with a Nepali speaker, I would have someone to translate for me in case more form-filling or negotiations were required. Also, given the fact that dogs were often treated like vermin in this country, I was unsure if a local taxi driver would be happy to travel with a caged-up dog in his car.

Ashok remained eerily quiet as we drove to pick up Tom the next day. When I'd asked him to bring me to the airport to collect my dog, he entertained this unusual request with nothing more than a dutiful nod. His lack of communication made me cringe when I considered what he must have been thinking. Ashok must have worked out already that I had spent more than his monthly wage transporting Tom to Kathmandu. He must have wondered what kind of dog was this that he was getting such preferential treatment. Most Nepalese haven't even had the chance to fly in an airplane. What was so special about this dog that he was allowed a boarding pass?

Or maybe Ashok, who had worked with foreigners for years, was thinking this was just another crazy thing expats did: they demanded things like constant water and electricity, expected to live in houses with proper toilets and separate kitchens, and they flew their pets in from exotic locations. Then, once their foreign pets were in place, such expats would feed them expensive imported food, tie them to themselves and take them for random walks, and even let them sit up on their own sofas, inside their own homes. Maybe that was why Ashok never said much; he was probably in a constant state of shock dealing with these crazy foreigners and their array of eccentric behaviours.

We drove in silence until we reached the arrivals terminal. I was too nervous to make polite conversation with Ashok, while Ashok thankfully seemed lost in his own random thoughts. On my lap I had printed-out copies of all the documentation Pete used to get Tom out of Vietnam. I held on them to them tightly, fearing that losing even one single page may cause Tom to be stranded in no man's land forever.

As we pulled up to the airport's arrivals terminal, I asked Ashok to park the car.

'I'm not sure how long this is going to take, Ashok,' I said. He calmly stared at the steering wheel and gave a submissive nod.

I had no idea where I was meant to go, which building I was meant to enter to pick up Tom and his crate. Instead, I homed in on the nearest uniformed airport staff worker who I could see roaming outside the arrivals building. I approached him and showed him my paperwork. He barely looked at the contents before ushering me inside the arrivals hall, to the same place I had picked up my own baggage when I arrived in Kathmandu from Hanoi. I realised that he must have misunderstood me, but I didn't bother arguing.

I had successfully gained access to an area normally strictly reserved for passengers, which was all that mattered.

Once inside, I glanced around the arrivals hall to see if I could see anything that resembled quarantine or customs. Nothing caught my eye. Instead, I saw hundreds of weary-looking trekkers and mountaineers arriving off their flights. They looked exhausted after their long-haul journeys, yet seemingly bursting to embark on their mountain excursions, already decked out in their waterproofs and sturdy hiking boots in eager preparation for the start. I could see them hanging around large baggage carousels, waiting for their oversized backpacks to swivel around so they could drag them off the belt.

Already I pitied the poor porters who would have to lug these monstrous rucksacks around the mountain trails just so that they could earn a living, so that these tourists could have the most amazing holiday of a lifetime.

I gazed as these tourists were reunited with their luggage, wondering where I should search for my own precious cargo. Suddenly, I saw a box I recognised perched on a conveyor belt. It was a crate, uncannily similar to the shape and size of Tom's. The only difference was that this box was plastered in all manner of stickers, making it difficult to decipher its distinctive red and white colouring beneath.

'Tom?' I shouted. 'Tom, is that you?'

Immediately, the box began to shake as if a mini tornado was taking place within its confines. Its contents couldn't possibly be Tom. There must have been a Tasmanian devil inside, not a domesticated canine. It began to vibrate at such a velocity that it looked like the whole crate would topple over and tumble off the belt from a great height.

I ran towards it to break its fall, only to hear Tom yelping in desperation. I would know that bark anywhere, although this time it was a mix of sheer joy and abject fear. It was a desperate sound arising from being cruelly abandoned, tinged with the hope of being soon reunited with a loved one.

I grabbed the crate's handle and hauled it off the conveyor. I peered through the grating, only to see Tom's whole body gyrating wildly, his tail wagging at such a rate that it could easily power a few light bulbs.

'Tom, Tom, hello!' I shouted, sticking my fingers through the wire mesh. I wanted to reassure him with my touch but struggled to make contact.

Until that very moment, I hadn't realised how much I loved Tom. Not only had his absence made my heart grow immeasurably fonder but, seeing him like this, I felt incredibly protective of him. I had no offspring, but I couldn't help wondering if this was how mothers felt when being reunited with a long-lost child.

'Don't worry, I'll get you out of here soon.' I didn't dare take Tom out of his cage in case I couldn't force him back in there for checks that must surely follow. Instead I hauled Tom on to a baggage trolley and wheeled him as carefully as I could towards the passenger exit. Surely there must be some sort of customs or veterinary checks there that I missed on entry, I thought, where they would check Tom's health and paperwork. I was just glad that the Nepali government had no quarantine requirements, so I was in theory able to bring him home that same day.

I arrived at an X-ray machine, where beleaguered travellers were being forced to place their luggage before leaving the airport building. It was a strange protocol, having security checks once they had already taken a whole flight and had a chance to blow up the entire airplane. When I got to the front of the queue, I gestured to the attendant.

'Dog,' I said, pointing to the container on my trolley. He swiftly motioned for me to go around the machine and to skip the standard procedure. He was evidently uninterested in examining the skeletal structure and bowel contents of my pet dog. I gladly shimmied around it, keeping a tight hold of the top of Tom's crate in case he tipped off with my ninety-degree change in direction.

Once around the X-ray machine, I somehow found that I had already exited the terminal doors. I was standing outside the airport building, breathing in the warm Himalayan air. I looked around in a daze and saw Ashok coming towards me from across the car park to help me with my charge. 'But no,' I thought. 'I can't go yet. Where are the checks? Surely someone wants to see Tom's paperwork?'

Suddenly the airport official, who had told me where to go, appeared from out of nowhere. At last, some officialdom that could prevent Tom's authorised entry to the country. He looked down at the box on my trolley, before jovially patting its top.

'Dog?' he said, chuckling to himself. 'You bring dog to Nepal?'

I nodded at him, joining in with his growing laughter just to humour him along. He then turned and scampered off to tell his colleagues about this crazy white woman he had just seen, a lady who was bringing her dog along with her on her trekking holiday.

I was watching him disappear, wiling him back to give Tom the okay, when Ashok arrived at my side. Despite my initial anxiety about Tom going through multiple inspections, I was really disappointed that not even a single official had shown the slightest interest in Tom. Having said that, I also couldn't believe my luck that Tom had gained such easy entry.

'Come on, Ashok,' I said, as I quickly pushed Tom towards the car in case it was all a terrible administrative mistake. 'Let's get out of here.'

Ashok made a high-speed getaway at my request.

Once I was sure no one was following us, I opened Tom's crate. He jumped straight into my arms with unbridled joy.

'Tom-Tom,' I screamed, ridiculously happy to see him still in one piece. He seemed unscathed by his voyage, even though I could see he had touched neither the food nor water that Pete had so diligently placed within his cage.

Tom wriggled and writhed in my arms as I gave him a desperate hug. He covered my face in frantic licks, tickling my ears and nose with his rough pink tongue, making me burst into hysterical laughter.

I was ecstatic to finally see Tom, especially after all the trials and tribulations of transporting him here. I was also acutely aware that Ashok was sitting right beside us, witnessing these exuberant displays of canine affection. Even though his eyes were firmly fixed on the road ahead, it would have been impossible for him not to notice the intimate goings-on in his passenger seat.

His silence left me feeling slightly embarrassed. I had no idea whether Ashok was appalled or really couldn't care less. Whatever he was thinking, I decided to keep such dog-induced emotions behind closed doors from now on.

'Can you bring Tom and me straight to my house?' I asked Ashok once Tom had calmed down and was sitting quietly. It was on the way back to the office from the airport, so didn't involve a major detour. Ashok didn't respond to my request but I saw him subtly turning the steering wheel in the direction of my home.

I let Tom jump out on to the driveway as soon as Ashok stopped the car. Straightaway, Tom took off after an invisible scent that led him to the base of a tree, right at the bottom of the driveway. As he lifted his leg, I could see the obvious relief in his little face. Even though the water bottle in his cage was still full, meaning he didn't drink much on his travels, if any street dog had wandered past our gate that afternoon, he would definitely have known there was a new dog in town.

Tom started to sniff rampantly around the garden as soon as Ashok pulled out of our driveway.

'Tom, come on inside,' I called after him, as I walked up the steps to our home. I was searching around to find my key when I saw the neighbours' front door open up a fraction.

'Hi there,' a friendly female voice called from the other house, as the door swung open.

'Oh, hi there Julia,' I replied. Since arriving, I had met my Dutch neighbours a couple of times as we went to and from our respective homes. Just as my predecessor Phil had promised, they were a friendly young family who were pleasant to have around.

'Is that your dog?' she asked, pointing to Tom who was now scampering up the steps to join us. 'I saw him from the window.'

'Ah, yeah,' I said. 'I've just collected him from the airport. He flew out from Vietnam yesterday.'

'Oh, he's so cute,' Julia said, bending down and patting her knee to beckon Tom towards her. Tom jogged up to her for a quick sniff. He even consented to Julia giving him a brief casual caress.

'Come here guys,' she shouted back into her home. 'Come and see the new doggie.'

At the door appeared her two young children. Sophie, her curious three-year-old daughter, seemed immediately smitten with Tom. She lunged towards him, ready to kiss and cuddle this new toy that had unexpectedly arrived in the compound.

I had no reason to stop her. Before getting Tom, I had read that schnoodles could be great dogs to have around kids. Their usually playful and lovable nature means it is a wonderful breed to have as a family dog. Not that I had put this finding to the test directly with Tom; I just assumed that, seeing as Tom had always been friendly towards strangers, he would be just as affectionate towards children.

I couldn't have been more mistaken.

As three-year-old Sophie stopped and reached out to pet Tom's head, I noticed Tom freeze. She proceeded to bang her hand up and down on his furry skull with increasingly manic frequency. Tom's tail was lowered and motionless, not relaxed and swaying away as it had been seconds before when in contact with Julia's gentle touch.

Despite Sophie's good intentions, Tom did not seem to take kindly to this toddler-attention. I could see his lip move upwards ever so slightly, to expose his raw gums and serrated teeth.

Sophie was totally oblivious to the warning Tom was giving off.

'Ah, I think Tom should come inside with me now,' I said, trying to head off any confrontation that might fray good neighbour relations. 'He might need something to eat and drink after his journey. He's very tired, you know.'

Sophie was not interested in giving up her newly acquired pet that easily. She continued to manhandle Tom, and though Tom refrained from growling or biting, his body language was yelling at her to stop immediately.

I knelt down and placed my hand on his back, ruffling his coat reassuringly.

'Good Tom,' I said, trying to remind him that I was right there if needs be. Just as I went to slip my finger under his collar to escort him gently away, I heard a manic scream coming from my neighbours' doorway. It was wild enough to make even Sophie stop mid-caress.

I looked up to see Lucas, Sophie's one-year-old brother, at the entrance. He was just about standing up, hanging on to the door for dear life, having probably just crawled his way from the sitting room to where the rest of his female family members were busy admiring Tom.

'Look, Lucas. It's a doggie,' Julia said, gently coaxing her son to come over and join in with the dog-appreciation session. Fortunately Lucas, at the tender age of one, had far more sense than the rest of his family. He took another look at Tom and burst into bewildered, frantic tears.

'Don't be scared,' Julia said, reaching out to her son. 'Look, he's very friendly.'

No, Lucas, you are totally right, I thought. Be afraid, be

very afraid. If only your sister Sophie would take a goddamn hint that Tom really doesn't like children.

Julia straightened up and went to pick up Lucas to calm his fright away. I took this opportunity to extract Tom from Sophie's grasp and lead him inside our home.

Closing the front door firmly behind us, I placed Tom down on the wooden floor. 'Don't worry, Tom,' I said. 'I'll protect you.'

I was pretty sure that Tom would soon find his own way of convincing the children to keep the hell away.

While Tom got busy scouting out his new pad, I typed out a quick email, telling Pete that Tom had arrived safe and sound. I took great pleasure in divulging how frictionless his exit was from the airport's arrivals terminal compared to his Hanoi freight terminal and customs nightmare.

Once I saw that the coast was clear outside, and that Julia's children had been firmly locked away, I decided to bring Tom on a little adventure: a quick walk up our street. I guessed he might appreciate the chance to stretch his legs while checking out his new neighbourhood. I hooked his lead around his collar before we walked up to the towering front gates that formed our garden's boundary. The gates themselves were thick sheet metal, making them impossible for Tom to see out of before I pulled back the bolt and swung them both wide open.

'Are you excited, Tom?' I said, as we stepped out over our threshold. By the way Tom was straining at the leash, I could see that 'excited' was an understatement. He had barely taken two strides from our gate before he homed in on a smell that he wanted to inspect further. I stood there idly, his lead limp, waiting for him to conclude his in-depth investigation. Before we could actually embark on our short walk, I heard a deep guttural growling sound coming from the house directly opposite us, on the other side of the alleyway. Local Nepalese lived there and I had yet to make their acquaintance.

I looked up to see a small white ball of fluff hurl itself at the bars of the house's wrought-iron gate, followed by a vicious tirade of barking that even made me flinch and cower. In contrast, Tom kept going about his business, totally unfazed by this display. Tom's presence had somehow elicited a vehement reaction from this mutt, whose existence I had barely noticed when I was previously coming and going from the house on my own.

I figured that if the dog got to sniff Tom a little, she would probably back down. Minus the teeth-baring and malicious snarling, she actually looked kind of cute. Against my better judgement, I took a few steps towards this Pomeranian that was avidly defending her patch, but the closer I got with Tom, the more irate the pooch became. She tried desperately to jam her head under the gate, biting down on its metal bars, trying to get up close and personal with Tom to show him who really was top dog. I stopped short of formally introducing them.

'What a bitch,' I muttered to Tom, before turning away. 'That's no way to welcome someone.'

After his seamless entry at the airport, I assumed Tom was destined to have an easy life in Nepal. He had left the hot-pot ladies far behind in Hanoi. There was no chance of being eaten by hungry Vietnamese diners. Instead, right at that moment, it seemed as if Tom had swapped these dilemmas for a whole new set of issues. Now he not only had to fend off the avid affections of little children with whom he had to share the same garden, but also defend his right to peacefully stroll out of his house without being antagonised by some territorially possessive, deranged, psycho female.

13

Abandoned

Tom kept a low profile for the next few days and stayed firmly within our compound walls. During this time, I had several long drawn-out conversations with him and we both came to the conclusion that 'Evil Dog' across the street was far too stressful to deal with for the moment. With an entire garden now at his disposal, Tom really didn't need to breach our defensive perimeter to relieve himself anyway. In fact, gone were the days of walk-up apartment living and Tom's utter reliance on me for toileting breaks. I was safe in the knowledge that I could leave him at home while I was at work, when he could pee and poo in his own time and leisure.

Tom also had the added advantage of having his own personal maid at his disposal, someone who could tend to all his personal needs. When Phil, my predecessor, was living and working in Nepal, he employed a Nepali lady named Sita to clean and cook for him during the week. Rather than make her unemployed, I was more than happy to take over her services from Phil. Thanks to Xuan's excellent work back in Hanoi, I had slowly warmed to the idea of having a maid around the place. Xuan had definitely broken me in.

What made the arrangement perfect this time around was that I didn't work from home as I had a proper office to go to. I didn't have to contend with Sita scrubbing and sweeping around me, reminding me of all the mess I had made that she was cleaning up on my behalf. She also had her own key so she could come and go before I arrived home, leaving me a spotlessly clean house to return to. Tom's floating fur balls didn't stand a chance with Sita around.

The day after Tom's arrival, I delayed my morning's journey to the office so I could introduce Sita to my dog. I feared she would see this random hound from Hanoi in the house and, not knowing that he was mine, chase him away with a broomstick. After all the stress of bringing Tom into Nepal, such a scenario would be catastrophic.

Soon enough, I heard Sita rattling at the padlock as she tried to unlock the front gate. I was just about to explain to Tom who Sita is and how she would look after him when, all of a sudden, he bolted out of the house straight past my legs, barking and sprinting at full kilter at the stranger daring to enter his compound.

'Tom, come back here!' I shouted after him, to no avail. Tom was set on terrorising this invader, homing in on her shins with teeth bared.

This was not the formal introduction I had intended. I couldn't help but fear the worst. My only consolation was the knowledge that, if he did bite Sita, Tom was officially certified as disease-free. After the raft of vaccinations he got before embarking on his travels, his bite was probably sterile.

It was a little disconcerting though to see him acting so territorial. He never used to be this way. He must have picked up this behaviour from Evil Dog, who seemed to do nothing with her life except ward off random strangers, all day and all night, with her incessant yapping.

Tom skidded to an emergency halt at Sita's feet, letting out one last fearless woof for good measure. Sita glanced down at this miniature ball of fur that was now dancing around her feet. Much to my relief, she looked totally unfazed. Instead, it seemed like she was trying to make sure she didn't accidentally stand on this thing while making her way to work.

Tom sniffed her shoes before jogging back towards me, his chest puffed out with pride. He probably didn't realise that defending his territory didn't mean valiantly retreating as soon as someone had actually gained entry to his empire.

Sita knew no English, and my knowledge of Nepali was nil. Despite our ignorance of each other's languages, we had learned to communicate the basics.

I pointed to my ferocious dog and said, 'Tom.'

'Tom,' she mimicked in return, smiling sweetly at our new addition.

Then I pointed to the garden outside. 'Garden,' I said. 'Stay in garden,' as I proceeded to bend down and pat the ground.

Sita nodded again, though I was not entirely sure I had made myself crystal clear. Regardless, I figured Sita and Tom had at least made their acquaintance and would probably work things out between themselves. With that reassurance, I headed off to work.

I'm not too sure what Sita understood by my pointing and pidgin English that day but my short speech must have worked as, for the duration of my stay, I never once found a puddle or turd within the house. The only slightly disconcerting thing was that I never once found a pee or a poo in the garden either. Either Sita whisked them away as soon as Tom produced them, or Tom became very adept at hiding them. Or maybe Tom found a way to sneak out of our compound to strategically deposit them at Evil Dog's door, a thought that made me proud. Whatever Tom or Sita did, I never once had to deal with Tom's bowel movements while living with him in Nepal.

The other good thing about having a garden and maid was that there was no need to put Tom in boarding kennels when I went away. For a few extra rupees, Sita was happy to pop round to the house to keep an eye on him in my absence and to make sure he was well watered and fed. Not that Tom appreciated this added convenience. I reckon he enjoyed the chance to go on boarding-kennel weekend breaks in Hanoi so that he could learn new tricks of the canine trade, such as the finer arts of leg cocking and territory marking. For me, however, it meant I didn't have to go to the hassle of finding a safe and secure place to keep him while I was away, and I didn't have to fork out for the at-times exorbitant expat kennel boarding rates.

When I finally decided to take up my new trail running friends' offer to go to Pokhara the weekend after Tom arrived, I simply sat Tom down and told him I would be back in two days, then asked Sita to call in on him when I was away. Finally, I packed my running gear and hopped on a bus early on Friday morning, to make the five-hour journey westward from Kathmandu to Pokhara.

Pokhara town itself is the gateway to the Annapurna Circuit, an immensely popular tourist hiking route. My new friends, Roger and his gang, had helped organise a seventy-kilometre ultra-marathon race that coming weekend, taking in a small part of this trail.

I arrived just in time for registration in a local hotel's dining hall. As I took a seat beside Roger and co. for the race briefing I did a quick headcount and found, much to my horror, that there were barely fifty people participating. To make matters worse, the vast majority were local Nepali men, all of whom looked formidably lean and mean.

Roger noticed the wary look on my face as he caught me surveying the room. 'Don't worry,' he said. 'Most of these guys are training to become British Gurkhas. About three thousand apply every year, though there's only twenty places up for grabs.'

I slumped down in my seat, overwhelmed by a terrible feeling of inadequacy. I had convinced myself that I was going for a fast trek around the foothills with the lads from last week's Kathmandu run, only to discover I had stumbled into a Gurkha Army training exercise. I knew this could all end very badly.

Fortunately, Roger came to my aid, restoring my excitement for the trip once more. 'Seriously, you'll love the route,' he told me just as the main race organiser, an ex-Gurkha named Ramesh, stood up at the front of the room and demanded everyone's undivided attention. Holding a baton in a somewhat threatening manner, Ramesh proceeded to deliver the race instructions.

'Tomorrow morning, at 0630, you start outside this hotel,'

Ramesh boomed at his submissive audience. 'You then run up Sarangkot hill to Birethanti, then up Poon Hill, and then back to Birethanti. Any doubt?' His question was met with total and utter silence. 'Okay, no doubt,' he said, evidently pleased that he had made himself understood.

I had absolutely no idea where Birethanti village was, or the location of the hills Ramesh mentioned, but there was no way I was going to be the one to raise my hand and potentially suffer an onslaught from Ramesh's military arsenal.

'Don't worry,' Roger whispered. 'The route will be marked. Seriously, you'll love it. It goes through these amazing remote villages full of teahouses, and then along a beautiful valley lined with rhododendron forests that are in full bloom this time of year.'

I listened intently to Roger's description, excited that I'd have the chance to explore such remote scenery.

'Remember to stop and have a look from the top of Poon Hill once you get there,' Roger reminded me. 'On a clear day, you'll get views of the snow-capped Annapurna and Dhaulagiri mountain ranges.'

I was so excited about the prospect of delving into the Himalayas the next day that, when the race briefing finished, I headed straight into Pokhara town to find an Internet café. I couldn't wait to call Pete online and tell him all about my plans.

I eventually found a small place on the main high street, full of computers equipped with Skype and large padded headphones. It seemed a popular place with other tourists who were also hanging out, making calls to loved ones back home or uploading snaps to make friends and family jealous of their latest trek.

Pete picked up after a couple of rings.

'Pete, hello!' I said, mad with enthusiasm. 'Guess where I'm calling from?'

'No idea,' Pete replied with a certain dryness to his tone.

I must have caught him at a bad time. 'Sorry, do you want me to call back later?'

'No. Now is fine.'

'I'm in Pokhara,' I said, continuing with the conversation I'd intended to have. 'There's a race tomorrow in the mountains, on part of the Annapurna Circuit, and I'm going to take part.'

'Good for you,' Pete said.

An uneasy lull followed. I was hoping it was just a bad connection from Nepal to Vietnam that was causing this edgy silence.

'How are you doing?' I asked. I was guessing he must be jealous that I was having such a great time, discovering this beautiful country and doing a job I loved. I was betting he couldn't wait to join me.

'Oh, I'm doing fine,' he replied. 'Real fine.'

'Well...that's good, I suppose,' I said.

'Of course I'm not bloody doing fine,' he shouted, seething down the line.

'Sorry,' I blurted, slightly confused. 'Why, what's happened?'

'You've not called for days,' Pete said. 'Have you just conveniently forgotten all about me?'

'Why would you think such a thing?' I said, deeply hurt. I believed we were good, that our relationship was strong. I thought we had resolved all this before I left for Kathmandu when Pete asked if we were breaking up. As far as I was concerned, I was happy with where our relationship was, and Pete was equally content. Truth be told, I knew I was lucky to be with such an amazing guy as Pete, and I thought he liked being with me too.

Sure hadn't we planned to move together to Nepal to start a new life there? As far as I was concerned, this plan had not changed one iota.

A quick apology, I thought. That would probably appease him and put our Skype call back on course again. 'Sorry, but I've been really busy. I did email you a couple of times, but I suppose I just never really got round to calling.' As I said it, I realised I couldn't remember the last time we'd spoken. I had just been so caught up in the whirlwind of settling into this new country that Pete momentarily slipped my mind.

Perhaps Pete was right. Maybe I was to blame. I said sorry again one more time for good measure, but if I thought that would be sufficient, I was wrong. Pete was on a roll.

'Did you just use me to get the job you wanted, in the place you wanted, and then bugger off as soon as it all came through?' Pete said, my apology having evidently done nothing to lighten his mood.

'That's not fair!' I shouted back, but Pete had no interest in my protest.

'You deserted me and Tom when you left on that first plane,' he said. 'Then you have the nerve to take Tom away from me as well.'

'Tom?' I said. 'What's Tom got to do with any of this?'

'Tom has got *everything* to do with this,' Pete replied. 'You,

Tom and I were a family in Hanoi. Now you've gone and torn us apart.'

I couldn't help but let out an exasperated sigh. I had noticed back in Hanoi that Pete had started using the word 'family' when referring to himself, Tom and me. I hadn't taken it too seriously, though I refrained from using this term when talking about our household. As far as I was concerned, Pete and I had moved to Vietnam to test our fledgling relationship. We hadn't talked about getting engaged or married, let alone about one day having children. Calling us a 'family' seemed slightly premature. In my mind it assumed that we were married with kids, and that Tom was our *de facto* 'child.'

I'd consistently brushed it off, until one day back in Hanoi Pete began to refer to himself as 'Daddy' while idly conversing with Tom.

'Are you going to come with Daddy for a walk, are you Tommy?' Pete said one day before they were about to head out the door.

'Daddy?' I said, stopping immediately what I was doing. 'You're not his father. Look at him. Can't you see that Tom is a dog?'

'What do you think, Tom?' Pete said, looking down at Tom who was busy doing his manic pre-walk jig around Pete's feet. 'Am I not your Daddy?'

Tom looked like he couldn't give a rat's ass what Pete called himself. All Tom seemed focused on was getting out the door as quickly as possible for his daily patrol of the street.

'I don't think Mummy approves,' Pete whispered down at Tom, an exaggerated clown-like frown forming on his face.

'Excuse me,' I said, feeling I must take a firm stand at this point. 'I look nothing like Tom. I am not his mother. And *we* are not a family.'

Tom's lead swung limp from Pete's hand as I uttered those words.

'Well then,' Pete said, after a moment of deathly silence. 'What are we?'

I had no idea Pete would take this factually correct statement so personally. He looked bitterly wounded.

'I don't know,' I said, back-pedalling at speed, not wanting to hurt Pete's feelings further or damage our relationship in the process. 'I suppose we're a...cohabiting unit?'

There. Yes, we were living together, and yes, we did depend on each other for certain things. Therefore, in my mind, a cohabiting unit was a far more accurate description of our living arrangement, without the emotional connotations of 'family' or 'parenthood.'

'Is that right?' Pete said. 'We are a cohabiting unit... A CHU?'

I nodded, a little sheepish now. We were arguing over such small semantics. I had to admit though that concluding that we were a CHU did seem a tad ridiculous.

'And what is your alternative to Mummy and Daddy, pray tell?' Pete asked, a little indignant now. 'I just want to be totally clear on where we stand on all this.'

'I don't know,' I said, unable to make eye contact with Pete. 'Tom's Master and Mistress...maybe?'

Pete had had enough.

'Come on Tom,' Pete said, tightening his hold on Tom's lead. 'Let's leave *your Mistress* to her cohabiting unit. *Daddy* is bringing you for your walkies.' With that, Pete had stormed out the door in a massive huff.

From that day forward, Pete insisted on calling himself Tom's father.

Sitting in the Internet café in Pokhara with oversized head-phones on my head, I knew now was not the time or place to be arguing with Pete whether we were technically a family or not. I was also aware that my fellow Internet users in the café were firing furtive glances at me, trying to eavesdrop on the increasingly heated row I was having with my other half.

'I'm so sorry, Pete,' I said, adopting the most conciliatory tone I could muster. 'I didn't realise you felt this way.' Arguing with your partner over a phone line when you're both in different time zones, in my experience, is never a good idea. I needed to end the argument asap. 'Listen, Nepal really is a great place,' I said, trying to change the topic to a more upbeat one. 'I think you'll really like it here. And you know that I can't wait for you to come over and join Tom and me, for us to be all together again.' I heard nothing but silence on the other side. I just hoped that Pete was still there, that he was listening to what I was saying. 'I really love my job. I'm really grateful that you helped me so much with my application. You know I couldn't have done it without you, don't you?'

Pete grunted back when I said this, something resembling, 'You're welcome.' He didn't sound like he had forgiven me, but at least some of the anger had disappeared.

'And Tom,' I said, 'You wouldn't believe how happy Tom is here.' I told Pete how well Tom had settled into the new house. I spoke to him about the neighbours and the well-meaning children, who I was sure Tom would grow to love.

I described to Pete the garden and how Sita the maid was happy to care for Tom, going to great lengths to explain how Tom had found a most worthy adversary in the form of Evil Dog.

'Sounds like you've a great set-up there,' Pete said after a little while. I sensed he was a little calmer after my prolonged monologue.

'Yes, it is great,' I assured him. 'I think it will suit us better than Hanoi. All we have to do now is get you over here. I promise, we can talk through everything once you arrive.'

'Can we even talk about the use of the word "family" in our day-to-day conversation?' Pete said, hope and humour jumbled up in his voice.

'Sure,' I said. 'We can talk about all of those things when you get here. I promise.'

14

Reunited

Pete still had a couple of weeks of work to do before he could commence his onward journey to Kathmandu. I didn't envy him being the one left behind in Hanoi, especially after Pete told me how empty the apartment felt with Tom and me now gone.

It didn't take Pete long, however, to find ways to keep himself entertained. Soon he issued an open invitation to all his friends and family to come visit him before he left Vietnam. When one of his old buddies from his teenage years took him up on his offer, Pete forgot all his woes, and instead diverted all his energies into being his mate's tour guide par excellence. He brought him to exotic locations along Vietnam's coast, forcing his old roommate to drink cheap bia hơi with Pete in dodgy dives until the early hours, before hitching lifts on the back of rented motorbikes to their cheap and cheerful backpacker hostels. In my absence, Pete took the chance to relive his adolescence.

I might have complained that Pete was forgetting all about me while he gallivanted around the country with his old buddy. However, I was quite content for Pete to let his hair down if it stopped him from moaning to me about how I had abandoned him.

As for me, I was not suffering from any such bouts of loneliness. Much to my surprise, Tom was proving to be my perfect companion in Kathmandu. When I emerged from my bedroom first thing in the morning, Tom would be already standing to attention, waiting for me at the bottom of staircase with his friendly, waggly tail. After a quick scratch on his head, when I would take the opportunity to pat away his scraggly bed hair, Tom was content to wander back to his crate to continue where he left off with his morning snooze. Then, when I arrived back at the house after work, Tom couldn't wait to perform his signature welcome-home dance for me. His tail took hold of his body, shaking everything at such high velocity that I struggled to catch hold of him. A quick rub of his furry back was again sufficient for Tom to retreat for a late-afternoon siesta.

Tom wouldn't surface again until bedtime, when I let him outside for a quick pee. Unlike others in our cohabiting unit, Tom was proving wonderfully low maintenance.

As the time for Pete to relocate drew near, he started to sell off the household items we had accumulated in Hanoi. We both thought we'd get reasonable prices for the goods given that they were barely used during our relatively short stint in the place. It was only when prospective buyers arrived to inspect what Pete was selling that we realised that Tom had caused most items to depreciate substantially. An attempt to sell some armchairs was thwarted after the buyer lifted up their cushions to find paw prints all over the upholstery. I would have sworn that I had taught Tom not to jump up on to the seats, only to discover he was doing exactly that when we were not around. Pete had tried to sell our shoe stands, only for the prospective purchaser to notice teeth marks on the legs. In the end, Pete had to sell most of our things at knockdown prices, far below what we paid, just to get rid of them.

As the day of Pete's departure approached, three suitcases of possessions were all he had to show for his time spent in Vietnam. Neither of us was worried though, as we knew Nepal was offering both of us a new chance to work and live and accumulate a whole new range of assets. I was just hoping that Pete's stay got off to a good start. If he liked Nepal as much as I did from the get-go, then there was a good chance we would call this our home for a little while at least.

The day before Pete's flight was due to arrive, my plans for a smooth entry were abruptly ripped asunder. Nepal's Maoist leaders called a national strike, or banda, to take place on the day of Pete's flight.

Bandas are a regular occurrence in Nepal. I had slowly grown accustomed to them during my thus-far brief stay. It is one of the ways citizens express their dissatisfaction with the ruling party. Whenever there's a policy or person they don't particularly like, they call for a banda in an attempt to force change. In this case, the Maoists were using the banda to try and force the current prime minister to resign.

What it means in practice is that the country is forced into lockdown. Schools and businesses are also expected to shut up shop. No public or private vehicles are allowed to move, rendering the streets hauntingly quiet, and just in case anyone would dare ignore the banda, Maoist supporters patrol the streets to ensure the country is shut down until their political demands are met.

My own office had to close as well, or face violent repercussions. Although the protestors' grievances were understandable, such protests were highly inconvenient.

The only silver lining was that the airport would remain open. Not even Maoist demands could prevent international flights taking off and landing in Kathmandu. Once Pete arrived at the airport, however, there would be no taxis available to bring him back home. Instead, the government would kindly provide free buses to shuttle tourists to major hotels. The nearest hotel on this drop-off route was a two-kilometre walk from my home.

Of course, there was no way that Pete would be able to negotiate the complexities of this banda all on his own. I had to somehow find my way to the airport so that I could help him get on the government bus that would transport him and his luggage to within a two-kilometre radius of my house. Fortunately, I had learned that travelling by foot is allowed when there's a banda on. With the airport less than ten kilometres from my home, I decided to run out to the airport and meet up with Pete that way.

The only thing I needed to be careful about on my journey was potential riots. Public rallies were often held during bandas to protest against the latest political angst. A mass of discontented, idle people gathered together in one place provides a perfect opportunity for some well-orchestrated violence. I just hoped that the long, lonely road to the airport was not used as a venue for any such uprising.

An hour before Pete's midday flight was due to arrive, I put on my running gear, bid farewell to Tom, and stepped out of my front gate. Outside, it was eerily quiet. Normally the street would be bustling with motorbikes, taxis, vans, buses, four-wheel drives, lorries and rickshaws vying for precious road space. Instead the road was devoid of anything sporting wheels. Even Evil Dog seemed to be taking the banda seriously and had gone inside in solidarity with the protest movement.

I took my first few tentative steps in the direction of the airport. Normally, running on these streets at this time of day would be considered a fool's game. The narrow, broken pavements would be chock-a-block with pedestrians, fruit vendors and random sacred cows. Vehicles would be spread across every inch of tarmac, belching out blackened fumes that would choke my airways, but that day, the road was pleasantly clear of people and traffic, and surprisingly pollution-free.

It was only when I attempted to cross the Bagmati River that I realised trouble could be coming my way. Spanning the only bridge that could get me to the airport was a large, ominous barricade. It was a ramshackle mess of wood and barbed wire, adorned with several burning tyres to stop any potential vehicular transgressions. Nepali youth idled around their creation, eyeing up a scattering of riot police who were keeping close tabs on them. Despite the evident stand-off, I saw local people walking past the barricade in both direc-tions, as if oblivious to its threatening presence.

I packed in close to some Nepali women, who seemed adamant that a bunch of young lads and some riot police were not going to stop them going about their ways. Much to my surprise, as we passed the barrier, no one batted an eyelid. I kept my head down, just in case something kicked off. Before I knew it, we had crossed the bridge without incident.

Quickly, I glanced over my shoulder at the youth and police whom I had just passed. It seemed that neither side was interested in starting a fight just because some prime minister wouldn't quit his job.

I arrived at the airport and went inside the arrivals terminal just in time to welcome Pete off his plane. The airport itself was deserted. There were no cars in the car park, no taxis in the rank outside. Everyone had stayed firmly at home, fearing the wrath of the Maoists if they dared defy their command.

With the place so quiet, it was easy to spot Pete as he left immigration.

'Pete, Pete!' I shouted. 'You've made it!' I was ecstatic to see him again after so many weeks apart. I fell into his arms, drinking in his familiar manly embrace that always made me feel so safe. He hugged me tightly in return, thanking God as he did that he had finally arrived in one piece. I knew, however, that overt displays of physical affection are frowned upon in Nepal. I stepped back from him reluctantly, consoling myself that there would be plenty of time to get properly reacquainted once we were firmly behind closed doors.

Surveying him from arm's length, I saw that Pete was in a total daze. I had come to learn that this was how Pete normally looked after a long-distance flight: his eyes were bloodshot, his chin had stubble, and his clothes had that distinctive smell of stale sweat.

'Come on,' I said, taking control of his arrival. 'Let's get your bags.' I led him over to the carousel, which was idly turning round and round without any baggage on it yet. While we were waiting, I took the opportunity to deliver the bad news.

'Just to let you know,' I said, bracing myself for his reaction. 'There's a strike on today.'

Pete looked at me blankly. He evidently had no idea what this meant for him.

'So there aren't any taxis to bring us home,' I said, before taking a deep breath. 'We'll have to take the bus.'

'Are you serious?' he said. 'We're taking a bus home? Can't you see I'm in no state for that?'

Of course, I could plainly see that Pete would struggle, but there was really no other way.

'I just want to go home, have a shower, take a nap,' Pete slurred. 'Is there not a quicker way?'

I slowly shook my head. It was not my fault that the Maoists disliked the current prime minister, yet I couldn't help but feel guilty about the strike, like it was my fault Pete arrived into such a mess.

At this stage, I also decided it was best not to tell him that we had to walk for two kilometres with his luggage once we disembarked. Probably wiser to just get him safely on the bus, then divulge this other bit of travel info once I no longer had any choice.

Getting Pete on the bus proved traumatic to say the least. With the bus the only way to shuttle holidaymakers away from the airport, it was packed to the gills with tired, short-tempered travellers. Tourists were wedged into its interior wherever they could find space. People were perched on top of each other in seats, with the remainder standing uncomfortably in the narrow aisles, squashed together with barely enough room to breathe.

Pete hated crowds and started to have a mini meltdown as soon as we made it inside. I placed my hand on his to keep him calm, but it seemed to have little or no effect on his current state of mind.

To make matters worse, Pete's luggage was hoisted up on to the roof and strapped precariously to the top of the bus along with a treasure trove of other rucksacks. He darted urgent looks outside, paranoid that his life's possessions would fall off in transit and splatter their contents all over the ground.

'It's okay, Pete,' I said. 'We're not going far. The stop is practically down the road.'

Pete stared at me, his eyes pleading with me to magic him home, to shelter him from this ordeal. But there was really nothing I could do except hope that we'd look back at this situation one day and laugh.

Once the bus was full to capacity, it lurched out of the airport and down the road towards the city centre. I tried to engage Pete in idle chat but to no avail. He was too busy staring out of the bus window, watching in horror as civilians and police gathered around one of the many barricades we had to breach to reach our final destination. It looked as if I had brought Pete into a war zone, even though I was quite sure the conflict would be over come dawn. I had no idea how to start explaining to Pete about this country I had just brought him to.

Fortunately, the first hotel that we came to was the one where we needed to get off.

'Is this it?' Pete asked, before the inevitable, 'This isn't your house. It's a hotel.'

'Yeah, sorry about that,' I said, muttering below my breath. 'We have to walk a bit to get home.' I quickly disappeared around the rear of the bus to check if Pete's baggage had made it in one piece. I also wanted to momentarily escape Pete's growing exasperation with me and with the situation I'd placed him in.

'Three bags, is that right?' I called after Pete, in the most cheerful tone I could muster. They were three of the heaviest suitcases I'd ever seen accepted on to a flight. All of them had stickers affixed to them, warning prospective handlers that they weighed over twenty kilos. I had no idea how we were ever going to physically get them as far as my front gate.

Pete rounded the bus to check out the haul laid out before me, before confirming that all his luggage was present and correct.

'So which direction are we going?' he said, grabbing the two largest cases by their handles before pointing them, with some resignation, towards the hotel gate. I took the remaining case, taking a moment to thank God for small mercies, that all of Pete's luggage at least had wheels.

'Follow me,' I said, marching off towards the main road.

The dearth of vehicles thanks to the banda proved fortuitous at this stage. It meant that we could cross over the normally chock-a-block main thoroughfare without stopping, then proceed down a narrow side street while taking over both the left- and right-hand lanes. The luggage wheels struggled, however, to shoulder the burden of Pete's goods. They were designed for pushing along smoothly tiled airport-terminal floors, not for dragging long distances along pot-holed developing-country back roads. After a while, I found it easier to carry the damn twenty-kilogram case in the air rather than contend with the bumps and bangs it endured from the rutted road beneath.

We were less than a hundred metres into our trek before Pete stopped abruptly in his tracks.

'How far did you say we had to go again?'

'I didn't,' I replied, refusing to stop and talk in case I couldn't get Pete moving again. I could feel Pete's mood worsening with every step, fuelled by sleep deprivation. Better we keep going, I figured, so we could get this enforced march over and done with. It seemed to be a valid strategy, as I soon heard Pete moving off again, trundling his two suitcases behind him. It was only when I heard a clunk and a 'FUUCCCCKKKK!' that I realised my strategy may have had some inherent flaws.

'What's wrong now?' I shouted over my shoulder, too scared to look back and see for myself. I was trying to suppress thoughts that I should have just waited for the strike's conclusion tomorrow and I should have made Pete sleep at the airport, then collected him once the transportation networks were up and running again.

'The wheel has just feckin' fallen off my suitcase,' Pete shouted back at me, before unleashing on the ungrateful one-wheeled bag a well-deserved kick. So much for the luggage having castors. We were down one already and still had a way to go.

I was so close to breaking down, giving up, and running straight home without Pete. This was not how our first meeting after weeks of separation was meant to pan out.

Whatever happened to the tearful reunion I'd imagined, the hugs and heartfelt kisses, the tender words describing how much we had missed each other all this time? Instead it had been a steady tirade of silent stress, trying to lug ourselves and Pete's property safely back to my house.

To make matters worse, Pete looked like he was going to stage a sit-down protest right there in the middle of the road with his three bags. Part of me wanted to leave him to his infantile brinksmanship. Fortunately for Pete, there was also another part of me that knew that I was responsible for getting him home safely.

'Tom's waiting for you, you know?' I said, producing the last card I had at my disposal. 'I told him you're coming home today.'

Pete didn't move. I wondered if I had left it too late to play my final hand.

'Does he miss me?' Pete said, mournfully, as if searching for a reason to go on.

'Ah yeah, sure,' I said, trying to sound convincing. 'To be honest, he tells me he misses you all the time.'

My lie, that Tom had learned to converse in English since his departure from Hanoi, seemed to do the trick. Pete cobbled together his possessions and somehow we pushed, pulled, heaved and shoved them all the way to my door.

The familiar sound of Tom's bark on the other side of the gate was a godsend after the day's earlier events. As soon as I swung open the barrier, Tom was all over Pete like a rash. The two of them merged into a blur of emotion, Tom bouncing and bounding around Pete in a flurry of heated excitement. Pete threw himself down to Tom's level to embrace his long-lost doggie. Tom reciprocated, sticking his tongue deep down into the recesses of Pete's inner ear, provoking Pete to unleash a frenzy of unfettered laughter. All this time, Tom whimpered and whined as Pete whispered sweet nothings to his canine friend.

Gone were the days when Tom uncoupled from Pete after a heartfelt embrace, then, out of unbridled excitement, accidentally sprinkled some urine on the floor. No, this time, after weeks of separation, Tom disengaged from Pete to reveal that he had a huge canine hard-on.

15

Bad Beginnings

'Put that away, Tom, will ye?' I shouted as soon as I saw Tom's erection protruding from between his hind legs. Even Tom seemed a little confused and embarrassed by the emergence of his inch-long manhood. He immediately dropped to the ground, threw his head into his groin, and started frantically licking his red, wet lipstick safely back into its cover.

'Can't you see he's just glad to see me?' Pete said, apparently quite chuffed by his dog's reaction. I couldn't deny the fact that Tom was ecstatic to see Pete again. I just wished his affections for his master were expressed in a slightly less sexual manner. 'Don't you know that I'm glad to see you too, my woman?' Pete added, sashaying his way up to me and enveloping me in a crushing, comforting embrace. It was a sign that all was forgiven, that we were ready for a new start. Finally, I thought, we will have the time and space to figure out if we have a future together, and if so, what it could look like.

'I think you first need to take that shower you mentioned,' I said, pulling away from him to take in a gulp of fresh air. Much as I liked his masculine odour, it was a bit overwhelming at this stage after him travelling for so long. I took the chance to show Pete around his new home before directing him towards the bathroom.

As I left him in peace to wash, I couldn't help crossing my fingers that there was hot water in the house. Electricity and water supplies in Kathmandu had been erratic lately, even on non-banda days. I needed consistent supplies of both commodities for Pete to have a warm shower and I was not sure he could cope right now if there was no water in the bathroom or if the electric shower spurted out a freezing-cold spray.

I heard a gushing sound through the taps, and Pete letting out a sigh of pleasurable relief. Hurrah! The house had water, and it was actually hot. It was a blooming miracle. I was starting to get really worried that I would have to deal with a tired, grumpy and smelly partner who wanted to go straight back to Hanoi until all of Kathmandu's services started functioning again.

Pete soon arrived down the stairs, changed and clean-shaven. For the first time that day, he looked happy and somewhat relaxed. Hopefully he would soon forget all about his disastrous airport arrival saga, and we could start his stay afresh.

'Hungry?' I asked.

'Famished,' he replied.

'Well, the supermarkets are closed because of the banda,' I explained, 'so it looks like we're going to have to eat out.' I knew that hotels with international tourists were allowed to serve food, even if there was a banda on. Things like US dollars are too precious for even the Maoists to ban for an entire day.

We walked up to the nearest hotel, a mere five-minute

stroll from our house. When we arrived there, the place was bustling with other expats who had had a similar thought process to ours. We all seemed to be taking refuge in the hotel, to avoid the boredom of sitting at home twiddling our thumbs while waiting for the banda to end.

We sat down at a table outside on the patio and, as soon as I got the attention of a passing waiter, I ordered on our behalf.

'We'll have two dal bhat,' I said to the man. 'And two Everest beers.'

The beers arrived quickly, thick condensation dripping down their bottled sides. It was the perfect antidote to the heated morning we had just had.

'Cheers,' I said, pouring my beer and raising a glass to finally welcome Pete to Nepal. 'It's good to have you here.'

Pete's glass met mine halfway. 'Thanks, Moire. I'm sorry about the state I was in this morning, but God that was stressful.'

'No Pete, I'm sorry,' I said. Much as I would have loved to have called off the banda on the basis that it was Pete's arrival date, there was really nothing much I could have done about the situation in the end. This was the reality of this developing country that I was suggesting we lived in.

'It's just that, first impressions are important, whether we like it or not,' Pete explained. 'And my first impressions of Nepal…well, I suppose you can guess—'

'They're not great,' I interrupted, not wanting to hear the words from Pete himself. 'I know, I know, but can you give it a chance?' I didn't want to beg, but I really did like this place, despite its obvious difficulties. I thought that we could be happy living together in Nepal.

Pete didn't get the chance to respond. He was interrupted

by the waiter arriving at our table with our meals, placing before both of us a bronze plate adorned with colourful bowls of different foods and flavours.

'This is dal, or lentil soup,' I said, pointing to the largest bowl. 'The other one is chicken curry, and that's yogurt, pickle, spicy vegetables and rice,' I explained, my finger completing a tour of the plate's rim.

Pete wasn't lying when he said he was famished. He polished off the contents of each of the bowls, practically licking the underlying plate clean. Good job he had a palate for spicy food. Dal bhat or rice with lentils would probably be on the menu a lot now that we were living on this side of Asia.

We ordered another couple of beers and caught up on our respective lives. I had forgotten how nice it was to have Pete's company when going out for a meal. He was always full of the hottest gossip that I seemed to miss out on. He spent the rest of the afternoon regaling hilarious tales of Hanoi's latest goings-on. I sat there, not wanting him to stop as he divulged scandal after scandal that he felt he could entrust me with. I felt privileged to be part of his inner cohort, and to finally be with him again.

With the next day being Saturday, and the Maoists off strike duty for the weekend, I suggested we made a plan to show Pete around Kathmandu.

'Why don't we go for a hike up one of the hills on the valley rim?' I said, thinking a bit of fresh air and a stretch of the legs might do us both the world of good.

Pete was amenable to the idea. One of the ways I had originally sold him on Kathmandu was the allure of wide open spaces and nearby countryside where Tom, Pete and I would be free to roam. Such a hike would be a chance to showcase one of the best parts of Kathmandu to him.

The following day, Pete and I woke up bright and early to go for our leisurely hike. We decided not to bring Tom along with us this time in case we opted to go into town straight afterwards for a bite to eat.

The best way to get to the hills from the city is by taking a taxi out to the valley rim. When we arrived early on Saturday morning at the rank at the end of our road, it was bursting with taxis trying to recoup their losses after the national shutdown the day before. The drivers scurried towards us as we approached them, trying to attract our attention. I recognised one driver who was used to ferrying me around town, so I homed in on him.

'To Shivapuri,' I said. 'How much?'

'Eight hundred rupees,' he replied.

I laughed at his audacity. 'No. Five hundred.'

'Five fifty,' he pleaded. I nodded back in silent agreement. 'Come, please,' he replied, ushering us towards his car, a miniature white Suzuki with massive scrape marks gouged into its sides. This car, like all the others in the rank, had seen better days. Through the windscreen, I noted plastic figurines of Hindu gods glued onto the dashboard. Given the state of the car's external bodywork, these gods obviously hadn't been much help when it came to avoiding road-traffic collisions.

Our taxi man opened the rear door, allowing a waft of pungent incense to escape its confines. I coughed a little as I entered the cloud, before effortlessly sliding onto the plastic-clad back seat. Pete, however, struggled to bend down to leverage himself inside the vehicle.

'It's a bit small, isn't it?' he said, his knees wedged precariously close to his chest. I hadn't really thought about the dimensions of these taxis, which are the norm around the city. Because I am of a similar shape and size to most Nepalese, I had slotted in quite well. Pete, however, is a giant in comparison, with his six-foot height and one hundred and ninety pounds body weight. I shrugged helplessly, powerless again to change the situation I had placed Pete in. I just hoped Pete would put up with his crumpled-up state for the half-hour journey across town to the foot of Shivapuri.

Pete unfolded himself with only a minor grumble when the taxi finally deposited us outside the gates of Shivapuri National Park. He straightened himself up, inflating himself back to his full stature, before taking a moment to breathe in the surprisingly cool and fresh mountain air. We may have been standing on the cusp of Kathmandu, but already we had escaped the smog and soot that permanently clung to the city. Before us lay a whole mountain, cloaked in deep forest, that we were now free to explore.

I paid the entrance fee to the park before beginning our climb towards Shivapuri's summit. At 2,725 metres in height, it is a considerable way to climb from Kathmandu's 1,400 metre base. It is, however, nowhere near the altitudes of several-thousand metres found in the Himalayas, where the air thins the higher you climb and breathing becomes more constrained. Shivapuri would certainly be a challenging day's walk, but nothing that we both couldn't handle.

Pete strode alongside me as we began our ascent. The path meandered its way upward through dense woods, a whole world away from the hustle and bustle of Kathmandu.

'This is lovely,' Pete said, as we walked along. 'Exactly what I was looking forward to when moving here.'

'I know Kathmandu itself is a bit hard to take at times,' I replied. 'But when you know you have places like this on your doorstep, I think it makes it worthwhile.'

Pete didn't react to what I'd just said. I decided he just needed a bit more time to work out what he really thought of the place. I wondered if he'd be able to stand the water cuts, the power outages and the stagnant pollution that hadn't affected our lives back in Hanoi. While some may be bothered by these inconveniences, I tend to see them as a worthwhile challenge. If I can survive these shortfalls, then I know I'll reap other benefits, such as the amazing outdoors that are in plentiful supply in Nepal.

I was so lost in my thoughts that I failed to notice Pete falling slightly behind me. I stopped and waited for him to catch up, before continuing with our walk. Even when I purposely cut my speed in half, Pete struggled to maintain our pace.

'Are you okay?' I asked when I saw him stopping for yet another rest. 'Do you want something to eat or drink?' I reached into my rucksack for our supplies.

'No, it's not that,' Pete replied, his voice now a fraction of its normal strength. 'I'm just feeling really dizzy and slightly nauseous. Maybe it's just a bit of jet lag.'

He made to continue on, but physically couldn't. He had barely enough energy to sit himself down on the path's edge to rest.

He really didn't look well. I doubted it was jet lag at play, when Vietnam and Nepal were separated by a mere seventy-five minutes' time difference. Technically, these two countries should be separated by sixty minutes, with Nepal and India on the same time zone. Nepal, however, has a long history of disagreeing with India over pretty much everything, so have set their clocks fifteen minutes ahead just to prove the point.

Back on the mountain, it was only when Pete's breathing became increasingly laboured that alarm bells began to ring. We needed to get down off the mountain quickly. I didn't want Pete collapsing up here when there was no one around to help.

I got him back on his feet and supported him physically as we made our way back to the entrance gate. His symptoms seemed to point to altitude sickness, even though I knew it was not possible when we were still way below three-thousand metres with plenty of oxygen for Pete to breathe.

I had no idea what was wrong with him. All I knew for certain was I had to get him home immediately.

Pete made a vague recovery on the taxi ride home. When we got through the front door, however, he had barely enough strength to return Tom's greeting as he welcomed us prematurely back home.

'Why don't you go to bed?' I said. 'Maybe have a bit of a lie-down?'

My suggestion was met with Pete running straight to the bathroom. For the next thirty minutes, I heard him emitting a cacophony of painful noises from behind closed doors.

He emerged from the bathroom a shell of the man who had gone in. 'Oh God, I'm so ill,' he said, creeping towards the sofa before clambering into its arms. Tom crawled over to Pete's side, a little unsure of what was going on. A quick sniff of the situation was enough for Tom to work out his services were urgently required. He plonked himself down below

Pete's hand, which hung limply off the couch. Tom kept his head tucked between his two front paws, only occasionally glancing up through half-moon eyes to check that his master was still alive. There Tom remained faithfully stationed, prepared to keep an all-night vigil if need be.

I took a more proactive approach to Pete's sudden illness: I mixed together rehydration salts to help replace the unexpected evacuation of most of Pete's bodily fluids, placed a bowl at Pete's head so he could puke his guts up without having to make the momentous journey to the bathroom, then called the doctor, whose next available appointment was not until the following morning.

'I'm sure you'll be fine by then,' I said to Pete, as I sat on the sofa trying to comfort him.

'I may be dead by then,' he replied curtly, curling up into an even tighter ball, before rolling as far away from me as possible.

I was trying as hard as I could to be sympathetic, but I don't do melodrama. Of course I felt bad that he was sick, I just wished he'd brave it a bit more valiantly.

I crouched down to see Tom still stationed faithfully by Pete's sickbed. 'You deal with him, Tom,' I instructed our long-suffering dog. Even Pete's sickness could not sway Tom's undivided loyalty.

Pete's visit to the doctor the next day revealed the real cause of his vomiting and diarrhoea. He had not been in the country seventy-two hours, and already had contracted food poisoning. I didn't dare admit that it was probably the spicy dal bhat from the local hotel I brought him to that gave him his bout of bad bacteria.

Amazingly though, once Pete had seen the doctor and

had some tablets physically placed in his hands, he made a miraculous recovery in the waiting room without swallowing a single solitary pill. I couldn't help feeling that Pete's illness may have had some slightly psychosomatic roots. Who could blame him? His arrival into Kathmandu, less than four days before, had been bumpy to say the least.

Then again, there were some who would have considered the Maoist strike, the congested tourist bus and the long walk home just part of an amazing adventure. I knew of others who wouldn't have batted an eyelid if the power went out, the water ran dry and the Internet failed to work for days on end. Though getting sick is never fun, there are people I know who would have just battled on, valiantly emptying their stomachs and bowels out as they climbed Shivapuri mountain, insisting on keeping a stiff upper lip when faced with such trivial adversity.

Pete had showed no such resilience. I couldn't help wondering if all this was Nepal's fault, if the country was just too harsh to live in. If Nepal was really that difficult, would our cohabiting unit survive this place? Would Nepal really be the place where Pete and I could figure out our future, or would we spend all our time just fending off the various problems the country threw at us?

Part of me couldn't help wondering, however, if the real issue was Pete. Had Nepal revealed to me who he really was? Was he someone who couldn't cope when faced with adversity? If real problems happened later on in life, would he struggle to deal with them? And if so, was this really someone I wanted to stay with long-term?

16

Tom's Teething Pains

Within a few days of Pete's arrival, he happened upon a potential job he could do using Kathmandu as a base. However, to be considered for the role, he needed to undergo a week's worth of training back home in Ireland.

The idea of him going back to Ireland, even for seven days, consumed me with jealousy. I longed to go home, even for a short break, just to see if things had settled down after the economic travesty that had forced us to depart. I was growing a little tired of spicy lentils and rice, and would have done anything to swap them for Irish potatoes lathered in thick creamy butter. Much as I loved the Himalayan Mountains on my doorstep, I would have traded them in any day for the gentle rolling hills south of Dublin.

I wanted to know if there was potential to return home for good one day.

After a brief discussion, we agreed that Pete might as well do the course, to keep his options open. I also secretly thought it would be good for him to get out of Nepal for a little while, to recover from his recent traumas. Admittedly, I wanted a bit of space too, to figure out how I really felt about him. I genuinely had no idea where my future happiness lay.

My concerns around my relationship with Pete were shelved when Tom developed his own issues with our Nepalese living arrangements. I came home from work one day to find Sita, our maid, in a tizzy. I was surprised to see her still at the house so late on in the day.

'You okay, Sita?' I asked, putting down my laptop bag and slipping off my work shoes.

'Tom,' she replied. This was the only word I understood before Sita launched into a long distraught onslaught of quick-fire Nepali.

'What?' I said. 'Is something wrong with Tom?'

She ushered me over to the corner of the living room and pointed to something on the tiles. It looked like some water spilled on the floor, with some unidentifiable beige gunge in the middle. She then did an amazingly accurate enactment of a vomiting motion.

'Tom vomited this up?' I asked, even though I knew full well that, given our ongoing language impasse, there was no way of checking with Sita if this was what had actually transpired. It was right at this moment, in the middle of all this confusion, that I heard a faint knock on my door.

'Hello,' the voice said, a little meekly. 'Okay if I come in?'

I turned to see Julia, my Dutch neighbour, approaching us across my living room.

'Hi Julia,' I said. 'Sorry, we're just in the middle of something. I think Sita is concerned about Tom.'

'That's actually why I'm here,' Julia admitted. 'I think I can explain.'

I looked at Julia, perplexed. How would she know anything about Tom and his current bout of Delhi belly?

Julia and I had seen less and less of each other ever since the stand-off between Tom and her children. Despite our various contrived attempts to make them all become best friends, Tom had resisted every forced encounter. It meant that, to maintain some sort of neighbourly harmony, I had had to keep Tom and myself firmly behind closed doors when I saw Julia and her kids outside playing.

'It's just, there was a mouse running around our house this morning,' Julia started to explain. 'We were trying to get rid of it.'

'Did Tom just eat rat poison?' I screamed, jumping straight to conclusions. 'Is that what that beige stuff is?' Good God, was I about to witness my dog undergoing a slow and painful death, wriggling and writhing in agony as the poison got to work? I didn't even know where I would find a vet to give him an antidote. How the hell was I going to explain to Pete that after all the time and money and effort spent bringing Tom to Nepal, he came here only to meet an untimely death?

'No, no, it's not that at all,' Julia said, waving her hands frantically to stop me making such gruesome assumptions. 'I knew Tom and the kids are around, so I made sure we didn't use any sort of poison at all. No, I think what Tom is vomiting up is glue.'

'Glue?' My brain's cogs slowly started turning before suddenly spitting out what Julia had in fact done. Instead of poisoning the mouse and putting it swiftly out of its misery, Julia had instead used a cruel, though admittedly effective, way to rid a house of mice.

I had seen this medieval rodent-trapping method used before. You take a plate and put something Asian mice like to eat, like minced meat, in the middle. Then you pour thick, sticky industrial-strength glue around the food, before placing the plate somewhere the mouse frequents. The mouse tries to reach the food, but gets stuck on the glue halfway. Over the next few hours, it fights to escape, its movements only serving to entrench itself more and more in the glue. Eventually the mouse becomes so exhausted by the struggle that it slowly gives up and dies.

'So, what you're telling me,' I said, 'is that Tom managed to get to your mouse trap plate, ate the food you put in the middle and probably ate some of the glue at the same time?'

Julia kept her head down as she spoke. 'It's just that, I had put the plate on the ground, outside our back door,' she said, guilt oozing from her pores. 'I didn't think Tom would manage to get at it.'

I looked over at Tom, who had finally made an appearance out of nowhere before the three of us. Surprisingly, he was showing no ill effects from his recent encounter with the glue trap. Instead he was sitting down, his eyes fixed on us having this heated discussion, with a toy ball positioned right between his front paws.

How, after creating all this angst, could this dog possibly think this was an appropriate moment for us to play?

With the mystery now solved, Sita packed up her things and headed for home. Before Julia retreated back to her side of the compound, I urged her to find perhaps a more humane, less dangerous way to entrap her mouse.

After everyone had left, I sat on the wooden floor and petted Tom for what seemed like hours. I was very worried in case he suffered any more glue-related after-effects. He gazed up at me with his deep brown eyes, his teddy bear nose nuzzling into my hand if I stopped stroking him for even an instant. All I could think was, please let Tom live, I really don't know what I would do without him.

Tom was probably busy thinking that he should eat glue more often if it got him such undivided attention.

After a while, once I had realised that Tom was not going to die, I said to him, 'Let's go for a walk.' I felt the need to escape the house, in particular to get away from my neighbours after this seismic near-death experience.

The mere mention of the word 'walk' saw Tom spring into action. Gone were the days when walks were a non-negotiable necessity for Tom, a reluctant exercise on his part. Instead, Tom now viewed them not only as an exciting chance for him to explore his immediate environs, but as a way to make his own distinctive mark on the neighbourhood.

I produced his lead with a flourish, dangling it enticingly above his head. He bounced up and down like a jack-in-the-box on ecstasy as if he believed that, by executing a big enough bounce, the lead would magically attach itself to his collar.

What with Tom having his own garden at his disposal, walks had become an increasingly irregular event. It was easier to just let Tom out the door, allow him to wander round the garden and come back in at his leisure. But there was a far more insidious reason why I failed to take Tom on a daily basis outside the safety of our compound: Tom's presence seemed to have the unfortunate effect of resurrecting street dogs from the shadowy confines of hidden laneways. Unfortunately, these dogs were not the submissive type. They lived hard lives, and they fought everything they conceived as a potential threat to their survival.

It meant that, if I was to venture on to public thoroughfares with Tom by my side, I had to do so well prepared. Once upon a time back in Hanoi, Tom might well have been on the path to becoming just like these street dogs, and could have held his own. Unfortunately, a year of pampering from Pete and me had made him soft and inexperienced when it came to street brawling.

It was with this in mind that I led Tom out of our front gate, holding him firmly by his lead. In my other hand, I brandished a large, wooden stick, ready to fight off any potential adversaries on Tom's behalf.

We were no further than fifty metres up the road when the first of Tom's enemies appeared: a large brown and black dog that tended to shout at Tom with intermittent snarls. This one I was well used to by now. One menacing point of my wooden baton combined with a threatening shout, and this dog would soon back down. The problem was that, once I rounded the corner, I was never too sure what canine creature we would confront next. Street battles often took place in this part of town, with different animals claiming top spot at different times.

We soon passed a rather sad looking female, with her tits hanging half way down her legs. It looked like she had been milked incessantly by a non-stop supply of pups that had hungrily sucked her mammary glands. She had no interest in Tom, nor had the energy to chase him off her patch. She knew only too well where confronting male dogs had got her in the past. She let us walk by without batting an eyelid.

It was not long, however, before we approached a pack of dogs that patrolled the local grocery store. When I was on my own, buying household supplies, these dogs showed not the slightest interest in me, but when I had Tom as my companion, my presence was quickly noted. They woke each other up from their apparent slumber, ominously alert within seconds. My stick would be no match for their menacing walk and violent talk which was fast approaching us.

'Come on, Tom,' I said, making a rapid U-turn. 'Walk's over. Let's get out of here.'

Tom reluctantly followed suit, oblivious to the ructions he had just caused. I frogmarched him the short distance back to our home. It was a very brief walk, less than ten minutes, but it seemed to have cleared both our heads.

I breathed a sigh of relief when I caught sight of our front gate. This relief was short-lived, however, when I noticed that Evil Dog's gate was lying wide open, with an unobstructed view all the way up to her house. Someone had just driven through its entrance, but had forgotten to shut the nine-foot, barbed-wire gates behind them. Evil Dog was lurking somewhere, watching, waiting.

Tom failed to register my heightened stress levels. We needed to get behind our own gates before Evil Dog noticed we were out there in the open. Plunging my hand deep into my pocket, my fingers fumbled around desperately trying to find my keys. I needed to unbolt the padlock on the inside as quickly as possible and retreat to the safety of our compound.

Too late. Evil Dog spotted us and came charging at us full pelt, hunting us down when we were at our most exposed and vulnerable. With no gate blocking her path, she was able to accelerate, reaching within two seconds the peak speed that is possible for the Pomeranian breed. Brandishing my stick at her snarling snout had no effect on this rabid animal. She had her sights on Tom, and as far as she was concerned, Tom was minced meat.

As Evil Dog dug her deadly fangs into Tom's rear leg, I didn't know whether to beat the living daylights out of this bitch or make a hasty retreat. 'Get away you feckin' animal,' I screamed at the top of my lungs, to no avail.

Poor Tom was too shell-shocked to defend himself from this stealth attack. All he managed to do instead was squeal like a little piggy.

I managed to yank Tom into my arms by pulling him up via his lead, briefly strangling him in the process: a minor discomfort when faced with having his rear leg chomped in half by a toy-sized pooch.

Eventually, I managed to force our gate open. Tom and I threw ourselves inside before I delivered a well-timed kick to Evil Dog's ribs to stop her from gaining entry. She withdrew hastily from her attack. Once safe behind our metal gate, I bent down to inspect the damage done to poor Tom's leg. Fortunately, there were no puncture marks, just a clump of hair missing that would grow back in time.

'Looks like walks are cancelled for the foreseeable future,' I said, patting Tom on the head. I had had enough of risking Tom's life and limbs for one day.

When Pete arrived back from his week's hiatus, he seemed in infinitely better form. The training had gone well, and he reported that the mood in Ireland wasn't as bad as when we left the place the year before. I couldn't help but hold on to these words, that Ireland might recover one day.

I also hoped that Pete was happy to be back in Kathmandu, together with us again after our brief break from each other.

On Pete's return to our house early on a midweek morning, he received his usual warm welcome from us all. Tom, of course, upstaged my own greeting, delivering his customary manic rave movements around Pete's feet by way of salutation. As was the norm by now, Tom's enthusiasm caused his manhood to become aroused. However, instead of licking it away like he normally did, Tom rolled over and started to lick a different part of his anatomy, his rear right paw.

'That's weird,' Pete said. 'I've not seen him doing that before.'

'Yeah, you're right,' I replied. 'Now that you mention it, I've seen him at that paw recently. I figured that he was just cleaning it.' I had been so busy coming and going with work that week that my interactions with Tom had become somewhat limited.

'Come here, Tom,' Pete said, beckoning him gently to his side. Tom jogged up to Pete with complete and utter trust. Pete then lifted him up on to his knee and sat his faithful dog on his bum like a baby. 'Let me have a look at that leg.'

Pete's mere touch of the limb made Tom retract it at supersonic speed.

'You're all right, boy,' Pete reassured him. 'I just want to see what you're licking at.'

It took Pete a few attempts before Tom finally agreed to such an intimate examination. Once Pete had peeled back Tom's foot locks, he saw what was attracting Tom's undivided attention.

'Oh my God! Come here and have a look at this, Moire,' Pete said, holding Tom firmly in his grasp while trying to gently reassure him.

'Oh no,' I said. 'That's disgusting!'

Tom's rear toenail had grown to such an extent that it had doubled back on itself and, in the process, embedded itself right into the middle of his paw pad. The area around it looked sore and infected. I was surprised Tom was still able to walk without a significant limp.

'So you're telling me that you didn't notice Tom had this foot issue,' Pete said. 'But I see it as soon as I come through the door?'

I sat there dumbfounded. How did I miss this? Did I not care for Tom at all? Was I really too busy at work, or was I just negligent when it came to looking after Tom, a dog that I wanted in the first place? Even when Pete made this painful discovery, I didn't have time to deal with it.

'I'm sorry,' I said, 'but I gotta go to the office right now. I'm late already. Can you try and get Tom treated?'

I grabbed my stuff and made a hasty exit, leaving Pete home alone to deal with Tom's poorly foot. I couldn't help wondering, however, if Pete hadn't been around, how much more Tom would have suffered while in my care.

When we lived in Hanoi, the Vietnamese ladies were wonderful at grooming Tom regularly. I didn't know it at the time, but they probably gave Tom immaculate pedicures, preventing his nails from ever growing long enough to impale themselves in his flesh. Here in Kathmandu, such pampering was unheard of. The fact that Tom had a home, and that he was fed and safe, meant he was practically spoiled in comparison with the rest of the local Nepali canine populace.

When I got home from the office later that day, Pete had already resolved Tom's in-grown toenail. He had managed to find a local vet and brought him along for treatment as soon as an appointment was available. The vet swiftly cut the nail in two, before yanking out the part that had self-embedded. The nail itself was covered in flesh and pus, and if it had been left a couple of weeks more, the vet warned, could have got highly infected and potentially turned gangrenous.

Once Tom's paw was wrapped up with a clean white bandage, Pete had lovingly carried Tom all the way back home in his arms, before installing him safely back in his crate to recuperate in peace. When I arrived home, I found Pete standing guard by Tom's side, making sure that he came to no further harm. Pete quickly informed me of what had happened at the vet and how Tom had endured the treatment valiantly.

I crouched down to see Tom curled up inside his box, his miniature bandage tucked safely away under his body. I felt so horribly guilty. I reached out to pet Tom, my way of apologising to him for being a terrible dog owner.

'Will you leave him in peace?' Pete growled at me, leaping to Tom's defence. 'Can't you see he's traumatised?' I pulled my hand swiftly away as if Tom himself had tried to bite it, but it was Pete who had snapped instead.

'I'm so sorry Pete,' I said. 'I just didn't—'

'That's right,' Pete interrupted. 'You didn't take care of Tom. In fact, it seems like the only one who looks out for him is me.'

Pete's words hurt deeply, but there was no way I could deny them. I stepped back and walked away from them both, knowing that there was nothing more that I could say or do. The incident shook me to the core, making me question everything I had believed up to that moment. Was it really fair for me to keep Tom in Nepal when all he seemed to endure were attacks and neglect? And seeing as Pete gave Tom so much more of his love, time and attention, would it not be best if Pete and Tom were allowed to go somewhere else, where they would both be much healthier and happier?

It wasn't long before the penny dropped. Maybe Nepal wasn't the issue at all. Maybe this country only helped expose a more insidious defect in our relationship? I had convinced both Pete and Tom to come with me to Nepal. It was obvious that Pete wasn't happy here. Tom couldn't be happy either, what with the abuse he suffered on such a near-daily basis. Maybe *I* was the problem in this unit, not Pete or Tom. Maybe they would both be happier if I were no longer part of the equation.

17

If You Go Down to the Woods Today

In the end, I didn't have much time to fret about what was best for us all. Sometimes, life takes unexpected turns, and Pete was now the one faced with the question of which way to go.

It was a lazy Saturday morning and I had had a particularly long and hard week at the office. Pressure was mounting to finish projects and complete reports before our office closing date in two months' time. I had still to decompress from the week's workload, so much so that I barely heard Pete's phone when it started ringing. It was only when I heard Pete answer it that I realised something must be up. Saturday morning was an unusual time for either of us to receive a call.

Pete spent a good half an hour speaking on the phone. Though I couldn't make out what he was talking about, he spoke in a highly animated manner, the way he does when trying to strike a business deal. This was not his run-of-the-mill catch-up chat with family back home in Ireland.

It was only when Pete hung up and came to find me that I

could see how bowled-over he was by the conversation. 'You're not going to believe this,' he said. 'I've just been offered a job.'

'That's great news,' I said, rushing to congratulate him. I was so relieved that, after so many long and thus-far fruitless searches, something had finally paid off. 'What is it?' I asked, wrapping my arms tightly around him. His heart was beating super-fast.

'CEO of AMK Microfinance Bank,' he said, barely able to contain his excitement. 'I can't believe it. This is totally my dream role.'

My heart sank. Damn it. I knew exactly what that offer meant. Pete would have to relocate to Cambodia to take up the position. His days of living with Tom and me in Nepal were over, like it or not.

Maybe it was for the best.

'In your dream country too,' I reminded him. It all sounded too familiar. Hadn't I said something similar back in Hanoi earlier that year when I chanced upon this job vacancy in Nepal? If ever the shoe was on the other foot, it was right now.

Both Pete and I had visited Cambodia numerous times before for short work assignments. Pete loved everything about the place. He really enjoyed working with Cambodians, who we both found quick-witted, diligent and smart. Their resilience never ceased to amaze us both, especially given that many of them lived through the Khmer Rouge era and suffered greatly at the regime's hands.

Pete also adored the sleepy feel of Phnom Penh, the capital, with its wide-open French boulevards and palm-fringed promenade lining the banks of the Mekong River.

There was nothing he liked more than retiring to the Foreign Correspondent's Club on the water's edge after a hard day's work, watching the sunset over the river from one of its terraces while he downed several happy hour Tiger beers.

I, on the other hand, was not a huge fan of the place. I found it unbearably hot and humid, the tropical climate making me so lethargic that all I wanted to do was lounge around all day. Phnom Penh is also located in the middle of unending flat terrain. After living in such a mountainous country as Nepal, with the entire Himalayas at my disposal, I was not attracted to the idea of living in endless, monotonous plains as far as the eye could see, covered in nothing but paddy fields.

'I assume you'll take the offer,' I said, wanting to sound as supportive as possible. I didn't want my own feelings about Cambodia to influence the decision Pete had to make there and then.

'I'd like to,' Pete replied, before quickly adding, 'what do you think?'

'Of course you should,' I said. 'Without a doubt. You'd be perfect for the role.'

'No, that's not what I meant,' Pete said, putting an abrupt stop to my lavish praise. 'What I want to know is, once you're finished up here in Nepal, will you come and join me in Cambodia?'

I couldn't help but breathe a heavy sigh. Did we both really want this relationship enough to uproot and move to Cambodia together? Could he put up with me if I was stuck at home, unemployable and dying with boredom? Did Pete still really want to be with me, what with my jealous tendencies and impatient, uncaring streak that had come to the fore over the previous year?

This was his chance to escape me and bring Tom with him. Why wasn't he taking it?

'Well, it's not exactly Nepal,' I said, avoiding the real issues at stake. 'Anyway, what would I do there?'

It was a moot point. My job in Nepal was finishing and I had nothing else lined up once I was done. I had also heard that Nepalese work permits were becoming more and more difficult to get, so jobs for expats were increasingly scare.

'My salary will be plenty to cover us both,' Pete explained. 'As you know, it's pretty cheap to live there. Anyhow, there are loads of charities working in Cambodia. I'm sure you'll find some work to do.'

I knew, however, that a potential move to Phnom Penh represented something far greater than yet another move to another city for another job. Over the past year, we had truly tried and tested our relationship and somehow, despite all the ups and downs, our relationship had genuinely weathered everything. This was now our chance to commit to each other, to say that we wanted to stay together long-term – or a perfect excuse for us to go our separate ways, if that was what Pete wanted.

'Are you sure you want me to come with you?' I said, deciding to no longer put off the topic that was teetering on my tongue. 'It's not like I've been the most patient with you since you arrived.' Pete looked back at me quizzically. 'I mean, it's not like I was the most sympathetic girlfriend when you were on your deathbed.'

Pete stood there silently, slightly dumbfounded. He

seemed to be waiting to hear what else I wanted to blurt out.

'Maybe I should have been more understanding when you stepped off the plane into a nationwide strike.' Pete couldn't help but smirk a little when I apologised on behalf of the Maoists. His suppressed smile, however, unearthed in me my ongoing frustration that he couldn't cope with a little hardship. 'But you do know that having limited water or electricity really isn't the end of the world?' I couldn't resist adding. 'Millions of people cope fine with that reality on a daily basis.'

Pete thoughtfully considered my outpouring before delivering his response. 'I'll be less stressed in Cambodia,' he promised. 'It's more my kind of place. Seriously, I'll be easier to live with once we're there.'

I looked at him, still somewhat sceptical.

'Please, come with me,' he said at last. 'I don't know about you but . . . I think we make a good team.'

I considered what he said. He was right, we *were* a team, and a good one at that. Maybe I didn't have to be as brilliant as him when it came to job prospects and career, and maybe it was okay if I was the hardy one, willing to rough it, while Pete was our couple's softer side.

I took Pete's hand in mine and looked at him long and hard. I thought of everything we had been through and marvelled how we had come this far. Of course, I had no idea what the future held, and what other adventures and adversities we would face. What was clear though was that it was better living life's unexpected events together rather than apart.

If love is about making that commitment, then yes, I

did love Pete. 'Of course I'll come with you,' I said softly. 'I wouldn't miss it for the world.'

We soon realised that Pete would have to move within the next couple of weeks if he wanted to take up the offer. I still had two months left of my contract, so would have to finish that before relocating. Soon we became so busy plotting and planning our now entwined future that we completely neglected to ask Tom his opinion on the matter. Did he even want to move to Cambodia, after his traumatic relocation to Nepal from Vietnam?

'What do you think, Tom?' Pete said when he saw Tom gazing up at him from the floor, looking all forlorn. Tom's tail beat out a slow and steady rhythm against the tiles, as if trying to communicate with us in some sort of dog Morse code.

'Is that a yes, Tom?' Pete said. 'Do you want to come with us to Cambodia?'

I was still surprised how, despite Pete being apparently so in tune with Tom, that he failed to guess what Tom *really* wanted half the time.

'Tom doesn't care about Cambodia, Pete,' I replied. 'Don't you see? It's the weekend. What Tom really wants is … a proper walk!'

The mere mention of the word made Tom spiral into a frenzy. What with casual, impromptu wanders up the road prohibited due to the presence of Evil Dog and her associates, walks were now confined to weekends when we could physically transport Tom further afield to safer, quieter trails.

'I'll get my shoes,' Pete said, once he had finally got with the plan. We had lately got into the habit of taking a taxi out to a random part of Kathmandu's rim at the weekend and going for a walk there. There was an area on my map that I had been meaning to explore for some time around Champadevi ridge. Tom didn't really mind where we brought him, as long as there were some interesting smells and some trees for him to mark.

We took a taxi out to the place marked on my map. It was a quiet rural area, with some houses dotted around the place that were linked together with a network of crude dirt paths. The only problem we had encountered recently was that the monsoon rains had arrived. It meant some hill tracks had turned into slippery mudslides, so we needed to be careful when selecting which one to take.

'Let's try this track into the forest,' I said, once I had got my bearings. I was hoping we'd be able to hike up onto the ridge and see what views there were from up there.

Pete and Tom were happy to do as I suggested. All they were truly interested in though was having some quality time together before our cohabiting unit was temporarily strung out between Nepal and Cambodia.

The forest track narrowed in places, forcing us to push back nettles and bushes that momentarily impeded our way. Instead of thinning out, however, the forest only thickened as we tried to forge our way further up the hill. It seemed as though the monsoon rains had made the foliage undergo some rampant growth.

This was not turning out to be the leisurely stroll I had hoped for.

'Maybe we should turn back and try to find a different track?' I said, trying to sound upbeat.

I glanced at Pete, who had a wretched look plastered across

his face. Thanks to our earlier feedback session back at the house, he was trying to heroically suck up this current hardship. However, it seemed like he needed some more practice as he was failing at it miserably.

Even Tom didn't seem to be enjoying this outing. He was straining at his leash, trying to stop us from delving any deeper into the forest.

'Yeah, this track is getting far too slippery,' Pete said. 'I can barely keep upright.'

I too was getting sucked into the forest floor by the monsoon mud. I looked down to examine the state of my own shoes, only to see a gang of tiny little worms wriggling towards my laces.

'I wonder what these things are,' I said, amazed by how furiously they seemed to be working their way up and around my runners. I looked over at Pete's shoes, which were also covered in these seemingly harmless worms. Some of them had managed to burrow through the mini holes in the shoe's side fabric. My eyes were soon diverted up Pete's ankle, to what resembled to be a massive slug stuck to his ankle.

'Yuck, there's a slug on your leg,' I shouted, bending down to flick it off before Pete got grossed out by it too. When my finger rebounded against the slug without budging it in the slightest, alarm bells began to ring.

'Oh God,' I said. 'I think that's a leech...you've a bloody leech on your leg!' I had never seen a leech in the flesh before. I had only seen them on the TV, on programmes where nineteenth-century doctors used to treat patients with a good dose of leeches to cure them of minor ailments. Reruns of *Blackadder* came quickly to mind.

'Oh shit,' Pete screamed, jumping around like a man possessed. 'Get it off, get it off!'

'I'm not sure how to get it off,' I said. 'Aren't these things properly stuck on?' I vaguely remembered hearing something about them being impossible to remove until they had drunk their fill of your blood. I also recalled something about their fangs getting lodged into you and getting highly infected if broken off. Or was that ticks, not leeches, that did that fang trick?

While Pete and I were trying to solve this leech dilemma, Tom was just content with the fact that we'd stopped walking deeper into the woods. He sat down on the muddy trail, happily panting while he waited for Pete to finish receiving emergency first aid. Soon, however, I couldn't help Pete any more. Leeches had appeared on my own ankles too, making me unleash a mighty roar.

'Let's get out of here,' I yelled, beating a hasty retreat back through the foliage. After what seemed like forever, we emerged back on to a wide Jeep track that had no undergrowth from which leeches could spring a surprise attack. Pete and I sat down on the ground and yanked off all our shoes. The outsides of our socks were steeped in blood from leeches that had dropped off after having their fill. Peeling off our socks, we then discovered what could only be described as Armageddon.

Between us, we had around a hundred leeches clinging for dear life to anything they could find below knee level. The fact that these beasts unleashed an anaesthetic on first bite meant that neither of us had felt the full extent of their initial assault.

Now that we were sitting down in one place, they proved remarkably easy to pull off.

'Total feckers,' I couldn't help but mumble to myself as I flung them back into the forest. If I thought removing the leeches from my legs would put an end to the terror, I was very much mistaken. As soon as the leeches disengaged, fresh blood started teeming from my legs. The leeches had had plenty of time to pump the anti-clotting enzyme, hirudin, into my system. Blood oozed from our legs as it refused to coagulate. Pete and I looked like extras from a particularly gruesome horror film. No sticking plaster would stem this tide.

Despite my ignorance of relevant wilderness medicine, I did know that the bleeding would eventually stop all by itself after a couple of hours. It was a case of just waiting it out.

Once we were satisfied that we had rid ourselves of the very last leech, Pete and I decided that we both needed to go home and get a stiff drink to calm us from the stress.

'Come on, Tom,' I said. 'I think we've all had enough walkies today.'

Tom stood up to leave, but as he turned to follow Pete, all I could see was bright red blood dripping from Tom's backside.

'Oh no,' I shouted to Pete. 'I think a leech has gone up Tom's ass!'

We both looked at each other, wondering who was going to be the one to remove the offending leech from Tom's bum passage. I was hoping that the fact that Tom's blood was visibly flowing meant that the leech had already disengaged and was already drunkenly wandering off down the road in the search of its next victim.

'It must have been when Tom sat down in the forest,' Pete said. 'Poor Tom, what have we gone and done?'

Pete eventually volunteered to inspect Tom's behind. He took Tom into his arms and tugged his tail out of the way. Blood was flowing copiously from Tom's rear, but there was fortunately no sign of any black beasties lodged up Tom's rectum. We then all decided just to limp home, where we spent the next three hours mopping up the never-ending blood spillage from our veins.

It took another seven days before the sores the leeches gave us healed up enough for us to stop itching the hell out of them.

Poor Tom. It seemed like he couldn't have a walk anywhere these days without being attacked by something that wanted a piece of him. Maybe it was indeed time for him to get the hell out of Dodge City.

18

On the Move (Again)

Pete and I were both adamant that, at all costs, we wanted to avoid the trauma we had endured when moving Tom from Hanoi to Kathmandu. We agreed, therefore, that Pete should first move to Cambodia and settle into his new job there. Then, as soon as he found a suitable home for us all to live in, I would bring Tom over on a weekend trip to Phnom Penh before returning alone to Kathmandu. Then, once I'd finished up with my own job, I would relocate and join them.

It meant that we could time Tom's departure so that it was not contingent on Pete's or my departure. This strategy was devised to help us avoid several stressful scenarios. We didn't want Tom to go with Pete immediately in case Pete couldn't find suitable accommodation for Tom while Pete started his new job. It would be practically impossible for Pete to look after Tom if he had to live in a hotel for the first couple of days he was there.

We also didn't want to delay Tom's departure until my own time was up in Nepal. If Tom was prevented from boarding the plane when I was already packed up to leave, I would be forced to overstay my visa just to make alternate travel arrangements. Or, in the worst-case scenario, Tom would be left permanently behind in Nepal, to face forever the wrath of Evil Dog. None of us wanted to even contemplate such a cataclysmic scenario.

The dilemma we were faced with was terribly reminiscent of the puzzle where a farmer tries to transport a fox, chicken and bag of grain across a river. Pete and I had to figure out how to move all these things from one side of the continent to the other, without anything getting lost or eaten on the way.

Within a couple of days of Pete's arrival in Phnom Penh, he was fortunate enough to happen upon a cute traditional wooden house located in the popular expat area of Boeung Keng Kang. It had a walled-in front area where a car could be parked, or if need be, Tom could be kept safely when no one else was at home. We would have preferred to have a garden with grass where Tom could do his business, like in Kathmandu, but in the interim this concrete enclosure was good enough to signal we were good to start Tom's emigration process.

I opted to fly with Thai Airways again, seeing that we already had intimate knowledge of their dog-transportation policies and procedures. This time I had all of Tom's medical documentation ready well in advance so I could receive his Nepali-issued government medical certificate in time. This in turn allowed me to get clearance from Thai Airways' head office in Bangkok three days before our flight's departure date, as should have happened when I originally moved to Kathmandu. It was amazing how, when I knew what to do and when, Tom's emigration process could be so wonderfully smooth and simple.

As before, I planned to take Tom physically into the cabin with me, seeing that he was just the right shape and size. When I arrived at Kathmandu airport, the check-in staff suggested that Tom might be more comfortable if he went into the hold.

Alarm bells began to sound. 'No, I want to keep him with me on board,' I protested, clinging desperately to Tom's cage. I was still traumatised from hearing Pete's account of his Hanoi customs experience. There was no way I wanted to lose sight of Tom for even a second before or during this flight.

Even Tom seemed to be still working through the memories of that previous ordeal. I noticed symptoms of post-traumatic stress disorder as soon as I started to pack up his belongings before leaving the house. When he saw me putting the water bottle back in his cage together with some dried food in a container, Tom immediately knew something was up. When I replaced the mesh door on his crate and added some more freight stickers, he ran and hid under the sofa, refusing to come out.

Only the promise of future walkies with Pete made him surface long enough for me to grab him by the collar and escort him swiftly, somewhat forcefully, into his crate.

Fast-forward to Kathmandu airport, and the Thai Airways staff had to summon up all their powers of persuasion for me to relinquish Tom. They told me that he would be safe in the hold, and that I could even go down and check on Tom in Bangkok when we had a flight connection.

'As long as you promise me that he's on the flight,' I said, reluctantly handing him over. I had terrible visions of him being left behind, spending the whole weekend going around and around on one of Kathmandu Airport's luggage belts.

I need not have worried. With the paperwork in perfect condition, Thai Airways diligently transported Tom all the way to Phnom Penh without the slightest hitch. Just like back in Kathmandu airport when I first collected him, his crate was ready and waiting for me in the baggage carousel area as soon as I disembarked.

I placed him on my luggage trolley in Phnom Penh airport and wheeled him out through the double doors. As in Nepal, not even the Cambodian customs official stationed at the exit had the slightest interest in checking my foreign dog.

There must be so much rabies running rampant around Asia, crossing borders willy-nilly, that there's no need for laborious checks or quarantine. Either that, or the Cambodian government trusts so profoundly Nepal's Directorate of Animal Health and Thailand's national airline that, if they say Tom is good to go, there are no further questions asked.

Pete was standing outside the terminal, arms open wide, waiting for us to arrive. The broad, beaming smile spread across his face revealed a mixture of happiness and sheer relief. 'So, you've come in the end,' he said, giving me a huge welcoming hug. 'I was wondering if you were going to back out of our plan.'

I shook my head, amazed that he could doubt me. I wondered how I was ever going to convince Pete that I was very much intent on sticking around.

'Of course we've come,' I said. 'Tom and I have missed you.'

I really meant what I was saying, and I was pretty sure Tom didn't mind me speaking on his behalf.

At the sound of Pete's words, Tom's crate, still balanced precariously on my trolley, leapt into action.

'Come here my dog, come here!' Pete said, freeing Tom from his cage. Tom squirmed his way straight into Pete's arms, licking him desperately. It seemed as though Tom wanted to ensure it really was Pete there present in the flesh by having a quick taste.

The two were so focused on each other that they were oblivious to the growing number of stares from the Cambodians around them. They too were waiting for loved ones to appear through the double doors, but they weren't anticipating their relatives to lick them on arrival.

We all crammed into a tuk-tuk, a type of open-air chariot pulled along by a motorbike, to ride back to Pete's new place. It's an exceptionally cheap and relaxing way to be transported around Cambodia. Pete got into the tuk-tuk then placed Tom on his lap, giving Tom the best possible view from our wagon.

Once the tuk-tuk driver took off, Tom looked infinitely happy. The wind was flowing through his locks, his ears were bristling in the breeze, and his nose was thrown out the side to capture the new array of exciting smells conjured up by this brand-new country.

Sitting there, with his dog on his lap, I could see that Pete was content as well. Maybe it was indeed the stresses and strains of Nepal that had caused me to question our relationship. Maybe all we needed was a change in scenery to help reunify and strengthen our cohabiting unit. I even found myself wondering if this would be the place where our CHU could potentially morph into a family? It seemed a pretty big step, but I couldn't help thinking to myself, maybe one day.

Our transit to Pete's house in the tuk-tuk was considerably easier than the crammed tourist bus and enforced death march back from Kathmandu Airport. I didn't dare mention that incident, however, in case it spoiled our currently tranquil drive. Hopefully the ease with which we were being transported home was a sign of good things to come in our new life in Cambodia.

The tuk-tuk driver eventually dropped us directly outside Pete's pad on street fifty-seven, as opposed to the Kathmandu tourist bus that left us two kilometres down the road. The house looked like something that had been airlifted from the countryside and dropped in the middle of this urban setting. I could see that it had originally been built on stilts, presumably a safeguard against the floods that often hit Cambodia. The area underneath had since been bricked in, providing a small kitchen and sitting room area that just about fitted two adults and one seven-kilogram dog. Upstairs the original floorboards and wooden walls remained intact, providing two bedrooms and a bathroom. It was cute, cosy and slightly claustrophobic. I was surprised Pete liked it, when confined spaces such as the narrow streets and miniature taxis in Kathmandu tended to freak him out.

'Welcome to your new home,' Pete proclaimed as soon as we were behind the large barbed-wire-topped, heavy metallic gate that guarded our wooden shack. I threw my bags down, before flopping into the cheap rattan furniture that decorated the entire place. Inside, the place looked remarkably neat and tidy. I complimented Pete on being able to fit in housework when he must be so busy at work.

'Ah, I meant to mention that,' Pete admitted. 'I've already hired a maid. Sorry, I meant to run it by you, but I urgently needed someone to iron my shirts.'

Gone were the days when I objected to employing a maid. Thanks to Xuan and Sita, I had unfortunately grown accustomed to arriving home to an immaculately and magically clean house. In fact, if I was forced now to clean up after myself, I'm not sure I would know how.

Chanteoun was the name of the Cambodian lady who had made Pete's house spotless for our arrival. She was also the one who would check in on Tom when Pete was out at work and I was back in Nepal, finishing off my own assignment.

It was only when I saw Pete seated in one place, out of the bright sunlight, that I realised how tired he looked.

'So how's work going?' I asked, purposely leaving the question open-ended. He was two weeks into the job already, and I had barely heard from him. It felt incredibly familiar, though our roles were reversed. The difference was that I wasn't giving him a guilt trip that he'd not made contact more often. To be honest, I felt more secure in my relationship with Pete now than I ever had.

'Oh man, it's crazy,' he replied. 'I'm working every minute of every day. This is the first weekend I'm having off since I started.'

'Do you like the job?' I said. 'Is it, like, what you expected?'

'Don't get me wrong, it's great,' Pete replied. 'I get a real sense of achievement from the stuff we're doing. I think we're making a big difference.'

That surge of pride that I had felt towards Pete in Ireland and Vietnam resurrected itself from the recesses of my mind. When Pete is busy, working hard, getting shit done, I feel so proud of him. It was at times like this that I was truly amazed such a gifted individual chose to be with me.

I was still basking in Pete's accomplishments when I heard a scratching sound right above our heads.

'What's that noise?' I asked Pete.

'Oh, I wouldn't worry about that,' he replied. 'I think there's a family of rats living up in the attic.'

I stared back at Pete, who seemed remarkably relaxed about sharing his wooden home with a gang of rodents. I couldn't help wondering if this was his attempt not to freak out about little hardships after me lecturing him about this back in Kathmandu but I wasn't convinced that a rat infestation is a hardship one should bear stoically.

The only thing that stopped me from insisting Pete get rid of them was my traumatic memories of the glue trap back in Kathmandu. I had no desire to see Tom vomiting up industrial glue again, or watching a rat writhe its way to an early grave just because I didn't like the scurrying sounds it made above me. As long as the rodents promised to stay in the attic and not venture downstairs, then I supposed I was fine with sharing our living space with them too.

'Don't worry,' Pete said, as I silently came to terms with the idea of having rats living above us. 'Once you finish off in Nepal, we'll try and find a proper villa we can rent, one with a garden where Tom can hang out.' On our journey from the airport, I had noticed many old French colonial-style homes lining the streets of the neighbourhood. Admittedly many of them looked large enough to accommodate three generations within their walls. Pete didn't have the time or energy to find something that would suit our unit's size, so it would be up to me to find somewhere once we were all Phnom Penh-based.

'Why don't we take a walk and check out the neighbourhood?' I said.

Tom was ready and waiting by the gate as soon as he heard the W word. Even if Pete wanted to stay indoors for the rest of the day, Tom had decided otherwise. We stepped outside on to the main street with Tom firmly on his lead. The district of Boeung Keng Kang, like most of Phnom Penh, is arranged into a regimented grid system. All we had to do was keep turning left when we reached a junction, and eventually we'd complete a lap of our block and return safely back to base.

Tom made a beeline for the first tree he saw, its trunk bursting out from between the paving slabs. Tom cocked his leg, and let out a long, satisfying pee.

'He must have been desperate after getting caged up all that time,' Pete said. 'Good job we brought him out for a spin.'

Soon it became evident, however, that Tom's peeing strategy had nothing to do with his bladder level. He had barely finished before he turned around one hundred and eighty degrees, cocked the other leg, and proceeded to go again in exactly the same spot. In the process of turning, Tom succeeded in rubbing his whole left side in urine.

'Tom, you silly dog,' Pete shouted, yanking Tom away from the tree mid-piss. 'You're going to stink.'

Tom didn't seem to care about how he smelt. Instead, he looked back at the tree that Pete had pulled him away from, despondent. Fortunately, there was a particularly stained wall further ahead that seemed like a doggie calling card. Tom peed on it again and again, just to make sure that it was truly his. He was like a kid in a toyshop, wanting every tree, wall and car tyre in Cambodia to be 'mine, mine, mine!'

With the amount of scent that Tom had just emitted, I was surprised no stray dogs had come running, on red alert. The further we walked around the block, the more I realised that there were actually no abandoned street dogs living in this part of town. Tom had lucked out.

Outside one particularly grand-looking villa, Tom chanced on a piece of grass. What with the hot sun and seasonally dry climate, green grass was particularly hard to come by. Some gardener must have been employed to take care of this foliage so that the villa's dwellers could drive past it as they entered through their huge stately gates. It meant that, as they waited for the gates to be opened by their security guard, they could look out of their Lexus SUV windows and enjoy this mini meadow effect.

Tom was so excited by the blades that he twirled around excitedly, just like a cat would do if on the verge of settling down on a nice comfy chair. It was only when he arched his back that I understood that he was defecating all over this villa's prized lawn.

Neither Pete nor I had a bag to pick the offending crap up from this immaculate turf. Instead, we yanked Tom away from the grassy area, pretending we didn't see what was happening, and hoped that his excrement would desiccate and disappear before the gardener returned.

We frogmarched Tom home, dragging him along a little faster whenever he tried to cock his leg. He'd not even been in the country twenty-four hours, and already he was trying to provoke his canine neighbours with unending scent marks.

Little did we know that Tom already had an adversary waiting for him, directly opposite his new home.

As soon as our wooden shack came into sight, I heard what sounded like a rumble of thunder from the gates opposite us. It sounded like an ogre, but when I peered through the steel bars I caught sight of a black and white patchwork brute of a dog, four times the size of Tom. Evil Dog must have radioed ahead to one of her Cambodian associates to warn them of Tom's arrival.

I didn't know whether Tom was being bullish or incredibly thick when he tried to take territorial control of the neighbourhood. Regardless of his motivation, he was a marked dog now and had better watch his back.

I returned to Kathmandu a few days later after an emotional, too-short stay in Phnom Penh. My house was noticeably quieter. I hadn't realised how much of a presence Tom was until he had flown the nest.

It was only when my house was burgled a week later that I realised how much I missed Tom. He would have heard the external mosquito netting being cut back, the window being pushed open, and the intruder jumping into my bedroom while I was downstairs watching TV. Instead, it wasn't until I went upstairs to bed that I realised my money and some electronic goods were gone.

If only Pete had also been there during the robbery to provide me with moral support. Instead, I had five Nepali cops barge into my house to investigate the break-in. I got the distinct impression that they just wanted to have a nosey around my home rather than collect valuable evidence that might actually help catch the villain. Despite my repeated suggestions that there was nothing more to see, the police failed to listen to me. Pete would have kindly escorted them out the door and thanked them for their all help.

Even though the robber only took a few dollars, a camera and a watch, I could no longer sleep easily in the house. I felt too unsafe, now that I was a female living all alone in a foreign country. I dearly missed the security and companionship that came with Pete and Tom.

This incident, combined with getting a good dose of food poisoning on a final swansong trek, made me long to leave Nepal as soon as possible. It may be a wonderful country to visit, to witness its amazing sights and sounds, but it was time I got out of there.

19

Decompression

After six long weeks of separation, I joined Tom and Pete in Phnom Penh.

During this time apart, Tom and Pete had grown accustomed to living together and had slotted into a daily rhythm that suited both of them quite nicely. Offices open bright and early in Cambodia to avoid much of the day's heat, probably a habit left over from the country's French colonial past. Starting at the crack of dawn allows workers a two-hour siesta lunch break at twelve o'clock, when the sun is at its worst. This meant that Pete had to be at his own office at the ridiculously early time of 7.30 a.m.

Before leaving his rodent-infested residence, Pete would take Tom on a quick walk to do a full inspection of his dominion. By 7.10 a.m., Pete's own personal tuk-tuk driver swung up right in front of Pete's door. For the grand sum of two US dollars, Chandara chauffeured Pete to his place of work. For no extra charge, he could detour via Pete's favourite coffee shop if Pete felt the need. Chandara would patiently wait outside while Pete collected his double-shot flat white and still-warm and melt-in-the-mouth croissant, before escorting him swiftly across town to his office block. This gave Pete ten minutes to recline in the rear open-air seat, calmly checking his blackberry and sipping his coffee while waking up to the warm, sunny climes of South-East Asia. It definitely beat the drudgery of a long commute in a crowded train through a cold, wet and dreary Dublin.

Having such highly personalised services at his disposal did mean Pete was able to focus solely on work-related matters. He was so absorbed, indeed overwhelmed, by his new role that he often forgot to stop for his midday break when the rest of the Cambodian staff were either eating or snoozing. Typically, it was only when Chandara appeared outside of his office at 6 p.m. that Pete realised it was time for him to go home. That didn't stop Pete answering more emails and setting up more meetings on the short tuk-tuk journey home.

When Pete pushed his hand through the front gate to unbolt the padlock, Tom's short, sharp lick of his fingers thankfully transported Pete back to reality. During the day, all Pete could think about was net interest margins, interest yields, return on equity and portfolio at risk. Only Tom could bring him out of this microcosm of microfinance and remind him that there was a whole other world out there that didn't involve spreadsheets or figures.

'Hello my dog, my good, good dog!' Pete would exclaim once he was through the gate. Tom would twirl on his two hind legs, whining with excitement. He was always dying to welcome Pete home by performing the most spectacular dance show ever seen, even better than the exact same one Tom had performed for Pete only the day before.

Every day, Tom would land his front paws on Pete's expensive trousers, clamouring for Pete to bend down to receive a doggie kiss. Poor Chanteoun: she would be scrubbing those paw prints out of Pete's trousers the following day. Seeing that this had turned into a daily ritual, she was probably well used to it by now.

If Tom won Pete's particular favour with his wonderful dance rendition, Pete would take him into his arms and carry him triumphantly back into the house. The only problem was that Tom was petrified of heights. So, as his final climactic move, Tom would do a pirouette in Pete's arms before leaping out of them, back to the safety of the floor. Once firmly back on terra firma, Tom would scurry away to his dressing room until it was time for tomorrow's repeat show.

God help us all though if Tom wasn't around to welcome Pete back home. One day, soon after joining them, I took the initiative to get Tom's fur back under control. I found a dog grooming service, temptingly named Happy Hound. I brought Tom there to get a short back and sides, and for a diligent manicure. The groomers thought that Tom's hair and nails were so unruly that they told me to call back in two hours' time. I left Tom there, returning to the house empty handed, for me to welcome Pete home instead.

Unfortunately, my welcoming routine paled in comparison to Tom's display. Pete noticed Tom's absence straightaway, immediately wondering why no one licked his fingers when he undid the padlock.

'Hi there,' I said when I saw Pete materialise inside the house. 'How was work?'

'Fine,' Pete answered curtly before quickly enquiring,

'Where's Tom?' He dropped his laptop bag inside the door, got down on all fours, and peered under the sofa for his missing dog.

'Tom's at the groomers,' I said. Pete muttered something incomprehensible before righting himself back to his feet, digging his hand deep into his pocket, and pulling out his blackberry. He then threw himself into a chair and started tapping madly on its keyboard.

'Want a glass of wine or something?' I asked, trying to attract his attention. Pete was still so absorbed in the world of work that he seemed incapable of hearing me.

'Busy day then, so?' I said, a little hurt. He was blatantly ignoring me.

'What? What did you say?' Pete bit back, in a voice that was totally uncalled-for.

His tone was not worth starting a fight over. All I had to do was wait for Tom to come home from his hairdressing appointment and work his magic to distract Pete from his various work dilemmas.

Once they were done with Tom, Happy Hound handed a shorn sheep back to me. As soon as Pete saw Tom, he forgot all his woes.

'Look what they've done to you!' Pete said, gazing at Tom proudly, holding him aloft to behold his wonderfully clean dog.

Tom looked more akin to a skinhead rat than a meticulously groomed canine to me. Fortunately though, with him back home, peace was soon restored to our household.

Though Tom was not as soft and cuddly as he was before, his razor cut was probably far more practical given how hot and humid Phnom Penh is. Days later, however, we wondered if they had taken a bit too much fur off. In the middle of the night, Tom started coughing so badly that we were convinced he was going to choke to death.

At 2 a.m., Tom's hacking was so serious that I got up and checked if he had something stuck inside his throat. Pete got up too and held Tom tight so that I could pry open his jaws and glance briefly down his gullet. I saw nothing in there except a pink tongue and rows of jagged teeth. Despite this, Tom continued to cough and gag, as if he was desperately trying to vomit up something.

'Maybe we should call an emergency vet, or something,' Pete suggested.

'And where exactly would we find one of those?' I asked. 'If you got sick at night, I'm not even sure where I'd bring you. And you're not a dog.' The absence of twenty-four-hour medical services for humans and canines in developing countries was something that had never really bothered us up to then.

Tom braved his near-death experience valiantly. In between severe coughing bouts, he would meekly wag his tail as if trying to comfort *us*, to reassure us that everything would be fine. He wanted us not to worry, when it was him who was suffering.

We soon concluded that Tom's condition was dire, but stable. 'He's probably just got a really nasty cold,' I said, hoping that I was right, and that Tom held tight and made it through the night.

The next morning, I found Tom curled up in his bed, thankfully still alive. 'Don't worry. I'll bring him to a vet,' I said to Pete.

Once Pete had gone to work, I happened to find a vet three blocks away from us, who told me I could bring Tom in straightaway. I was relieved that I didn't have to wait for an appointment after the night Tom had just had.

Tom was fine to walk the short distance to the vet under his own steam. Our route took in a different set of streets to the ones he usually frequented, which helped distract him from his mysterious, potentially fatal illness.

Within five minutes of arriving at the vet's, the receptionist ushered us into a treatment room. Inside, a tall French man greeted Tom and me before introducing himself as Pierre. He got down to business straightaway. I explained the symptoms Tom had developed during the night. As I spoke, he hoisted Tom on to his table and begun to scrutinize Tom's still-alive corpse.

Tom didn't have the energy to fight off Pierre's advances. Instead, he froze to the spot, afraid to move even a single muscle. He didn't even wince when Pierre shoved a thermometer up his rectum.

'Have you put Tom in kennels recently?' Pierre asked while he waited for the thermometer to deliver its reading.

'No,' I replied, surprised by the question. I'd never had to place Tom in kennels in Nepal, as Sita was always there to keep an eye on him if I was away, and since arriving in Cambodia, we hadn't left Phnom Penh. What did kennels have to do with Tom's coughing and aborted vomit attempts? 'I just thought that maybe Tom caught a bad cold or something, seeing that he's recently had a haircut.'

It sounded such an amateur diagnosis from a sentimental owner, but I figured I might as well throw my theory out there and see if I was even close.

'Haircut?' Pierre said, homing in on that piece of information. 'Can I ask where you got him groomed?'

'Happy Hound,' I replied, slightly embarrassed by the business name.

I looked down at Tom, whose back leg had started to vibrate like a pneumatic drill. On the other end, a never-ending torrent of drool streamed from Tom's mouth. Soon the torrent developed into a substantial puddle directly under Tom's chin.

I prayed that Tom wasn't going to become mentally scarred by this examination. It was a far cry from the veterinary table in Hanoi where he was hand blow-dried by three stunning Vietnamese girls.

'Okay, so I now know your problem,' Pierre said, gesturing for me to put Tom back on the ground. Tom shook his head, then his body, and finally his tail in sequential order to demonstrate his relief at being out of Pierre's reach. 'Tom has kennel cough. He probably caught it from Happy Hound. I've had a couple of dogs in here this week who also got groomed in that place. I've already called them and told them to clean up their place, but they don't listen to me. They're just interested in getting money and don't care about the animals, as far as I'm concerned.'

I couldn't help but feel guilty about bringing Tom to Happy Hound, though how was I to know the place was riddled with kennel cough? Where were the regulators responsible for checking on such businesses and shutting them down? Did such authorities even exist in developing countries like Cambodia?

'So, how do we go about treating his kennel cough?' I asked, fearing that I was going to have to force-feed Tom medicine.

'No medication is necessary. He just needs to rest, and to be well watered and fed,' Pierre said. 'And, whatever you do, keep him away from other dogs so they are not infected as well.'

It took Tom a full two weeks for his kennel cough to clear up. We then got Tom vaccinated against the disease in case he came in contact with an infected dog in the future. And, despite its alluring business name, we resolved never to darken the doors of Happy Hound ever again.

While Tom was busy recovering, I set about trying to find us a new home. In theory, it was simple enough, as houses for rent usually had a sign posted outside their front door indicating their availability.

I decided the best thing to do was to walk up and down all the streets in Boeung Keng Kang to find something suitable. I started by walking down the rest of street fifty-seven, then up street fifty-one before going back down street sixty-three. When the vertical, odd-numbered streets had nothing on offer, I decided to go horizontally and to the even-numbered streets. I headed along street 306, 310, 322 and 334, before giving up and going back home.

There were houses galore on these randomly numbered and named streets, but nothing that looked even vaguely appropriate. Most places for rent were palatial mansions way beyond our budget. Those that were affordable turned out to be cavernous terraced houses that tried to keep out the Asian heat by excluding any light, hidden behind distinctly unwelcoming gates and sky-high walls. Compared to those vacant properties, we much preferred to remain in our rat-ridden shack.

What kept us in the district, however, was the amazing range of dining options within walking distance of our place. On my hunt to find our dream home, I happened upon a mouth-watering selection, from French fine dining to wholesome Italian fare; there were Japanese sushi restaurants and Australian tucker bars; there were ice-cream parlours, cafés offering fry-ups for hungry backpackers, and beer-swilling sports bars. I found Nepali and Indian eateries offering curries for a couple of dollars and, in the midst of all these culinary delights, there were fabulous Khmer restaurants serving up delicately prepared fish and rice. If we lived in this neighbourhood, we would never have to cook for ourselves again.

If food wasn't enough of a draw, Pete had found another reason to stay within a few streets of where we lived. He had found the most relaxing place ever to go for an hour-long foot massage, just up the road.

Going for massages had become our weekend 'thing' while living and working in Asia. In Hanoi, every Saturday morning, we used to attend a nearby Japanese Buddhist centre for full body massage. It was an excellent way to unwind after the week. For ninety minutes, tiny Vietnamese ladies half the size of Pete would smooth our bodies with long, oily, gliding strokes. Typically Pete would fall asleep halfway through his massage, his gentle snores rippling through the thin blind that provided us with a modicum of privacy. It was only when his masseuse found a knot that needed undoing that Pete's snores would be suddenly interrupted by a blood-curdling scream.

The first time I heard Pete yelling from the adjacent cubicle, I was convinced that he would forbid us from ever returning to the place. The lady was trying to unravel a particularly tight knot in his calf muscle. It took a few minutes before she untangled his muscle, signified by Pete simultaneously sobbing and laughing. It was only later that I learned that, according to Pete, the more excruciatingly painful the massage, the better. Pete evidentially couldn't get enough of this pain and faithfully returned to the centre every weekend until we left.

In Kathmandu, I found a massage place that would only touch me if I were fully clothed head to toe in thick cotton pyjamas that they themselves provided. It turned out to be a Japanese form of rubdown known as Sotai. This entailed three individuals positioned around me, simultaneously kneading my legs, back and shoulders using their hands and feet. It was an explosion of senses that made me return on a weekly basis. Pete enjoyed the massages too, but got a bit weirded out when they suggested he should also drink his own urine and occasionally iron himself on his back to improve his circulation.

Having a foot massage in the spa up our road in Phnom Penh was thankfully in safe territory. With no requirement to strip off, there was not even the slightest risk of any hanky-panky, unlike in some less reputable parlours in other parts of town. All Pete and I had to do was sit down on large reclining armchairs while polite Khmer ladies bathed our feet and lower legs before tending to them for an hour. What made the experience even more enticing was the fact that an hour's worth of unadulterated attention cost less than ten dollars.

There was also the possibility of popping straight into the beautician's right next door afterwards for a ten-dollar manicure and pedicure, should Pete be unsatisfied with this level of pampering. When I initially discovered Pete's propensity for grooming, I wasn't sure how to react, but when I saw how beautifully his nails and feet turned out after such sessions, I was also tempted to indulge in this once exclusively feminine practice.

I was starting to understand why Pete loved Phnom Penh so much. With chauffeured tuk-tuks, personal maids, luxurious massages and fine dining options at his beck and call, he was getting thoroughly spoiled. With his dog at his side, and me on his arm, could it be that Pete had worked out how to have it all?

20

Tom's Villa

Despite my initial reservations about moving to Phnom Penh and indulging in its laid-back lifestyle, I slowly converted to Pete's pampered way of life. It was indeed pleasant to be Pete's companion as we dined out in sumptuous restaurants every night. It was lovely hanging out with him in massage parlours, as our bodies were alternately beaten then caressed for a fraction of the price such attention would cost back home in Ireland. Maybe Pete was on to something when he suggested we moved to Phnom Penh. I hated to say it, but I knew I could well become accustomed to, and indeed expect, this lifestyle from now on.

Pete was also right about me finding work in Phnom Penh. There were plenty of charities based in the capital that needed people to do short assignments for them. These freelance jobs suited me down to the ground. It meant I could work flexible hours, as well as pick and choose the type of work I wanted to do. In reality this meant I sat for hours in my favourite coffee shop, ordering endless lattes while writing up long reports I considered to be literary masterpieces.

I hadn't realised it when Pete originally suggested this move, but maybe *this* was really my dream job in my dream location. Maybe Pete knew what was best for me after all.

Just when I didn't think life could get any better, I got a call from an estate agent who I had recently co-opted in our search for our dream home. A villa had become available on street 302, just four blocks from where we currently lived. It had three bedrooms and a garden, in the heart of Boeung Kang Kong. Pete and I didn't hesitate, and agreed to visit it that very day.

Our estate agent, David, met us outside the house during the lunchtime break. There were no signs outside saying that it was up to rent, hence why I hadn't known it was available. David may have been an expat from Australia, but he had a crack team of Cambodians out patrolling the streets, knowing the status of every property in the capital. The current occupants wanted to move, so were planning to vacate soon. As soon as David swung open the gates, I couldn't fathom why the present tenants would ever want to leave such an amazing place.

The villa was beyond perfection. To the right of the gate, a lawn stretched out under a myriad of palm trees swaying in the warm afternoon breeze. The scent of frangipani flowers wafted gently through the air as we made our way towards the cool, shady veranda and in through the front door.

Inside, a high-ceilinged open-plan room stretched out before us, with fans rotating lazily above our heads. They provided a welcome remedy to the heat outside, transforming the room into a haven where I could picture myself chilling out.

Slipping off our shoes at the entrance, I noticed the intricate floor tiles beneath my feet. They were from the French colonial era, with deep rich colours and fleur-de-lis beautifully preserved within this tranquil residence.

We continued to wander through the villa, taking in the en suite bedrooms and small yet functional kitchen. Then David led us outside to a small, narrow stairway hidden away behind the house. It brought us up to the most incredible, palm-fringed veranda perched on top of the roof. From up there we had an amazing view of our garden, a hidden tropical paradise.

'A perfect place for parties,' David suggested as Pete nodded enthusiastically. I could already see Pete installing a fridge crammed full of ice-cold Tiger beers and inviting round all the neighbours. I, on the other hand, couldn't wait to hang a hammock and escape under these fronds. I could sway the weekend away, sipping on a glass of chilled wine while indulging in a novel from the local second-hand bookstore, where backpackers dumped all the latest bestsellers.

'So what do you think?' David said, dragging us abruptly back to the present.

I didn't dare gush about the place in case it raised the rental price. I *had* to find something negative to say so we had a reason to bargain hard. 'Well, the tiles downstairs look a bit worn.' As soon as I said the words, I cursed myself for uttering something so profoundly stupid.

Pete fortunately ignored me and thankfully took charge of the negotiations. It was at times like these I thought I'd be quite adrift without him.

'How much is the landlord looking for?' Pete asked. Much

to our surprise, it was not an astronomical amount, well within our budget. There was no need to quibble over a few dollars when they were offering us exactly what we wanted. David went away and told the owner on our behalf that we accepted the suggested terms. Within a couple of weeks, we could vacate our wooden hut and move into a proper brick-and-mortar house.

Tom was ecstatic when we took charge of our new home a few weeks later. He scurried through the gates and headed straight for the green, glistening lawn to give it a good test. He galloped around it in circles, carving up sods as he skidded around its ninety-degree corners until his little legs couldn't take it any more, his tongue lolling out of his mouth with sheer exhaustion and dehydration.

'Come on, Tom,' Pete called from the veranda, where he had been watching his dog perform his laps. 'Let's get you some water and check the place out.'

Tom trotted over to the house and straight in through the door. He then proceeded to do an extensive sniff of all the rooms, making sure the place was in order. Once he had completed his inspection, he pronounced it safe for us to live in. Not that there was much for Tom to smell. The previous tenants had stripped the place of all their belongings, leaving the villa nothing but a bare shell.

'We should go buy some nice furniture for this place,' Pete suggested once he had seen for himself how empty the villa was.

I did a double take. Pete could be pretty cheap when it came to things like furnishings. He was happy out lounging on cheap bamboo back at the wooden hut, preferring to spend his money on more frivolous activities like drinking and dining out. I was not sure where this change of mind had come from, for him to actually hand over hard-earned cash for something useful and concrete.

'Buy proper furniture?' I said. 'Like, spend more than five dollars on a chair?'

'Yeah,' Pete replied. 'I don't know about you, but I was hoping we'd be able to stay here…for a while.' He took an anxious gulp. 'I just thought, it would be nice to maybe have some proper tables and chairs in our house…like, you know, a proper couple would.' He stopped just short of saying the dreaded 'family' word. He probably didn't want to rock the boat.

The resultant silence between us could have been cut with a machete. It seemed like we were on the cusp of something big. Joint ownership of quality household items was a major step in our relationship.

'Ah, sure,' I said, not wanting to make a big deal of this suggestion. 'I'll have a look around, see what I can find.'

Pete nodded silently, and left me to get on with it. In hindsight, suggesting to me that we were a 'proper couple' with common property must have been quite nerve-wracking for him.

It didn't take me long to find out where expats typically purchase their interior fittings: I was soon told of a local Cambodian carpenter who produced the most exquisite furniture. When I tracked him down, he drove me to his secret warehouse, down a hard-to-find pot-holed alleyway near the Russian Market. It was packed to the rafters with thick chunks of timber waiting to be transformed.

When I saw the quality of these fine woods in his warehouse, I couldn't help but wonder if these deceased trees were derived from the rampant deforestation that Cambodia was often accused of. I hesitated, before pointing to a particularly fine heavy slab that would make a remarkable dining table.

'Good choice,' he told me. 'This, old Khmer bed.'

I sighed with relief. I loved the idea of this bed having life breathed into it once more by this carpenter's aging hands. It would have weighed heavy on my mind if it were from a virgin forest, chopped down in its prime. I couldn't help but wonder though who used to sleep on this hard plank of wood and, given the country's sordid history, what had become of them.

I was also given the contact number of a seamstress who could sew bespoke curtains for our villa. A small, elderly Cambodian lady, with noticeably slender hands and the slightest, most delicate frame, she came especially to our house to take her measurements. She spoke no English and I no Khmer, but somehow we managed to communicate through broken French, which she must have picked up during the country's colonial past.

As the lady drew out her tape and gently noted down our windows' proportions, I couldn't help but wonder how she managed to survive the Khmer Rouge regime that had ruled Cambodia in the 1970s. Back then, an estimated quarter of the country's eight million population died, many of whom were mass buried in what have become known as the Killing Fields. Anyone with a modicum of education was massacred at their hands. Her knowledge of French and her delicate sewing skills must have made her a target in their eyes.

I didn't dare ask her any questions about this painful period in the nation's history, in case my query elicited too many heartbreaking memories.

An awkwardly shaped living room meant I was directed to a boutique décor shop to acquire a handmade sofa. For a few hundred dollars, we could have a seating area designed to fit precisely into its corner. Unfortunately, Pete came along to participate in the design process. Though he had no prior experience of interior design, he took control and insisted on covering the entire couch in a plain creamy white fabric.

'But Pete, if Tom jumps on the sofa, there's no way we'll get his paw prints out,' I said, trying to convince him of his folly.

'He won't jump up,' Pete said, coming to the immediate defence of his best friend. 'Tom's a good dog, so he is.'

'I'm not denying he's a good dog, Pete,' I replied. 'But one paw print will immediately halve its resale value.'

I was trying to jog Pete's memory of how Tom's secret sofa-sitting destroyed our armchairs in Hanoi, but the more I objected, the more Pete insisted Tom would remain on terra firma now that he was an older and wiser dog.

When the sofa eventually arrived, Pete went to great lengths to demonstrate Tom's obedience. Pete sat on the pristine white covers, patting them enticingly to show Tom how comfy they were. Tom padded over to Pete's legs, placing his warm snout on his knee. All credit to Tom, he wasn't tempted in the slightest by Pete's beckoning, and remained with all four paws firmly on the tiles.

Later on, Pete didn't think I was watching when he brazenly lifted Tom physically off the floor and placed Tom on his knees, before giving him an impromptu massage.

Tom's paws were millimetres from the cushion covers. I was just about to shout at Pete for this breach in the household rules, when I noticed Tom looking distinctly uneasy with the current arrangement. Normally, Tom would be all on for a deep-tissue rub and this heightened degree of affection from Pete, but it seemed as if Tom knew the rules better than his own master and didn't want to be caught infringing them. I watched as Tom successfully squirmed out of Pete's grasp, and dropped to the floor like a lead weight.

The sound of Tom's thud gave me with an excellent excuse to come out from my hiding place. It was obvious to all what had just transpired. Leaning hard against a wall, I folded my arms and stared silently at Pete, trying hard to suppress a grin.

'What?' Pete said, all innocence. 'Tom was touching my knees, not the fabric.'

'I'll bar *you* from the sofa, Pete, if you're not careful,' I said.

Much to my surprise, Tom continued to prove that he was a very obedient dog despite Pete's repeated attempts to lure him into deviant doggie behaviours.

Back in Hanoi and Kathmandu, Tom had stuck religiously to the rule that he was not allowed upstairs to the bedrooms. The stairs were a very clear demarcation zone for Tom that helped him adhere to this rule – which had admittedly been in place more for Pete, so that he wouldn't start sneaking Tom upstairs to sleep with him. However, the bedrooms in our Phnom Penh villa were on the same level as the main living space, so it was up to Tom to work out where he was and was not allowed.

For some interior décor reason, the living room and bedrooms were tiled with slightly different designs. It meant that our bedroom doorway's boundary was designated by a slight change in the floor's hue and design. Tom soon determined that he was allowed on the brown tiles but not on the orange and yellow ones.

Pete, however, couldn't help but put Tom to the test. One morning, Pete opened the bedroom door, hopped back into bed, and called Tom by his name. Tom obediently appeared at the bedroom doorway, standing to attention. Tom then placed his bum within the living room's jurisdiction and waited for Pete to come into the living room, to welcome him to the start of a brand new day.

'Tom, Tom, come here Tom,' Pete called from behind the bed sheet. Despite Pete's calls, Tom knew his place. He danced across the door's opening, hoping to entice Pete out of bed. When that didn't work, Tom yelped at Pete desperately, telling him to get up, to not be so blummin' lazy.

Throughout all this torture, not once did Tom place even a toenail on an orange bedroom tile, remaining firmly on the brown living-room ones. Pete was vindicated.

Unfortunately, there were other dogs residing close by that were not as well behaved. We had assumed that our villa did not have any street dogs within its vicinity, and that any dogs that did live in the neighbourhood were firmly locked behind closed gates. That had been the case when we'd lived in our wooden house, just a few blocks away. What we didn't count on was a family of small white Shih Tzus being allowed to roam freely outside a local shop a couple of doors down from our new house, completely unrestrained.

Neither Pete nor I even noticed this gang of animals when coming to and from our house. When us humans passed them by, this pack barely batted an eyelid. It was only when Pete and I decided to take our canine companion for a walk one day that this dog mafia revived themselves from their fake slumbers. Within seconds, Tom was identified as a legitimate target.

The first thing I noticed was three short white furry figures scampering across the road at speed, causing traffic to stop dead. Tom continued to trot along on his lead by Pete's side, taking no heed of the warning barks.

The ringleader, a butch bastard of a dog, got up close, barking halitosis into Tom's face. Tom, in ignorance, ignored this explicitly threatening behaviour. Instead he peed all over what they considered their personal property.

Tom only escaped physical harm thanks to Pete practically choking him to death as he dragged him determinedly away up the street at speed.

We were sadly mistaken if we thought that keeping Tom behind our own gates would resolve this turf war. The next morning, as I stepped on to the pavement outside, my flip-flop came within millimetres of standing on a strategically positioned piece of dog crap.

There were no other pieces of poo dotted along the side-walk. The tiny turds were only lying in front of our entrance. They were exactly the right shape and size to have come from a Shih Tzu's rear end. The little feckers from across the street had started to shit directly outside our house.

It was not long before this episode in Tom's life became known as Shit-gate.

While Tom was dealing with the excrement of his canine rivals, Pete and I were dealing with a different poo problem.

We had begun to notice that the external walls of our house were increasingly covered in what looked like bird droppings. What I couldn't understand was how, as birds did not frequent our garden. They couldn't have been responsible for the mess being made of the house, given that the number of splats ran into the hundreds, if not thousands.

It was only when Pete and I were having pre-dinner drinks one evening that the provenance of this poo was revealed. The sun had gone down, but the night air was still warm enough for us to sit outside on the veranda. I was curled up on a large bamboo sofa, sipping chilled red wine, contemplating how pleasant life in Phnom Penh was.

Then I noticed a flicker in the streetlamp outside. 'Did you see that?' I said to Pete. 'I could swear I saw something fly past that light.'

Pete shook his head, uninterested in engaging me in a conversation about unidentifiable flying objects. It was only when the light flickered a second time that Pete happened to be looking in the right direction.

Pete put his wine glass down before walking out into the pitch-black garden. He stood there a while, letting his eyes grow accustomed to the dark. It was only then, watching him, that I saw a black thing swoop past the top of his head, letting out a subtle shriek.

'Bats!' I shouted. 'There's bats out there.'

Pete ducked just in time as a volley of bats performed a display worthy of the Red Arrows directly over our lawn. With my attention now fixed on them, I saw that their final acrobatic display involved a fly-by over our house, where it was bombs-ahoy with their stool.

'We've bats living in the palm trees,' Pete said, as he retreated back into the house. 'How do we get rid of them?'

A quick Google search suggested that mothballs might successfully scare them away, but when I spoke to a medical friend of mine, she suggested leaving the bats well alone. The bats eat mosquitos, she told me, and can help prevent the spread of Dengue fever. So if we wanted to keep free of this mosquito-borne disease, the bats had to stay where they were.

Letting the bats live in our palm trees didn't solve the dilemma of our poo-streaked house. We came to the conclusion that if we couldn't stop the source of these splats, we just had to clear up the resultant mess.

Fortunately, a Cambodian friend of our maid, Chanteoun, came to our aid. For a small weekly fee, an elderly gentleman named Mr Sonny agreed to come to our home and clean up the bat shit. For no extra charge, he tended the lawn that had started to suffer from Tom's extensive use, as well as cared for any potted plants around the place. With Mr Sonny added to our payroll, we now had a driver, a maid and a gardener at our disposal. It was quite a formidable team of staff assembled to tend to our every need.

I couldn't help wondering how Pete and I had come to acquire such a cushy, pampered lifestyle, when all we originally intended to do was escape our birth country's economic hardships. Would all this easy expat living render us too soft to ever return to Ireland?

21

Teenage Tom

Life continued in Phnom Penh, weeks blurring into months. Before we knew it, we had been in Cambodia for a full calendar year.

'We should go away for a weekend sometime,' Pete said after we spent yet another long, lazy weekend lolling around the capital.

I was surprised by Pete's suggestion. We had been at pains not to leave Tom alone after the unfortunate kennel cough incident. However, over recent late-night dinner parties, expat friends had regaled us with the wonders of the Cambodian coastline. I had become increasingly jealous of their stories, and had wanted to take a look at it for myself.

'Okay then, why don't we go to Kep?' I said, not wanting to miss this rare opportunity to escape the city's confines.

Pete had also heard of this relaxing, luxurious seaside town a few hours' drive from Phnom Penh. It didn't take much to convince Pete to leave for the coast that very weekend.

I soon found out from these same friends the best places to eat and stay in Kep. All we had to do before we left was find a safe place for Tom to stay. Fortunately, during a recent trip to the vet for Tom's annual vaccinations, I discovered a fine kennelling establishment that Pierre, Tom's vet, deigned to approve. Run by a fellow Frenchman, Pierre swore there was no risk of Tom contracting any infectious diseases in this place.

Pete and I decided therefore to send Tom to the exotically named Pet Resort while we were out of town. Situated in an expansive area on the outskirts of Phnom Penh, it boasted kennels covered by traditional straw roofs, built in the shade of mango trees. The dogs stayed in carpeted abodes, a rarity for even Cambodia's humans. Outside these homes, there was a substantive sandpit for the dogs to frolic about in. For smaller dogs, presumably those Tom's size, there were bungalows available complete with mosquito nets, as well as hammocks and piña coladas no doubt. For an additional ten US dollars, we could even have Tom picked up from the nearby vet's office and personally chauffeured to Pet Resort.

Reading the literature made me wonder if Tom was going to end up having a more luxurious break than ourselves. It's a bad omen if you're jealous of your pet's vacation arrangements.

We ended up paying for the extra taxi service to avoid having to drop off Tom ourselves. 'At least you know you don't have to worry about him,' I said to Pete as we stood watching Tom being whisked away from the kerbside for his weekend stay. Pete looked on as Tom's transportation drove down the street and disappeared out of sight.

'I sincerely hope we don't have to worry,' Pete replied. 'Seeing how much we're paying.'

Pete's disgruntlement at Tom's kennel fees thankfully

dissipated once we arrived in Kep. The town was as idyllic as everyone had said. Old colonial houses peppered the roads we journeyed along towards our hotel. Our room itself overlooked the clear blue ocean through a myriad of swaying palm trees. The sunny climes and the sea views made it unnecessary to venture far from town.

After settling ourselves in, we sauntered down to the seafront to Kep's local crab market to indulge in some lunchtime seafood. There were a variety of vendors, spread out all in a row, so we took pot luck on one. Inside the restaurant of our choosing the décor was basic, with plastic chairs and tables cloaked in vinyl. We were able to overlook this tackiness when faced with the restaurant's mouth-watering and extensive menu. The seafood selection was rich with shrimp, crab, squid, red snapper, calamari and tuna – the finest fish caught fresh from the sea that very morning.

We picked out a couple of dishes to sample and share. While we waited for our food, Pete and I ordered a couple of ice-cold beers.

'This is nice, isn't it?' Pete said, leaning back on his cheap plastic stool, breathing in the fresh salty air.

'Yeah.' I took a swig of my chilled-to-perfection Angkor, its bitter fizz instantly relaxing me and giving me that 'I'm-on-holiday' feel. 'Probably too nice, to be honest.'

Pete raised one eyebrow. I cursed myself under my breath. I hadn't meant to say that out loud. Unfortunately, I had caught Pete's attention and he was waiting for me to clarify.

There was nothing for it now except for me to come clean. 'Don't you think we're getting spoiled by Cambodia? That this place is making us ... soft?'

'Hell yeah!' Pete said, slamming his beer can down, spattering me with the puddle of condensation that had since formed beneath it. 'Cambodia is great! It's cheap, it's got excellent service, it's sunny and warm – what's not to like?'

'It's not reality,' I mumbled back. 'Seriously, life is not meant to be this easy. If we ever go back to live in Ireland, I'm not sure we'd be able to cope.'

Pete stared back at me. This topic was our elephant in the room. I knew Pete was happy hanging out in Asia; he wasn't ready to go back home just yet. I, on the other hand, knew that if we were committed to each other, we had to start thinking seriously about where we were going and what we were doing with our lives. For example, I wanted to know if our future involved things like marriage and kids? If so, would it be best to raise our children closer to family and friends, in a culture we were both familiar with?

'Look at us. Neither of us cook or clean for ourselves any more,' I said, trying to make my case. 'We're ferried around in tuk-tuks like royalty. We're pampered every weekend with massages and manicures.'

'I know,' Pete said, grinning manically. 'Isn't it great?'

I wasn't sure I agreed. The only chore that we could possibly complete on returning to Ireland was a weekly supermarket shop, and only because Pete insisted we go there ourselves so he could wander up and down the dog-food aisle. He didn't trust our maid, Chanteoun, to pick out Tom's daily meals.

While Pete took great pleasure in spending several hours selecting a wide and balanced range of flavoured dog food pouches for Tom, I took the opportunity to maintain my shopping skills by purchasing toilet rolls and bananas.

'It's fine for a while,' I replied, conceding slightly. 'But it's like we're on permanent holiday. There's just no way I want to live here forever. What about Ireland? What about our friends and family over there?'

After his training back home the year before, Pete had admitted to me that Ireland was starting to emerge from the worst of the recession that had forced us abroad. People were no longer losing their jobs. The talk of house repossessions seemed to have lulled. I had begun to cling on to this lifeline: that Ireland might actually recover soon and we could finally go back home.

'What about Tom?' Pete said, throwing down his standard trump card. 'I doubt there's a Pet Resort back in Ireland.'

'Come on, Pete,' I said. 'In which universe does a street dog get chauffeured to his weekend kennels?'

The issue of Tom had, however, weighed heavily on my mind. After the traumas of his inter-country transportation within Asia, I was not sure I could cope with the stress of sending him to the highly protected island fortress of agricultural Ireland. When a human steps off a plane in Dublin, they have to declare to customs if they've been near any farm animals while abroad in case they're infected with some contagious disease. Imagine trying to bring a former street dog into the territory? Tom would be put down before he could even reach the baggage carousel.

Regardless, Pete and I *had* to have this conversation about what happened next. Pete had originally come to Cambodia to turn around the business that currently employed him. It was made clear to him from the start that, once he had accomplished this mission, he was to hand over to a Cambodian.

With Pete being so good at his job, such a handover was fast approaching. We had to work out whether Pete would find a different job in Cambodia, or whether we declared mission accomplished and headed elsewhere.

As soon as our grilled seafood platter arrived, we shelved the discussion for another day. Part of me didn't want this difficult conversation to ruin our sumptuous meal. The other part knew that we had to let our thoughts and words settle before we could safely revisit the subject later.

After one short sleep, we were back in Phnom Penh, after a wonderfully relaxing weekend away. We went straight to the nearby vet's office to pick Tom up at our pre-determined rendez-vous time. Surprisingly, it was not a Cambodian who dropped Tom off. Instead, a finely dressed and remarkably handsome white-skinned gentleman got out of the Pet Resort van. Tom immediately jumped down on the pavement right behind him.

'You are Tom's owners, I presume?' the distinguished man asked in a distinct French accent. I quickly surmised that this was the owner of Pet Resort.

Pete and I nodded as we looked at our long-lost dog. Tom seemed content, if a little fatigued after his weekend away. I guessed he must have been glad to be reunited with us, seeing that his tail was wagging so happily.

'I hope Tom was no trouble to you,' said Pete.

'Tom is a good dog,' the man pronounced in return, pressing Tom's lead firmly into Pete's palm. I could feel the heat of Pete's cheeks radiate beside me as they reddened with immense pride.

'In fact, there is only one issue I have seen with him,' the owner went on.

My heart skipped a beat. Tom had an issue? 'What would that be?'

'Tom is a good dog except that he tries to fuck everything that moves,' this genteel Frenchman stated without batting an eyelid. 'He fucks my leg, he fucks all my staff's legs, and he tries to fuck each and every dog he can get close to.'

I was utterly mortified. How exactly did one reply to such a statement?

I looked down at Tom once more and realised his apparent fatigue was due to thirty-six hours of hip gyration. When I glanced over at Pete to check if he was as mortified as me, instead of shame, the same look of pride he'd had on hearing Tom was a good dog was still emblazoned across his face. If anything, that pride seemed to have amplified since being informed of Tom's sexual efforts.

I apologised to Pet Resort's owner for Tom's inappropriate behaviour and promised him that it would never happen again – that is, if Tom was not already permanently barred from his kennels.

The French man seemed to shrug it off as if he had seen it all before. Perhaps that was what all pets at his place tended to do. Seeing as neither Pete nor I had visited Pet Resort, I couldn't help wondering how exactly Tom was housed while he was out of our care. I had assumed dogs were purposefully segregated to avoid any possible confrontations or occasions for hanky-panky. Now I was starting to think that Pet Resort was more of a communal affair. I couldn't help wondering too if Tom actually had hit the mark on his weekend rampage and inseminated some poor bitch in heat.

As soon as Pete, Tom and I got home, I made my views

explicit to them both: 'Tom is to be neutered,' I told Pete, stating it as if the decision had already been made.

'Hold on a minute,' Pete said. 'Tom was only having a bit of fun. Didn't we pay enough for him to have a little something extra on the side?'

'Seriously Pete, what if some poor dog owner finds in a couple of months' time that there's a brood of mini Toms running around their house?'

'Sure wouldn't a few extra Toms in the world make it a better place?' Pete replied, this image doing nothing to convince him to give Tom the snip. 'Think about it, Moire. Tom is – what? Two years old now. Around fourteen in doggie years. Tom is going through dog puberty. No wonder he's so randy!'

Pete looked over at Tom lying lifeless on the grass. Tom's eyes were practically at the back of his head, he was still so crazed with amorous thoughts. Pete was gazing at Tom as if Tom was his personal protégé. 'Anyhow, neutering male dogs can change their personality. I've heard it can quieten them down and make them fat and lazy.'

'My understanding is that only a handful are affected,' I said. 'It might be good if Tom calms down at little.'

'I'm sorry, but that's a risk I simply don't want to take,' Pete said. 'If Tom's personality changed and he stopped greeting me the way he does when I come home from work, I don't know what I'd do.'

Pete had a point. Tom's frenzied greetings were the only thing that decompressed Pete after a long and hard day's work. If Tom was no longer able to fulfil this role, I was not sure what *I* would do.

I finally relented and agreed that Tom's reproductive organs could be left intact, at least for the moment.

Tom was noticeably depressed after his brief stay at Pet Resort. He barely ate, he slept almost all the time and when awake, he moped around the garden. Pete was so worried about Tom that he barely left his side. I on the other hand was convinced Tom would snap out of it eventually. He was just being a teenager, sulking when he returned home to his parents after a wild weekend away with his mates.

When I suggested we go out for dinner one evening after our return, the only way I could convince Pete to accompany me was to agree to bring along Tom as well. Pete point-blank refused to leave Tom at home alone.

Fortunately for us all, there was a restaurant close to our house that welcomed children and animals. We arrived at Le Jardin and took a seat on one of their reclining sofas in their expansive, relaxing garden. Children were already running around the grounds, but the place was large and so well designed that we barely registered their presence.

Pete tied Tom's lead to the sofa leg, somewhat unnecessarily. Tom was so uninterested in roaming that he slumped down at Pete's feet straightaway while we made our dining selection. Tom looked as if he would have preferred to stay at home and play console games rather than be dragged out to dinner. Perhaps he was secretly plotting how to escape our grasp and make his own way back to Pet Resort.

I was so busy perusing the menu, trying to work out if I wanted crêpe or salad for dinner, that I barely saw the black streak careering past our table. Tom, though, was on it. Suddenly, he was standing up straight, ears raised, tail erect, straining at the leash. It was the most attentive I had seen him since his Pet Resort release.

The black object whizzed past our chairs again in the opposite direction, a blur of frantic energy. Tom was now prancing on his two hind legs, yelping excitedly.

'What's up boy?' Pete said, patting Tom's elevated head.

Tom seemed uninterested in this affection, his attention totally elsewhere.

The black blur finally came to a halt at the table of another couple. Once it had slowed, I could see that the object of Tom's interest was a small black puppy dog.

The couple soon noticed the commotion at our own table. 'This is Lucy,' the man called over to us, when he saw all three of us staring in their direction.

'This is Tom,' Pete reciprocated, proudly showing off our own canine. 'I think Tom wants to play with Lucy, don't you boy?'

Tom salivated in response.

What transpired next is the closest analogue I've seen to two men trying to make their kids become best friends. With Lucy's master's consent, Pete unclipped Tom's lead and let him run after Lucy. Tom took off at high speed. The next thing we saw was a white blur chasing a black blur round and round the garden.

I was amazed the restaurant owners didn't come out to put a stop to this frantic doggie game.

With our two dogs now fully occupied, Lucy's owners invited us to join them at their table. 'I'm Milan,' the man said. 'And this is my wife, Jenny.' We learned that the two were originally from Sweden but were now working in Phnom

Penh. Soon enough talk turned to our respective dogs and their provenance.

'We found Lucy in China,' Milan said. 'She was just a street dog there.'

'No way!' Pete exclaimed. 'Tom too! Only we found him in Vietnam.'

Pete and Milan then swapped horror stories of trying to transport their beloved dogs across various borders. While Pete recounted his Vietnamese customs trauma, I watched Tom chasing after Lucy. Despite being the same shape and size as Tom, she was far too fast for him. As Tom whizzed past us on his umpteenth lap, I realised he had that same ecstatic face as when he stepped out of that Pet Resort van.

All of a sudden, the penny dropped. Tom probably never even came close to impregnating another dog when he was at Pet Resort. My guess is he just sprinted after random females and humped off later when approached by the kind French gentleman's leg.

If Tom thought this was the way to get laid, he still had a lot to learn.

Pete and Milan swapped phone numbers and agreed to meet up again. Their pledge was based on the promise that they would bring their dogs along as well. Pete was ecstatic at the prospect of Tom having future doggie dates with Lucy, his new Chinese mongrel sweetheart.

I was not sure, however, if Lucy had been informed or would be okay with this plan. Once Milan and Jenny were finished eating, I noticed that Lucy used her last ounce of energy to escape Tom's desperate grasp. She sprinted towards their Vespa motorbike, hopping on to the footplate under

Milan's legs just as he revved the engine and sped out of Le Jardin's gate.

The scene was reminiscent of our Vietnamese teacher, Ms Phuong's, dramatic departure from our apartment in Hanoi. Tom would need to learn from Pete that it is fine to look, but you're not allowed to touch such beautiful Asian creatures.

22

Doggie Dates

As promised, Pete and Milan met up quite regularly and became quite good friends. It was obvious though that they both had the ulterior motive of matchmaking their dogs. I got the impression that Milan loved Lucy so much that he wanted to breed her with a fine young male like Tom to make some mini-Lucys. But while Lucy started to see through this flagrant set-up, Tom continued to wander after her totally oblivious, a lovesick puppy dog.

When Milan brought Lucy over to our house, the cute Chinese female quickly figured out how to use our house rules to her favour. Working out that Tom was only allowed on brown-coloured tiles and prohibited from orange ones, she firmly planted her paws on the orange tiled section within our bedroom and refused to budge. Tom drooled and yelped at her from afar, perched on our brown-coloured living room doorsill.

I felt so sorry for Lucy being pestered by Tom that I let her hang out in our boudoir to get a modicum of peace from his presence.

Eventually it became clear to us all that Lucy was sick of Tom. When she emerged from our bedroom's safety to make her way home with Milan, she did so with teeth exposed. Even with Lucy emitting such a stern warning, Tom still chanced his luck. He tried to mount her, but this move was only met with a warning snap delivered in the direction of his goolies.

After several aborted attempts, Pete finally concluded that a long-term relationship between Tom and Lucy was not on the cards. 'Tom at least deserves some sort of company,' Pete said once Milan and Lucy had gone.

To some extent, I agreed Tom needed some companionship. His chance meeting with Lucy managed to drag Tom out of his post-Pet Resort depression, but now that Lucy was a non-runner, Tom's dark moods had returned. Some days he barely made it out of bed.

The problem with getting Tom a playmate was our uncertain future. If we remained in Cambodia, having two dogs posed no problem. However, if we did decide to move home or to another country, then having two dogs would place us in the same situation as Susan, Tom's original owner back in Hanoi. We would have to bear the expense and stress of moving two close-knit dogs. Or we might find the cost and trouble too much to bear and end up giving one up.

Despite this uncertainty, we kept an eye out for a spare dog. Phnom Penh has a similar expat online network to Hanoi where general information is shared and unwanted items bought and sold. We didn't have to wait long before an ad appeared on the forum from an American family who had inherited a dog from a departing neighbour. Unfortunately, they had discovered that caring for the pooch was too much for them and they wanted to find a good home for her. I got in contact and we arranged for their dog, Matilda, to come and stay with us for the weekend.

The family brought Matilda over late one Friday afternoon. She was a pleasant little brown dog, around the same size as Tom, with a soft, kind demeanour. When I called her, she immediately trotted up to me and let me stroke the short, smooth hair on her back.

If Tom hadn't been in the picture, I would have taken her in a heartbeat. She was one of the cutest things I had ever seen. But this wasn't about me finding a dog – this was about Tom. It was up to him to decide whether Matilda was a suitable playmate or not.

Straightaway Tom did exactly what he had done with Lucy when they first met: chased Matilda round and round the garden. This time it was a brown rather than a black blur followed by the familiar white streak. Just when it looked as though Tom was tiring, Matilda exited the circuit they had carved in the garden and came over to work on befriending me.

I soon found that Tom wasn't too choosy about female company: Matilda's slowing provided him a chance to make a rear assault. Like Lucy, Matilda had zero interest in mating with our dog. Unlike Lucy, however, Matilda had no qualms about inflicting bodily harm on Tom to keep him away.

Tom retreated instantly, yelping and screaming from the love bite Matilda had planted on his neck.

Neither Pete nor I could understand why Tom was so unpopular with the ladies. It wasn't as if he was a bad-looking dog. We thought him quite a handsome specimen, with his long white locks, dark brown eyes and a silky-smooth tail. Was it that Tom has certain canine characteristics humans are oblivious to but female dogs find repulsive?

I would be the first to admit that I can easily overlook Tom's jutting-out lower jaw and his overcrowded teeth but, when he licks me, I've noticed that he also has pretty bad breath.

Watching Matilda's reaction to Tom, I wondered if Tom was the dog equivalent of a nerdy lad who's desperate to lose his virginity. Just like his human peer, the more Tom tried, the less successful he seemed to be.

If only he were a tad more subtle. Not everyone loves a trier.

The rest of the weekend proved incredibly stressful for our entire household. Tom didn't know whether he was coming or going. He couldn't seem to work out if the bite was a sign that Matilda was just playing hard to get or if it really meant that she wanted nothing to do with him. Though Matilda was the picture of grace around Pete and me, she turned into a demonic bitch when Tom was in her vicinity.

By Sunday, Tom wasn't even welcome within his own home. He sat cowering in the corner, afraid to move anywhere close to Matilda in case it was misconstrued. If Matilda were going to remain with us, we would have had to strictly demarcate zones for where Tom was and wasn't allowed. This was not the type of companionship that we had envisioned for Tom. Matilda had to go, and Tom's deep dark moods soon returned.

However, instead of retreating to the confines of his bedding, Tom decided he was going to exert his masculinity another way. One morning, as Pete headed out to work as normal, he bid farewell to Tom before swinging open our gate. Without Pete even realising it, Tom darted out between his legs and ran straight across the street, directly towards the shop where the three mongrel Shih Tzus lived.

As soon as Tom reached their Shih Tzu stall, he unleashed all his pent-up anger. Lifting up one hind leg, he pissed all over their shop front. His woman trouble and the as-yet unresolved Shit-gate saga were obviously weighing heavily on Tom's mind.

The three Shih Tzus had to do a double take. Not in their wildest dreams had they thought the meek and mild Vietnamese schnoodle who lived across the street would dare pull such a stunt.

The angry growls and vicious snarls that ensued attracted Pete's attention. He glanced over at the dog brawl that had broken out across the road, with no intention of getting involved. It was only when he heard an all-too-familiar yelp that he looked again, this time more closely, to see Tom slap-bang in the middle of the fight, getting the shit kicked out of him.

'Oh good Jesus, Tom!' Pete shouted, dropping his laptop bag outside our gate with a thud. He bolted directly across the road, straight towards the pack of dogs.

At least when Evil Dog attacked Tom in Kathmandu, Tom could claim he was a victim of an unprovoked attack. This time, however, Tom was wholly to blame for inciting the violence being inflicted on him.

Once Pete arrived at the outside of the mêlée, he tried to pull the gang of Shih Tzus away from his beloved dog. 'Get the hell off him,' he shouted, throwing the mutts to the side one by one. Though Pete managed to clear the scrum momentarily, the Shih Tzu gang remained undeterred. Instead of scampering off down the road with their tails between their legs, the Shih Tzus hurled themselves back into the maul with even greater vigour.

Unfortunately, Pete's presence had also served to arouse the interest of other dogs further down the street. Two members of the Shih Tzu rapid response team were soon deployed as reinforcements and before Pete knew it, five dogs were tearing Tom to pieces. Their attempts to teach Tom a lesson soon spilled over to Pete. Both suffered puncture wounds as canine jaws came at them from all angles.

The blood-curdling screams emanating from Tom meant Pete had no choice but to intervene more drastically. He plunged his hand deep into the mass of bloody fur and located the familiar feel of Tom's collar. He grabbed the leather band and hoisted it aloft, shaking off the foreign dogs that had latched onto Pete's arm in the process. Bloodied and beaten, Pete carried Tom back across the threshold on to Tom's confirmed terrain.

'Tom, you idiot!' was the first thing Pete could muster up once he had slammed the solid-iron gate behind them. His frustration at Tom's kamikaze attack on foreign territory soon dissipated when he saw the carnage that had been wrought. 'Those feckin' mutts, what have they done to you?' The bite marks on Tom and Pete were too numerous to count.

I came out into the garden to find out what all the commotion was about, screaming when I saw the state of them both. 'Oh my God! What happened?'

Tom didn't explain that he was just trying to assert his manhood. Instead he quickly set to work, licking his open wounds.

For my benefit, Pete launched into great detail explaining the war that had been waged outside just then.

'Regardless of whose fault it was, you're both going to have to get checked out,' I said, trying not to sound hysterical. 'I'll take Tom to the vets, but you need to get yourself to the doctor. I'm sure you'll need shots.'

Pete went inside to the bathroom to scrub clean the cuts crisscrossing his arms and legs. While Tom had recently been vaccinated against rabies, Pete needed to get additional vaccines. In the end, Pete parted with a hundred US dollars to protect him from contracting this potentially deadly disease. Tom's attempt to exert male domination and relieve his frustrations had come at a significant cost.

It was not long, however, before Tom identified something else that could be his new best friend. One night, Pete and I were sitting out on our veranda, watching the nocturnal bats from our palm trees circling closely above our heads. The sharp squeaks of these flying vermin were soon drowned out, however, by other squeals: Tom had spotted something on top of the perimeter fence separating us from our neighbours and was sitting to attention, tail wagging profusely, letting out the occasional yelp.

'What is it, Tom?' Pete shouted over. Tom was too distracted to provide Pete with an in-depth explanation, but it didn't take Pete long to work out what Tom had set his heart on.

Sitting atop our nine-foot brick wall was a pussy cat. She was looking down at Tom from its vantage point, giving Tom a perfectly executed death stare. She had places to go and things to do. She was not interested in this over-curious dog that was interfering with her nocturnal plans.

For his part, Tom was too excited to realise the kitty didn't want to be friends. Instead all his body language seemed to convey that this was to be his new playmate.

'That's a cat,' I shouted over to Tom. 'Don't get too close.' I had no idea why I said this when Tom rarely heeded my advice.

Much to my surprise the cat jumped down from the safety of the wall, landing silently in our flowerbed. Now that this feline was on the same level as Tom, our dog could barely contain himself. He lunged towards the cat, who proceeded to go berserk, arching her back and hissing for all she was worth.

Most cats back in Ireland would have run a mile by now, but this Cambodian street cat seemed to be well used to dealing with bothersome dogs. The cat evidently had business to conduct in our garden, and there was no way that Tom was going to thwart her designs. Using her full artillery of feline fending-off skills the cat advanced towards our lawn, stopping only to give Tom a well-aimed swipe with her claws fully deployed if Tom got too close.

'Tom, will you leave the puddy cat alone?' Pete shouted over, though he was undeniably enjoying watching this charade.

'That poor cat,' I said. 'Why can't Tom just leave it in peace?'

Maybe the owner of Pet Resort was right. Maybe Tom did try and fuck everything that moved. Or maybe, what with being the only animal in the household, Tom was just lonely and needed a platonic furry friend.

'Don't worry about puddy cat. She is well able to handle

herself,' Pete pointed out. 'It's Tom I'm more worried about. I don't think he realises how sharp cat claws are.'

Eventually, the cat successfully completed her covert mission, whatever it was, and hopped back on to the wall. All Tom could do was bounce up and down like a madman, pleading with his new feline best friend not to go. Unfortunately for Tom, the cat ignored him and, with one lick of her paw, slipped back into the dark from whence she had come.

Tom was so taken by this feline encounter that he kept an eye out for her for days. In fact, the mere mention of the words 'puddy cat' by Pete or I subsequently sent Tom into a flurry. But it was a one-sided relationship. Tom had to find something, anything, that would put up with his enthusiasm and love him for who he truly was, even if it meant down-grading his search to a mere platonic relationship.

Finally, after months of searching, Tom found the perfect bosom buddy. I was clearing out a spare bedroom in our house so a friend of ours could stay over. From the crayon scrawls on the wall, I guessed this used to be a child's bedroom. I pushed back a bed that hadn't been shifted since we'd moved in, to clear the dust from underneath it. Next thing I saw was Tom darting behind the mattress, emerging with a small brown fabric object in his mouth.

I barely thought anything of it as Tom quickly disappeared, leaving me to my cleaning chores. It was not until much later on that I noticed Tom had been unusually quiet that day. I sauntered over towards Tom, who was hanging out in our living room. He was curled up in a tight ball, with the same brown object now lying underneath him, barely poking out from under Tom's paws. Somewhat surprisingly, Tom seemed quite uninterested in mating with this object. For once, it seemed like Tom just appreciated its company.

'Come here, boy. What have you got there?' I said, bending down to take a closer look. Tom curled up tighter over his newly acquired possession, as if trying to hide it from my grasp. Thankfully he knew better than to bite me when I reached out to pick it up.

Tom had found himself a stuffed toy to be his new best friend. It was a little brown mouse, no larger than my hand. The former tenants' kids must have left it behind after they moved out.

Sadly the cuddly toy had seen much better days. Bits of woven stuffing hung out from breaks in stitching across its stomach. It was also completely blind, having lost both of its glass eyes. Despite its decrepit appearance, Tom seemed to love this little mouse very much.

'What shall we call him?' I asked Tom. 'If he's going to stay, he needs to have a name, no?'

Tom wasn't interested in the naming process. He just wanted his new best friend back straightaway. He jumped up and down, hurling his mouth at this little brown toy mouse trying to rescue it from my hand. It seemed that an inanimate object was the best kind of companion for Tom.

'Jerry,' I said, remembering the cat and mouse cartoon from my childhood. 'That's what we'll call him. You're Tom and he's Jerry.'

That's how Tom found Jerry, his forever friend.

23

Should We Stay or Should We Go?

Now that Pete and I had been in Phnom Penh for more than a year, we had managed to accumulate an impressive group of friends. This extensive network meant that most weekends we were invited to some dinner or drinks or nocturnal social gathering taking place around the city.

Lately we were increasingly receiving invites to farewell parties. The longer we stayed, the more it became clear that most expats leave in the end. Only those people who had married Cambodians seemed to remain long term. Most other foreigners seemed to be on assignments lasting a couple of years and, at the end of their contracts, they would up sticks and go to work in another exciting foreign destination. We were slowly learning that this is what expat life generally entails. The question for Pete and me was whether this was the type of lifestyle we really wanted for ourselves?

At one such weekend gathering, I posed our 'should we stay or should we go' quandary to one of our good friends,

Andreas. Pete's contract was due to finish in three months' time. After that, we had no idea what we were going to do or where we would be, and Andreas was no stranger to this dilemma. He had worked for many years around the globe for the Red Cross/Red Crescent, a formidable international movement well known for its emergency placements, many of which are short-term. Although Andreas wasn't that much older than us, I always had the impression that he had already lived several lifetimes. Surely he would have some good advice for Pete and me.

Andreas and I were not long into our 'where to live and work' conversation when I revealed our ongoing concern around Tom. Moving him from Vietnam to Nepal to Cambodia had been a huge undertaking, I told Andreas. I wasn't sure if I could cope with shifting Tom again to another country, especially if that jurisdiction required him to go into long-term quarantine.

'I had a dog once,' Andreas divulged unexpectedly. On one hand I was not surprised that, amongst Andreas's multitude of life experiences, he'd once owned a dog. On the other hand, I was curious how he'd managed to look after a pet when he never stayed in one place for very long.

'What happened to him?' I asked.

'It was back in Tanzania,' Andreas replied. 'His name was Akili. That's Swahili for wisdom, intelligence. I gave him that name because he was a very wise dog. He was such a wonderful companion, and my daughter Jenny's best friend. When we were leaving Tanzania, we had no choice but to leave Akili behind. I gave him to another German couple who we hoped would bring Akili back to Europe with them.

They didn't, and instead handed Akili to some other expats who swore they would look after him.'

'And did they?' I asked.

Andreas breathed a long, heavy sigh. 'I suppose they tried their best. But Akili was smart. It wasn't long before he escaped from them, probably trying to find me.'

'But you had already left the country?' I said, now fearful what Tom would do if put in a similar situation to Akili. If Tom was as clever as his own namesake, he'd probably put himself on the first international flight out of Cambodia and track us down via Interpol.

'Yes, I was long gone from Tanzania,' Andreas admitted. 'Over a year later, I had to go back to do some follow-up work. I returned to the town where I had left Akili, though I figured he would be long gone by then. I passed my old house, and was whistling like I used to, remembering the good old times when Akili and I were together. Then suddenly, something jumped out of the bushes at me. A stray dog.'

'You're not serious,' I said, somewhat sceptical. 'Was it Akili?'

'Yes it was!' Andreas shouted triumphantly. 'I told you he was a clever dog.' Andreas's happy demeanour didn't last long, however. 'He was so malnourished, covered in ticks and very weak. I barely recognised him. I felt so guilty about leaving him there in the first place, but there was really nothing else we could have done. For the next five days, I nursed him back to health. It was so nice having him sleeping by my bed for that short amount of time while I cared for him. I also set about finding Akili a new owner and managed to convince an American nun to look after him. He stayed with her until he passed away peacefully a couple of years later.'

Though Andreas's story had a happy ending, it was enough to convince Pete and me that whatever we did next, wherever we travelled to, we would take Tom with us.

While Tom's future was now firmly decided, Pete and I still had to work out where exactly that future lay. The imminent end of Pete's contract ultimately forced the conversation.

Pete came home from work as usual. Less usual was that he immediately grabbed a bottle of wine from the fridge and carried it outside to the garden with a glass in each hand. It was a sure sign that it was time to talk.

'What's up?' I asked, once I had taken a seat and swallowed a good slug.

'They want me to stay on,' Pete replied, matter-of-fact.

I couldn't help but shudder at the thought. I hadn't realised until then that the prospect of living much longer in Cambodia would be so upsetting. 'I thought you were meant to hand over to your deputy? Surely Borann is dying to take over your job?'

'He is,' Pete admitted. 'Borann knows the job is his, but he also knows how much work is involved, so he's happy for me to stay on for a while.'

'For how long?' I was starting to feel very nervous. I had been looking forward to my farewell party. Was it never going to happen? In my head, I had already started planning where I was going to source the balloons and canapés.

'Another six months?' Pete said, surprising me with his inflexion. It was as if he was seeking my permission to stay on for an additional half year.

I was torn. I knew how much Pete loved Cambodia and enjoyed working here, but I was also finding that, with every day I remained in this country, all I wanted was to return to Ireland. It was the random things I missed. I wanted to be around people who spoke my language and who understood me in turn. I longed for a cool day of soft Irish rain and to get soaked to the bone. Now that we were certain that Tom would be coming with us, could we not just make plans to get out of Cambodia?

'What do you think?' Pete said.

I hesitated. I knew I was going to stay with Pete, come what may, but I also needed time to mull this over. Whatever I said in the next few moments would ultimately forge my future happiness.

'Six months?' I said. 'You promise? You promise that after six months we can leave Cambodia and go back home?'

Pete sighed. 'Yes. I promise.'

I may have won the battle that day, but I couldn't help feeling as though everyone had lost. I was forcing Pete to leave a country he loved, while I was agreeing to stay longer in a place all my instincts told me to leave. I had grown lazy and bored with the easy lifestyle that Cambodia offered expats and I just wanted to go home.

They say relationships are all about compromise, but sometimes all that compromise does is ensures no one is happy in the end.

While Pete got busy extending his contract, things started happening in the capital that unexpectedly worked in my favour. Phnom Penh was changing. Investment was filtering into the economy and with it came visible signs of prosperity.

More and more cars and motorbikes and workers were spilling on to the roads, causing a phenomenon that was once totally foreign to Cambodia: a morning rush hour.

While the roads got progressively busier, the city's skyline was also being transformed. We noticed elegant French colonial villas in our own neighbourhood being torn down to make way for twenty-storey apartment blocks. Even our former wooden house around the corner didn't escape the formidable march of progress and was demolished to make way for a new bar and restaurant welcoming customers who had just moved into the newly constructed high-rises. The building that replaced our wooden home was concrete, neon and crass, though admittedly it was better rat-proofed.

Slowly but surely, Phnom Penh's increased pace of life started to affect Pete. One of the main reasons he had originally liked living in Phnom Penh was because, for a capital city, it was remarkably quiet and relaxed. Now, with all the construction going on, it started to feel like every other major Asian city.

I began to notice Pete's change in heart when he arrived home late from work one night, after getting stuck in yet another traffic jam. His sombre mood forced Tom to perform his welcoming dance for an extra-long time.

'Good day at work?' I asked Pete as he slammed shut the front gate behind him, trying to sound as upbeat as I could.

'Hm,' Pete mumbled back as he swept past me straight into the house, kicking off his shoes with an unusual amount of force. He walked straight over to the dining table, pulled his laptop out of his bag and threw it down on the surface. I knew better than to disturb Pete when he was at his computer.

However, it was very unusual for him to physically bring work back to the house. Normally he tried to complete everything in the office before returning to the relative sanctity of our home.

I left him alone to tap at his keyboard and double-click on his mouse. I saw him staring intently at his screen for over half an hour. Finally, he banged his laptop shut.

'Six months,' he said out loud.

'I'm sorry,' I replied, assuming his statement was directed at me. 'What's six months?'

'Tom will have to go into quarantine for six months if we bring him back to Ireland,' Pete replied. 'That's what Ireland's Department of Agriculture's website says.'

My heart soared and sank in equal measure: soared because Pete, of his own volition, for the first time ever, had brought up the subject of returning home. But six months? That seemed like forever. It would be cruel to put Tom under lock and key for so long.

'It says that Tom would have to be vaccinated on arrival, then have additional blood tests to confirm that he has already been vaccinated against rabies,' Pete explained. 'Then he would be put in quarantine for six months. Apparently it could cost us anything up to 3,000 euros in kennel fees.'

I heard Tom's tail beating softly against the tiles behind us. I turned around to see him lying submissively on the ground, eyes fixed intently on us both. He knew we were talking about him.

'What's brought on this change of heart?' I asked. 'Why are you suddenly googling how to bring Tom back to Ireland?'

'I was in my tuk-tuk, on my way back home just there now,'

Pete said. 'The dust, the noise, the congestion really got to me. All I could think about was how nice it would be to go home to my Dad's farm, to wander down the fields and pick stones out of the ground together with Tom, just like I did with Reggie when I was growing up.'

I dug my nails deep into my palm, trying not to react. Pete could be surprisingly sentimental sometimes. If this image of picking stones with Tom in rural Ireland made Pete want to go back home, then this was the image I had to remind him of if I wanted him to follow through.

Neither Pete nor I liked the idea of placing Tom in quarantine for a whole six months as soon as we arrived home. While I was resigned to this depressing bureaucracy, Pete was wondering if there was some way of avoiding this scenario.

After another extensive trawl of the Internet, Pete declared he had found the perfect solution. 'We can bring Tom to the USA and live with him there for a couple of months,' he suggested. He had found out that the USA was on Ireland's list of low-risk countries that had less stringent entry requirements. 'The USA doesn't require dogs to be kennelled if coming from Asia. Then we could bring Tom in to Ireland from Cambodia via the USA without ever putting him into quarantine,' Pete said with a spectacular flourish, proud of himself for finding this ridiculously complicated workaround.

I looked at him, wondering how I should even begin explaining to him that this was a non-runner.

'Nice try,' I said. 'Definitely original. But no. I'm not travelling halfway around the world just to get Tom home.' I had to at least give Pete credit, though, for thinking outside the box.

Initially disheartened by my tepid response, Pete set about finding a more realistic way around Ireland's quarantine rule. Part of me wanted him to quit wasting his time and just face the fact that, if we wanted Tom to return with us to Ireland, he would have to get locked up on arrival for a little while. After all Tom had been through already, I was sure our intrepid dog would survive this minor inconvenience.

Maybe I was missing the point. Maybe the real issue was that Pete wouldn't survive being separated from Tom for half a year.

After several more days of Internet searches, Pete emerged from behind his computer screen. 'This is it!' he shouted. 'Moire, come and have a look!'

I humoured Pete by making my way over to his computer and reading the webpage that he had loaded up: the UK Government's Department of Environment, Food and Rural Affairs, or DEFRA.

'But we're not bringing Tom to the UK,' I said immediately. 'We're bringing him to Ireland.'

'Northern Ireland is part of the UK,' Pete pointed out. We both knew that the boundary between Northern and Southern Ireland was notoriously porous. My parents, who live in Northern Ireland, would often drive from the north to the south and back again the same day, crossing the border to walk their own dog on the Republic of Ireland's superior beaches. Never once had they been stopped at the frontier to be quizzed about the nationality of their dog or its vaccination history.

It meant that, if we managed to get Tom into anywhere within the UK, it would be really easy to get him into Ireland.

'Okay, say we fly Tom into Northern Ireland,' I said. 'He'll still be subject to the same quarantine arrangements as the Republic of Ireland I'm sure. We'll still have to put him into quarantine.'

'Not from next January onwards,' Pete proudly stated. 'The UK rules are all about to change.'

I leaned further over Pete's shoulder and started to scrutinise the screen. I read that from the 1st January 2012, new laws would come into effect in the UK governing the transportation of pets. These new regulations, known as the Pet Travel Scheme, would harmonise the UK's laws with those already existing within the EU.

Little did we know at the time that we had a short, precious window when the UK would align with the EU before pulling the plug entirely. Back then, the word Brexit hadn't even been invented.

'That's all well and fine, Pete,' I replied. 'But how do we get Tom into the UK in the first place?'

'Will you just read the whole damn thing? Then you'll understand.'

I scrolled through the information. It was thick with details about moving animals into the UK from various jurisdictions around the world. My eyes began to blur with information overload. 'Can you just give the summarised version? Which set of rules applies if you're bringing your pet to the UK from Cambodia?'

Pete took a long, drawn-out breath. 'Okay, Cambodia is not in the EU, so it is formally classified as a "non-EU country"', Pete said, clearly and carefully. 'Then there is a list of countries that are not in the EU but have special status. If you look carefully, Cambodia is not on that list.'

'Okay,' I say, having followed thus far. 'So, what does that mean?'

I could tell that Pete was trying very hard to keep his patience. 'It means that Cambodia is classified as an "unlisted non-EU country",' he said as if it was the most logical thing in the world. Admittedly, the UK civil service's description of Cambodia as a double negative country was disappointing to say the least.

Clicking on the regulations governing 'unlisted non-EU countries', I got a raft of additional terms and conditions that came into effect on January 1st.

'I'm sorry, Pete,' I said, my head swimming by now with protocols and procedures. 'I'm really lost.'

'What it means,' Pete said, 'is that if Tom is vaccinated against rabies, all we need to do is get a blood test done in an EU-approved lab while we're still living here in Cambodia. Once the test result comes back to prove Tom doesn't have rabies, we are allowed to enter the UK together with Tom three months later, without ever putting him in quarantine.'

Pete stood there proudly, waiting for a rapturous round of applause. I had to admit, he had surpassed himself.

Just to make sure that this was not some Internet ruse, I made an appointment to see our vet, Pierre, to ascertain if this was for real. I brought Tom along as well so that, if the information was indeed genuine, we could start the process straightaway.

As soon as Tom saw Pierre, he started to get the shakes.

'It's okay Tom,' I said, bending down to deliver reassuring strokes. 'We just want to see if we can bring you home with us.'

Once inside his surgery, I provided Pierre with print-outs of the information Pete had already unearthed.

'Yes, this is all true,' Pierre pronounced on seeing these pages. 'I have already started the process for some other pets that are returning to the UK from Cambodia.'

Reassured that Pierre already had experience of this procedure, I listened intently as he explained the steps that must now be followed. 'Firstly, Tom must be microchipped.' I nodded, knowing this was already job done – it had been one of the first things we had to do before Tom could take his first flight out of Hanoi.

'Then we need to vaccinate Tom against rabies, today if you like,' Pierre said. 'In thirty days' time, he must come back to get another rabies vaccination.'

These two vaccinations came to a total of seventy US dollars. While I was aware that, when it came to transporting Tom back home, no expense would be spared, I hadn't yet realised that seventy US dollars was pocket change compared to the final bill.

'Thirty days after the second vaccination, you need to bring Tom back so that we can do a blood test,' Pierre continued.

'That's the one that has to be analysed by an EU-approved lab?' I asked.

'Exactly,' Pierre replied. 'The only reputable lab we have found that can deal with our blood samples is located in Scotland.'

Ironically, Tom's blood would land on UK soil before his body was allowed near it. This part of the process, what with the courier costs to and from Scotland, would set us back an additional one hundred and eighty US dollars. The bill was starting to mount up rapidly.

'We should get the blood test results back after another month,' Pierre said. 'Then, if they show Tom is rabies-free, three months later you can enter the UK.'

Though it did seem to be quite a lengthy process, it all sounded logical enough. There was no time to lose. I instructed Pierre to get Tom's immigration process started straightaway.

24

Certificates and Signatures

After receiving his series of rabies vaccinations, a minuscule capsule of Tom's blood was sent to Scotland for examination. It took a couple of weeks before the Scottish lab technicians gave Tom the all-clear. We then followed the UK's new immigration rules to the letter and waited for the stipulated three months to pass. By June 2012, Tom was finally ready to begin his long-awaited trip towards the UK and Northern Ireland.

With the clock ticking, I initiated the next sequence of events. The DEFRA website stated that we must use an approved transport company to import Tom into the UK. Before, we'd made all the necessary arrangements directly with the airline ourselves, but this time we had no choice but to use an intermediary. I had this foreboding that Tom's Asian exit was going to involve significantly more actors, and prove infinitely more complicated and costly, than any of our adventures to date. I was hoping that my gut instinct would be proved wrong.

Our vet, Pierre, suggested we contact INTRA Co., a freight-forwarding company based in Phnom Penh. I emailed them straightaway with details of our proposed plan and their manager, Han, wrote back stating they were happy to assist. In his email he outlined the medical steps we had to follow, all of which we had fortunately already started. Although this reassured me, the next part of his email threw a massive spanner in the works: 'You also need to find an approved airline to transport your dog. This might be difficult if your final destination is Belfast, as only a few airlines are authorised to transport pets out of Cambodia. I am not sure if any of these approved airlines go as far as Northern Ireland.' My heart tried to escape my body. 'I would like to ask you whether it would be an option to transport your dog as far as London?' Han continued. 'You could collect your dog from there, then make your own arrangements from London to Belfast.'

I burrowed my face in my hands. Why did our commitment to Tom make everything so complicated? If we disembarked in London, we would not only have Tom with us but all of our own luggage. How were we going to get ourselves and all our personal effects all the way from London back to Ireland? It was not totally impossible but it would be an immense logistical undertaking.

Despite enlisting Pete's superior Internet search skills to prove Han wrong and find an alternative routing, unfortunately Han proved to be right. We were unable to find an approved airline that would transport all of us across the Irish Sea to Northern Ireland. London was as far as any of the carriers would bring us. We would just have to get on with it and make our own arrangements from there.

Having a final destination of London threw up an additional problem. For any of the airlines to allow us to travel, we had to nominate someone in London who would act as Tom's receiver so that, if Pete or I got delayed or were unable to pick up Tom, the airline could contact this person and offload Tom on them. Fortunately, the Chairman of Pete's Board of Directors at his Cambodian Bank, Tanmay, happened to live in London. Having also lived in Cambodia previously, Tanmay was used to such idiosyncrasies. Pete contacted Tanmay, who was happy to act as our consignee.

With our routing now confirmed as Phnom Penh to London, we began our search for an approved airline. The choice turned out to be remarkably limited. In the end, we opted to go back with Thai Airways for this final leg of our Asian adventure.

I couldn't help wondering if this company was secretly waiting for us to settle down in one place and stop forcing them to transport Tom around the world.

Our freight forwarding company INTRAC Co. made the necessary arrangements so that Pete, Tom and I were all booked on the same flight leaving on Monday 16th July 2012. With this booking came yet more invoices. Pete and I had to pay around nine hundred US dollars each for our air tickets, which seemed a reasonable price for a human to travel from Asia to the UK. It was only when INTRAC Co. sent on Tom's flight bill that I couldn't help but let out a gasp.

'Pete, come look at this,' I said when I scanned down to the bottom of the page and saw the final price. 'You're not going to believe what Tom's flight home costs.'

As soon as Pete saw the amount, he let out a similar yelp. 'Seven hundred and fifty-five dollars! That's almost the same as my flight!'

There was a detailed breakdown of how INTRAC Co. had arrived at this fee. The actual flight was calculated at twenty-six dollars for every kilogram Tom weighed. Tom's only saving grace was that he is not a Great Dane. The additional monies were meant to cover customs clearance and handling charges, in addition to more paperwork: a customs export permit and sanitary certificate were all apparently required, whatever they were. Tom was so well documented by this stage, he probably could have written his own book about his Asian travels. When we queried INTRAC Co.'s charges, it turned out that they were quite reasonable. This was how much it costs to transport a dog halfway around the world. We just had to suck it up.

Our departure date was set. The clock had started ticking. I already felt sick with nerves, fearing that something was bound to go wrong. True to form, two weeks before our flight was due to leave, Thai Airways threw a spanner in the works.

I received an email from INTRAC Co.: 'Thai Airways is now waiting for you to send them your EU health certificate and import licence. Can you please advise when you will receive this documentation from your vet?'

I had no idea what either of these pieces of papers were, having never heard of them before, or even if our vet could provide them. I made an urgent call to Pierre.

'That EU health certificate they are asking for,' he said, 'is what we call here the third country certificate.' As if I was meant to know that the same piece of paper was called different things depending on your jurisdiction. 'I can only process it five days before the flight leaves when I give Tom the necessary treatments. It is not possible before that.' I could hear from the tone in Pierre's voice on the line that such bureaucracy bored him. He sounded exasperated that Thai Airways would even ask such a silly question, never mind that he had to inform them of the proper process.

'Okay, that's clear,' I said, scribbling this all down so I could tell INTRAC Co., who could then inform Thai Airways in turn. 'And what about the import licence?'

'Import licence?' Pierre replied. 'Oh, I know nothing about that.' With that, he abruptly bid me a good day and farewell.

All this bloody confusing paperwork made me want to scream. I looked around our house to see where Tom was, so that he could give me a reassuring hug and lick. I needed him to tell me that he appreciated all we were doing for him and that everything would work out all right. But Tom was nowhere to be found. He could probably sense my stress levels rising and was taking cover until I calmed down.

I didn't dare tell Pete about this new administrative quandary. He was already stressed out of his brain trying to hand his job over to his successor. I had to deal with this issue myself. I was also aware that if we didn't get everything in perfect order, Tom was going nowhere, and with Pete and Tom totally inseparable, this could mean we all got stuck in Cambodia forever.

I started emailing everyone I could think of who could clarify what this import licence was and where I could get hold of one. Eventually, I was referred to JCS Livestock in London, Thai Airways' nominated import agent for live animals in the UK.

Diane, the JCS representative, soon revealed the mystery of the import licence. 'As your dog is travelling under the new

Pet Travel Scheme that is effective from January 2012, you will not require an import licence. This is only for animals travelling under the old quarantine rules,' she wrote in an email.

It seemed like Thai Airways, on this side of the world, was still following an outdated version of the UK process.

I immediately forwarded Diane's email to INTRAC Co., begging them to share it with Thai Airways in Phnom Penh, Bangkok and London, and any other relevant city they saw fit, so that I was never ever again asked for an import licence.

Once this confusion was cleared up, I turned my attention to our own belongings. When we had left Vietnam and Nepal, we sold all our worldly possessions and relocated with just a couple of suitcases in hand, but during our time in Cambodia, we had acquired a wide range of household items that both Pete and I had grown quite attached to. Pete loved our white sofa, and impractical though its colour was, he wanted to bring it back home. I had bought a number of framed pictures and paintings that I didn't want to leave behind. Our former-Cambodian-bed dining table had to come with us too.

We sourced a removals company that could pack up our effects and place them all within a container which would then follow us back home on a ship, to be delivered to my parents' front door within two months of our departure. My parents had kindly agreed to store our stuff until we found a more permanent abode.

A week before our flight was due to leave, a team of packers arrived at our house. Tom immediately jumped to attention at the sound of the doorbell and rushed towards our metallic gate, barking with all his puny might to prevent the intruders from gaining entry.

'It's okay, Tom,' I said, bending down to stroke some calm back into Tom before allowing the crew to come in. 'They're just here to pack up our stuff so we can go back home.'

Tom's tail wagged back submissively. I was not even sure he understood what 'home' meant after all he had been through with us.

As the movers began their business of dismantling our house, a small piece of Tom seemed to die. With his familiar surroundings being removed and the edges of his dominion becoming less certain, he beat a hasty retreat. For the remainder of the day, he kept a low profile while, one by one, our possessions were subsumed within identical cardboard boxes, which were in turn individually carried off our premises with great care, before being loaded on to a truck.

It was not long before our once-beautiful villa was nothing but a shell. If Tom hadn't worked out already that his life was about to change forever, yet again, there was no hiding from it now.

I also couldn't help feeling a certain sense of loss. We were about to leave a set-up that would have rendered most rational people green with jealousy. We were leaving our jobs, our network of friends, a place that we had called home for nearly two years. It had all been dismantled and packed into cartons. There was no turning back now.

One of the hardest jobs we had to do before leaving, I refused to do alone. Together, Pete and I told Chanteoun, our housemaid, Chandara, Pete's tuk-tuk driver, and Mr Sonny, our gardener, that we were returning to Ireland and their employment with us was over. Despite having worked for us so diligently, there was no guarantee they would get new jobs once we were gone. There are so many Cambodian maids, drivers and gardeners working for the expat community that vacancies are few and far between. We did what we could, writing them excellent references, posting their availability online, telling our friends who were staying in Phnom Penh that we had staff who would gladly work for them. We gave them severance pay and wrote off any loans they had. Despite my deep feelings of guilt, I knew Chanteoun, Chandara and Mr Sonny were resourceful. I consoled myself that they would be fine without us.

Five days before our flight took off for the colder climes of London, we commenced the final stage of Tom's departure process. DEFRA required Tom to be treated by a vet for tapeworm, no less than twenty-four hours and no more than five days before his scheduled time of entry into the UK. I had already made an appointment with Pierre for Tom to have this final treatment and for us to receive the last remnants of Tom's paperwork.

I wondered if Pierre would be glad or sad to see us go now that our departure was imminent. True, I had bugged him with a lot of administrative issues around Tom's transportation but we had also provided him with a sizeable and regular income thanks to Tom's various vaccinations and appointments.

Pierre gave Tom his tick treatment as well as treatments for Echinococcus and heartworm. I parted with an additional forty-six dollars and mentally added it to Tom's bill.

'Now all I have to do is prepare Tom's papers and he should

be good to go,' Pierre told me, leading me towards the reception desk. 'I just need to send them over to the Ministry of Agriculture to get them signed and stamped.'

Signed and stamped by the government? A bead of sweat broke out on my forehead. I couldn't help but worry there would be some delay if some government officials got involved. We simply didn't have the time to wait for a vital piece of paper that could end up lying forgotten on some desk back at the Ministry.

'So when can I collect the signed papers?' I said, trying to conceal my anxiety.

'They should be ready on Friday, that is tomorrow afternoon,' Pierre said. 'Don't worry. I've dealt with this Ministry a few times already. They're normally pretty good.'

With Pierre's reassurance, I led Tom away from the vets and frogmarched him back to our empty villa. Although I tried to heed Pierre's advice to not worry, my brain was working overtime. What if we didn't get the documentation back within the next twenty-four hours? We were leaving on Monday and the government didn't work at the weekends, so I had to get them back tomorrow or else Tom would be a no-show.

Even when I tried to retreat from my worries on our return to the house, I couldn't shake them from my mind. I was so distracted by these thoughts that I failed to see Tom dry-heaving on the lawn.

'Oh God, Tom, what's wrong?' I shouted, running towards my poor sick dog once I finally registered his sudden illness. I was petrified that Tom had had a violent reaction to the tapeworm treatments and pleaded with him not to die. In fact, Tom *couldn't* die now given all the money we had just spent on him, with no possibility of refunds.

When I saw Tom had recovered slightly, I reattached his lead to his collar and took him straight back to Pierre.

'He's sick!' I shouted at the receptionist, barging into the office. 'He needs to see Pierre right now.' I had no time to make an appointment when it was highly likely my dog might breathe his last on her floor.

Pierre must have heard the commotion from the tranquillity of his surgery. He came outside to see me kneeling down talking to Tom, who had seemingly made a miraculous recovery. Maybe the sight of Pierre cured him.

'I swear, he was really sick when we got home,' I professed. 'He was trying to vomit something up.'

Pierre gazed down at Tom. 'He's stressed,' he said. 'You're stressed. He senses your stress. Stop being stressed.'

I hoped Pierre wasn't going to charge me for this additional piece of advice.

The next day, as mutually agreed, I found myself back at the vet. The Cambodian receptionist smiled sweetly at me as I stated I had come for Tom's paperwork.

'Here is the EU health certificate back from the Ministry,' she said, laying the form before me. I peered at it and saw a big red ink stamp with a squiggle of a signature. It was miraculously complete. Maybe I was wrong to doubt that the government officials would do their job. 'And this is the UK customs form,' she said, placing this piece of paper carefully beside the EU certificate. It was also stamped and signed. She also gave me a 'certificat sanitaire' issued from Pierre himself, with his own squiggle and stamp. I could hardly believe my luck.

'There is only one issue,' the receptionist replied, bursting my bubble with some reluctance. 'The official refused to sign this form.'

I looked back at her blankly. I thought I had everything Tom needed. What else was required?

'He needs to sign and stamp this form that gives Tom permission to leave Cambodia,' she said, pointing to yet another piece of parchment. A squiggle and red stamp were noticeably missing. 'He said that, because he has signed all the pieces of paper to get Tom into the UK and the EU, it is obvious that Tom is leaving Cambodia, so he doesn't need to approve this one.'

'But...but...of course he does!' I shrieked, before trying to regain my composure. I didn't want Pierre marching out of his office and telling me to calm down again. 'Does the official want a bribe or something?' I whispered at her now.

The receptionist shrugged her shoulders at my suggestion. She looked distinctly powerless.

'We don't bribe,' a familiar voice stated from over my shoulder. Damn it. Pierre had heard the commotion. 'If we start bribing them to sign documents, then they'll always want kickbacks. I refuse to go down that road.'

I was just as opposed to the idea as Pierre but at this stage of proceedings I would probably have sold my own granny just to get Tom out of here.

'So what should we do then?' I asked Pierre. I wondered who was more tired and frustrated with the whole situation, Pierre or me?

'Leave it with me,' the receptionist said, unexpectedly stepping into the ring. She pulled the unsigned, unstamped piece of paper off the counter. 'Come back in one hour.' I looked over at Pierre, who returned to his room to treat sick animals that were actually in need. He seemed glad that his receptionist was letting him off the hook.

I grasped this last-ditch hope and entrusted her with the document. One long hour later, I returned to the surgery to find the document autographed. The distinctive red stamp was missing. She told me not to worry, the signature would suffice.

I didn't care and didn't ask how that official's scrawl had miraculously materialised. All that mattered was that Tom's paperwork was complete.

It was finally time for Pete, Tom and me to embark on the last leg of our Asian adventure.

25

Homeward Bound

The day of our departure arrived, and Tom was the first of our trio to bid farewell to Cambodia. Five hours before our flight was due to leave, Pete, Tom and I arrived at Phnom Penh's airport's cargo terminal. Kheng, the representative from our freight forwarders INTRAC Co., met us at the loading dock to guide us through Tom's process. He seemed happy and relaxed. I tried to follow his lead.

'Tom's crate needs to be scanned before they allow it on the flight,' Kheng proceeded to tell us. Pete coaxed Tom out of his cage and handed the plastic box to Kheng. While Tom's crate disappeared into the recesses of the X-ray machine, Pete placed Tom on the ground so that he could have his last sniff of Asia. Tom must have sensed it was his last chance to stamp his ownership on the continent as he took his time.

'That's it Tom,' Pete said. 'It'll be a while before you're able to empty your bladder again.'

Having complied with Pete's command, Tom sat down on the ground to indulge in a leisurely pant, squinting his eyes as he took a long last look at the Asian sun.

'I wonder how he'll cope with the cold at home.' I had been so focused on getting Tom out of Asia that I had neglected to consider how Tom would cope with this new part of the world we were bringing him to.

'I'm sure he'll be fine,' Pete replied. 'You're always fine Tom, aren't you?'

Tom didn't have a chance to answer, as Kheng arrived at the loading dock entrance and motioned to us that Tom's chariot was ready and waiting. Tom scurried into his cage and plonked himself down against its very back wall. He knew the drill by now. Even Pete and I were less emotional about Tom's departure this time around. We all said goodbye to each other before slamming Tom's crate door shut and allowing Kheng to escort him away.

As Kheng and Tom's crate disappeared into the depths of the cargo warehouse, Pete and I suddenly found ourselves sitting on the loading bay alone. It was a bizarre feeling being without Tom. Already his presence was sorely missed.

'Come on,' Pete soon said, snapping me out of this stupor. 'We'd better head home and get our own luggage I suppose.'

A couple of hours later, we were back at Phnom Penh airport, only this time each of us had two suitcases in tow. Even though we had packed our container to the gills and only left out the bare minimum for our final days' stay, our luggage still took up considerable space. I breathed a sigh of relief when Thai Airways didn't accuse us of being overweight and accepted all our bags onboard.

The overnight journey to London passed without major incident. Despite its tranquillity, I couldn't help wondering how Tom was faring in the deep dark hold beneath us. That feeling was soon usurped by the abject fear that Tom was not actually in the hold but on some other flight, or even worse, stuck back in Phnom Penh airport. Unfortunately, I was unable to alleviate my unfounded suspicions by popping down to check on him. I had to wait until we disembarked at Heathrow to check on Tom's state and whereabouts.

We landed in London Heathrow early the next morning. I pulled on a jumper as soon as my skin hit the frigid summer air. If I had thought that going back to Europe in July would ease our transition, I was sadly mistaken. Nevertheless, it was still good to be one step closer to home.

Diane from JCS had already informed us via email about what would happen to Tom next. Upon arrival, Tom would be apparently collected from the aircraft and taken directly to the airport's Animal Reception Centre. There, DEFRA's State Veterinary Service would examine Tom and the reams of paperwork we had compiled on his behalf. Once they had completed their checks, JCS would be given another document to add to Tom's folder: a Common Veterinary Entry Document. JCS would then submit this to Her Majesty's Revenue and Customs, and once these final authorities were satisfied, we would pay an additional four hundred pounds for the pleasure. Upon receipt of our cash, Tom would be handed over to us. The whole process would take around five hours.

With our flight arriving in at 7 a.m., we had to hang around until noon for Tom to go through these administrative hoops. The last thing we wanted to do after such a long journey was wait around in Heathrow's arrivals terminal, sitting on uncomfortable plastic chairs and drinking expensive lukewarm coffee, so we booked ourselves into the Air Canada kerbside lounge that let new arrivals freshen up and chill out. If Tom was going to have all this money spent on him, we figured we should at least spend a little on ourselves.

Pete and I were too stressed and tired to make much conversation while we waited. Instead, our eyes kept wandering towards the lounge's wall clock, willing the hands to announce to us that it was finally midday. By 11.30 a.m., Pete could stand it no more.

'I'm going to wander over to the Animal Reception Centre,' he said. 'Can you stay here and mind our bags?'

'Yeah, sure,' I replied. 'You're okay going over there on your own?' I could see that Pete was emotionally fragile: he was always a bit grumpy if he travelled overnight and, truth be told, being separated this long from Tom was never good for his mood. I was less sure how he was coping with the fact that he could no longer call Cambodia his home.

'Yeah, I'll be fine,' Pete said. 'I just need to go get Tom.'

Pete was gone for what seemed like forever. I checked my phone every few minutes to see if there was any news, but nothing appeared on its screen.

I couldn't believe how worried I was, not just about Tom, but also about Pete's well-being. I needed us to be all in the same place once again. Maybe these were the kind of feelings and experiences you had to go through to make you realise you're not just a cohabiting unit. Maybe the amount of effort we were making showed that we had indeed become a family, Pete, Tom and I, without me even realising it.

It was only when I received a text from Pete that I was dragged back to reality. 'We're outside! Come see Tom.'

I bolted out of my seat, abandoning our assorted luggage to whoever was milling around the lounge. I threw myself through the sliding doors, which couldn't open quickly enough. There was Tom, out of his cage, dancing around wildly at the sight of his other family members. I bent down to pet him, but this was an insufficient greeting for Tom who instead lunged his two front paws on to my knees, then catapulted himself on top of my head so that his belly balanced on my cranium.

'Tom, what are you doing?' I giggled helplessly at his exuberance. He whimpered and whined and squirmed away as he rejoiced in being my new headgear.

Pete helped him perform a perfect dismount so that he landed safely back on his paws.

'So how was it?' I said.

'Not too bad,' Pete replied. 'By the time I arrived, Tom had already passed all the checks and he was ready to be picked up nearly straightaway.'

I refrained from telling Pete that my question was aimed at Tom. I really wanted to know how his journey was, what he saw on his travels, whether he met other dogs along the way. I wanted to know what Tom thought of Heathrow, whether the British Isles with their foreign language and temperate climate would suit his Asian tastes. Part of me also wondered what Tom thought about all he had gone through in these three short years, whether he was glad he had left Hanoi and agreed to come with us on our travels.

The final step was the ferry to Ireland, Tom's first ever boat trip. I don't think he understood or cared about the significance of this moment. Even Pete and I were too tired to work Tom up about this exciting prospect. We were so jaded, physically and emotionally, that all we could think about was getting home safely.

It was barely twenty-four hours since we had left Phnom Penh but it already seemed like a lifetime ago.

As soon as we boarded our train to Fishguard Harbour, I fell asleep on Pete's shoulder, lulled by the sound of train tracks echoing beneath our feet. Sleep proved to be the necessary antidote to all the stress that had led up to this moment. It made the five-hour train journey from London slightly bearable. It also gave me enough energy so that, once we arrived in Fishguard, I could sit around on the cold and dark platform without complaint while we waited to board our ferry.

Tom's passage to Irish shores from the UK went remarkably smoothly. As far as the authorities at both terminals were concerned, he was just another dog that had lived on the British Isles all his life. They requested none of Tom's documentation, even though we were willing to provide it. Instead, we hauled Tom and our luggage on to the boat and sailed across the Irish Sea in the dead of night, no questions asked.

Pete's father, Robert, was at Rosslare Harbour to collect us off the boat early the next morning. 'Well, will you look here,' he said as soon as he saw us walking off the ramp. 'Sure isn't it the returning immigrants?'

The weather was dark and dank as I stepped on to the wet and cold car park tarmac. Another time I might have been depressed by this overwhelming dreariness, but I couldn't help but drink in its familiarity. Finally, I was home.

'Hi Da,' Pete said, hugging his father with a couple of manly pats on the back. 'Thanks for coming to get us.' Robert extracted himself from his son and gave me a welcoming peck on the cheek.

'Who's this?' Robert asked, peering into Tom's cage. 'Is this the infamous Tom Dog?' Tom's tail beat out a friendly tune at the mention of his name. 'Are you the one that's been causing all this trouble?'

'I'm afraid so, Da,' Pete replied. There was no way Pete was going to divulge how much we had spent on Tom, however – Robert would have dropped down dead from a heart attack.

'I suppose we'd better be getting you home so,' Robert said.

Who would have thought that this would be our arrival procession? When Pete and I left three years before, we fled this small island with a mere forty kilograms between us. Now we were not only bringing home a ten-ton container full of memories, but also a small seven-kilogram dog that had been an integral part of our exiled time away and our newly formed family.

We received a warm welcome when we finally arrived at Robert's farmhouse, Pete's childhood homestead. The kettle was put on, teabags were thrown into mugs and warm buttered toast was passed round. Pete's brother was soon on the phone, promising to meet us for pints in the village later that night. The Aga stove was soon fired up, and I leaned against it for warmth. Generations of practice mean the Irish really do know how to welcome their kinsfolk back home.

As soon as he had had his fill of tea and toast, Pete said, 'Want to go for a walk, Tom?'

'You're not going out, are you?' I said, clutching my mug. 'It's about to rain.'

Pete didn't pay me the slightest heed as he clipped Tom's lead in place. He didn't need to tell me where he was going – I knew he'd be heading down the fields with Tom to pick stones in memory of Reggie.

They were gone no more than ten minutes before the heavens opened – and sure enough, I heard them traipsing back into the house not long after.

'Did you find any stones?' I said, as soon as they re-entered the kitchen where I was nursing another cup of tea.

Pete's shoes were covered in muck, and Tom's underbelly was caked in cow shit. They mightn't have shifted a single boulder between them, but they both looked content.

I'm sure at that moment, Reggie was looking down on them both from doggie heaven, wagging his tail happily.